CHARACTER

Profiles in
PRESIDENTIAL COURAGE

CHRIS WALLACE

RUGGED LAND | 401 WEST STREET · SECOND FLOOR · NEW YORK CITY · NY 10014 · USA

RuggedLand

Published by Rugged Land, LLC

401 WEST STREET • SECOND FLOOR • NEW YORK • NY • 10014 • USA

RUGGED LAND and colophon are trademarks of Rugged Land, LLC.

PUBLISHER'S CATALOGING-IN-PUBLICATION DATA

(Provided by Quality Books, Inc.)

Wallace, Chris.

Character : profiles in presidential courage / by Chris Wallace.

p. cm.

ISBN 1-59071-038-X

1. Presidents--United States--Biography.
2. Courage--United States
3. United States--Politics and government.
I. Title.

E176.1.W275 2004   973'.09'9
QBI04-200178

Book Design by
HSU + ASSOCIATES

RUGGED LAND WEBSITE ADDRESS: WWW.RUGGEDLAND.COM

SEPTEMBER 2004

1   3   5   7   9   10   8   6   4   2

First Edition

To my dearest Lorraine,
who teaches me about character—and courage—every day.

TABLE *of* CONTENTS

INTRODUCTION

I'm not sure when it was that I realized everything I thought I knew about being President was wrong.

I was covering Ronald Reagan as the chief White House correspondent for NBC News in the 1980s. And every day my conceptions about the presidency were stripped away one by one. It reminds me of those credit card commercials you see on television—

Intelligence: almost irrelevant.

Mastery of policy: helpful.

Judgment and steadiness of purpose: priceless.

I grew up during the era of John F. Kennedy, and I remember the stories about the dashing young President and his band of advisers. "The best and the brightest" they were called, and they weren't inclined to reject the moniker.

In 1962, Kennedy held a White House dinner for Western Hemisphere Nobel laureates. In his toast to the assembled group, the President said, "I think this is the most extraordinary collection of talent, of human knowledge, that has ever been gathered together at the White House—with the possible exception of when Thomas Jefferson dined alone." Left unsaid, but clearly shimmering in the air that special night, was the notion that Kennedy could have dined with Jefferson on equal terms.

No one ever mistook Ronald Reagan's brainpower for either Kennedy or Jefferson. When he came to Washington, longtime Democratic insider Clark Clifford famously called him "an amiable dunce." That may have said more about Clifford than Reagan, but even the President's own loyalists worried constantly that he would fumble—and felt they had to protect him from reporters, and himself.

I remember that in 1982, Reagan unveiled a complicated new arms control proposal to the Soviets. I happened to be the pool reporter in the Oval Office that day, and I asked the President, live on national television, to explain how the proposal would work. Looking back through the years, I can't remember any purpose to my question other than to stump him. And I vividly recall the President's men—standing in the wings off camera—literally gasping that I would have the temerity to ask Reagan about his own plan. They looked as surprised as I did when he explained his offer in perfect detail.

The point I want to make, the lesson I learned during the Reagan years, is that it didn't matter whether the President could discuss the intricacies of his plan. What mattered was that Reagan knew what he believed, had a keen strategic sense of how to achieve his goals, and never wavered.

It's easy to forget now how fierce the opposition was back in the 1980s to President Reagan's policy of "Peace through Strength." Millions of demonstrators took to the streets of world capitals, and American cities, protesting his plan to deploy medium-range missiles in Western Europe. It became a central issue in the 1984 presidential campaign. Walter Mondale accused the White House of having no constructive program to engage the Soviets. At a Rose Garden ceremony that fall, a reporter shouted at the President, "What about Mondale's charges?" "He should pay them," Reagan shot back, without missing a beat.

In the chapter that follows on Ronald Reagan, I'll take you back to that extraordinary time and recount how the President stood firm against all the doubters (some of the biggest in his own White House) and pulled off the diplomatic masterstroke that changed the world.

Unless you've been in the White House—and you get only the barest sense of it from the White House press room—it is impossible to understand the extraordinary pressures that swirl around any controversial presidential decision. It's so easy to be blown off course—by politics, by genuine differences of opinion over policy, by fear of failure on the grandest stage of all. Watching President Reagan, I saw that the presidency is not an exercise in intellect or ideology. It is a test of will and purpose.

When I began this project, I wanted to look at those instances when a President did the unpopular thing and saw it through because he believed it was the right thing to do. I wanted to tell of these historical events from a journalist's perspective—to try to capture the drama of the moment, to reveal the character of some of our best-known, as well as some of our least-known, chief executives.

The stories in this book are remarkable: the battle to bring down a corrupt national bank; a deadly labor strike that lit the city of Chicago ablaze; a dangerous air raid to "decapitate" an implacable foe. Even more remarkable, however, is the way these watersheds in American history brought out the strength and courage of the Presidents involved.

These are stories of Presidents acting against the advice of their counselors, against conventional wisdom, against political expediency, and often against the popular will. Each did so because he believed he had a mission, and a responsibility, to make the country, and the world, a better place.

Curiously, the distance of historical perspective largely erases partisanship. Republicans and Democrats have both served our nation well at times of great danger and committed themselves in ways their party politics would least indicate. A Democrat and lifelong supporter of workers' rights, Grover Cleveland put down a labor strike. A Republican and staunch anti-Communist, Richard Nixon opened the door to Communist China. These aren't stories of men who did their political parties proud—they are stories of men who thought first of their country.

In choosing a leader every four years, we have no idea what challenges will confront that President. Who knew in the fall of 2000 that the central issue of the Bush presidency—the central test of Western values—would be the clash with Islamic extremism and the forces of terror? In that sense, every election is a bet on a person. Who has the character to stand tall in the face of unimaginable pressures and fiercely competing interests in order to make the hard choices? Who can we really count on? There are 16 men in these pages who the nation had to count on at some of its toughest junctures—their insight and determination showed through. To further highlight this, at the end of every chapter I have included a primary source from each respective President related to the crisis he faced.

I have divided this book into four sections. The first, Internal Strife, looks at three Presidents faced with domestic problems of tremendous urgency. The second section, Executive Action, illustrates Presidents fighting the bureaucracy in Washington and rising above "inside the Beltway" politics—long before there was a beltway. Third, The Map for Peace highlights Presidents taking diplomatic action to secure tranquility and order on the international stage. And finally, Against the Enemy shows Presidents leading the United States during times of burgeoning conflict.

Winston Churchill once remarked, "Courage is rightly esteemed the first of human qualities because it is the quality which guarantees all others." One may or may not agree with the presidential decisions depicted in this book, but those decisions, undeniably, were brave. It is a blessing to our history, and a testament to our political system, that Americans have so often chosen leaders courageous enough to meet the challenges that awaited them.

if one is courageous they will preferaccount for those virtues

INTERNAL STRIFE

GEORGE WASHINGTON RECEIVING A SALUTE ON THE FIELD OF TRENTON, 1776.

Copy of a print by William Holl after John Faed, ca. 1860. National Archives & Records Administration.

CHAPTER 1

SADDLE UP

George Washington and the Whiskey Rebellion

In the autumn of 1753, the governor of colonial Virginia, Robert Dinwiddie, had a problem. The British had heard reports of French marauders in western Pennsylvania. King George II had instructed Dinwiddie to send an emissary to warn the French to get out of the territory. The journey would be perilous—the area was barely inhabited by Europeans, Indians were numerous, and winter was coming on. No one of appropriate rank wanted the job.

One afternoon a young man with reddish hair and gray-blue eyes finally appeared at Dinwiddie's office to apply. For the times, he was a giant; at over six feet, three inches tall, he towered over the short, rather plump governor. Physically he clearly qualified for a demanding trek through the wilderness. And though only 21, he had visited the frontier before as a surveyor. True, he had little formal education and no diplomatic training whatsoever. But as the third son of a modest Tidewater planter, the young man was obviously eager to make a name for himself, and he was the best option the governor was likely to find. George Washington left Dinwiddie's office with his first government job.

When Washington arrived in the foreign territory, a much older and experienced French officer treated him courteously but utterly ignored the British ultimatum. The young man rushed home to tell Dinwiddie. The next year the colonial government gave Washington, who had no military experience either, command of a ragtag group of soldiers and told him to go back to western Pennsylvania and defend against a possible invasion. Almost immediately, his inexperience came to light.

Washington's men happened upon a small party of Frenchmen lounging by their campfires. Even though Great Britain and France were not officially at war, the newly commissioned officer ordered his men to attack. In a quick skirmish they easily killed 10 Frenchmen and captured the remainder. But the prisoners claimed that they were on a peaceful diplomatic mission, similar to the one Washington had undertaken the year before. Word got back to Paris. Almost single-handedly, the young Washington had started the French and Indian War.

He wasn't particularly concerned: "I heard the bullets whistle, and, believe me, there is something charming in the sound." But he and his soldiers soon came to regret his aggressiveness. He directed construction of a fort to repel the inevitable French retaliation. Fort Necessity was woefully inadequate; it couldn't even hold all of his own soldiers. An observing Indian called it "that little thing in the meadow." When the French and their Indian allies did appear, and in much larger numbers than the colonials, Washington injudiciously insisted on fighting them. He surrendered the fort only after losing a third of his men and watching the rest drink themselves into a stupor to dull the pain of being scalped.

Washington fought for five more years in the frontier war and generally did not impress. He did show a knack for inspiring confidence in his men, and he demonstrated considerable physical courage. At one battle his soldiers, who had been split into two columns, began shooting at one another by mistake. Washington rode his horse between the two lines, pushing the firing guns up with his sword. But he constantly complained that British officers treated him poorly because he was a colonial native. He spent large amounts of his time away from troops under his command. He made unsolicited pronouncements regarding military and political matters that he did not understand. Dinwiddie accused him of ingratitude. More than one general had to brusquely put him in his place. At 26, Washington retired from the service, admitting that there was "much that I must strive to forget."

Thirty-three years later, in the fall of 1791, Robert Johnson rode his horse along Pigeon Creek in western Pennsylvania, in the same territory where Washington had once fought the French. Much, of course, had changed. Pennsylvania was now one of the United States. The disappointing young soldier and diplomat, meanwhile, had led the Continental Army to victory over the British and had become the nation's first President.

But western Pennsylvania was still wild country, and Johnson knew that his mission—collecting the new federal excise tax on whiskey—put him in danger. Many of the settlers in the region depended on the sale of whiskey to survive. All of them opposed the new tax. Only a few days earlier, representatives from neighboring counties had met and proclaimed the "obnoxious" tax the "base offspring" of the new Congress.

And out here, as Johnson knew, people sometimes expressed hostility to the law with more than just words. A few years before, Pennsylvania had enacted a state tax on whiskey. When a revenue agent tried to collect it in the western part of the state, a mob forced him to stomp on his own papers and curse himself. Not satisfied with that, they then cut off the hair on one side of his head and stuck the rest through a hole they cut in his hat. Chanting "Liberty and no excise!" and forcing him to take a drink whenever they came across a whiskey still, the mob paraded the humiliated agent through three counties. No one was punished, and Pennsylvania repealed the whiskey tax.

So when 16 men dressed in women's clothes suddenly appeared on the trail Johnson was riding, he feared they had more in mind than a practical joke. Ladies' bonnets framed angry, determined faces. The "girls" told Johnson to forget about collecting taxes in their county. To emphasize their point, they then tarred and feathered him, stole his horse, and left him to find his own way out of the forest.

But Johnson did not give up; he convinced a judge to issue warrants for his assailants' arrest. The deputy marshal charged with serving the documents, understandably afraid to do so, hired an illiterate cattle drover to do the job for him. The drover, for his pains, was whipped, robbed, tarred, feathered, and left tied to a tree. Western Pennsylvania did not intend to pay the whiskey tax.

Word of Johnson's mistreatment reached Philadelphia, the temporary national capital, a few days after he found his way out of the woods. Rumors circulated that the Secretary of the Treasury, Alexander Hamilton, wanted to raise an army to compel payment of the tax. Hamilton, the architect of the tax, believed passionately in a strong national government. Would a government's powers not be meaningless, he asked the President, if it declined to enforce its own laws?

But an older and now much wiser George Washington refused to be swayed by his aggressive former aide-de-camp. Especially in these early years, the President always had to consider national unity before taking any action on a significant issue. For Washington, the critical question was not whether the government could collect the whiskey tax but whether the young nation would survive at all. The Constitution had been ratified only three years before, and only after a bitter political struggle. The ties binding the United States together were still exceedingly fragile. Foreign observers believed that the republican experiment would soon fail. Hamilton was free to argue for strong measures, but in order to preserve the Union, Washington knew he had to steer a narrow middle course, asserting the government's authority while doing as little as possible to inflame still-active, and powerful, resistance to central governance.

Opponents of the Constitution had especially feared that military power would be used not to defend the nation but to suppress internal dissent. If the President raised an army because a tax collector had been tarred and feathered, Washington said, "there would be a cry at once, 'The cat is let out, we now see for what purpose an army was raised.'"

On a more practical level, his Treasury Secretary's grandiose visions notwithstanding, the fledgling national government simply did not have the power to compel payment of the whiskey tax all along the frontier. Citizens from Georgia to western New England were also resisting the tax. In many places the U.S. Treasury could not even find revenue agents to collect it. The President agreed with Hamilton that the situation was "a very unpleasant and disagreeable one," but for three years, despite intermittent violence, he refused to send an army to western Pennsylvania to enforce collection of the tax.

Washington had come away from his early experiences in the region with a healthy disdain for its people. The young soldier wrote of frontier settlers as "a parcel of barbarians . . . an uncouth set of people." Thirty years later, most easterners would still have agreed with him. Real estate promoters billed the west as "the Scripture Eden," but frontier life was brutally hard, even by the standards of the 18th century. The region was isolated from the rest of the country by the Appalachians. Harsh winter, especially in Pennsylvania, often made the mountains impassable. Wolves and panthers roamed the forests. Indians murdered settlers and then disappeared into the wilderness. Only six months before the mob attacked Robert Johnson, a family living near Pittsburgh had welcomed seven Indians into their home for a meal. When the guests finished eating, they blocked the door and then killed and scalped their hosts—four men, one old woman, and six children. Settlers often responded to such incidents by massacring peaceful tribes.

In addition to the unrelenting danger of frontier life, many people in the west were destitute. Despite promises in the brochures and an abundance of land, huge numbers of settlers did not own any property. Enormous tracts had been gobbled up by eastern speculators. Settlers who did own land used farming methods that were 2,000 years old; they were lucky to grow enough to feed themselves. The poverty appalled visiting easterners, who said frontiersmen lived like "so many pigs in a sty."

The existence did not appeal to, or suffer, the faint of heart. One visitor watched with horror as a man horsewhipped and then shot another man who tried to break up a fight between two dogs. Men met on Sundays not to go to church but to "try their manhood in personal conflict." One-eyed men were an everyday sight, eye-gouging being a customary tactic in such bouts.

The life bred a fierce independence. Frontiersmen in the late 18th century resisted the idea that a government on the other side of the mountains had any right to govern their lives. Throughout the 1770s petitions for separate statehood circulated in the west. Western Pennsylvanians tried to form a state they named "Westsylvania."

So when supporters of Hamilton's economic program introduced the whiskey tax in Congress, nearly every frontier representative argued vehemently against the measure. Many settlers opposed excise taxes (an internal levy on the sale of a commodity) in general. A large number had emigrated from Scotland or Ireland, and their ancestors had violently opposed, as a matter of principle, excise taxation in their home countries for centuries.

And even if they had accepted the idea of an excise, westerners would have opposed the whiskey tax because it was so patently discriminatory. The government taxed each gallon of whiskey produced, so even though whiskey sold in the west for half the price it did in the east, westerners paid the same amount of tax per gallon as easterners (the effective tax rate on whiskey in the west was over 25 percent, twice the rate in the east). In addition, while large commercial distillers predominated in the east, in the west, small farmers produced most of the whiskey. Many depended on its sale to make ends meet. The grain that farmers grew cost a lot to transport and often rotted before it got to market, but whiskey weighed considerably less and would not spoil. No less important, the economy of the cash-poor west functioned largely on barter. Most people just did not have the hard money necessary to pay the tax.

Westerners also believed that revenue from the tax would do little, if anything, to benefit them. In the 1790s the two most important issues for frontier settlers were protection from the Indians and the opening of the Mississippi, then controlled by Spain, to frontier shipping. The government had proven unable to stop attacks by Indians, and it had done nothing to force Spain to open the Mississippi. Why, westerners asked, should they pay a tax for which they would receive nothing in return?

Finally, Hamilton's decision to tax whiskey rather than another commodity showed an utter lack of concern for the culture of the frontier, where whiskey played a fundamental role in daily life. In a land filled with disappointment and horror, almost everyone drank, and "old Monongahela rye" was often the only choice. Church congregations paid their ministers in whiskey. Landowners could not retain workers without keeping them drunk. Westerners bristled at the idea of paying tax on a product so central to their existence and that many produced and consumed on their own property. James Jackson of Georgia thundered that frontiersmen "have long been in the habit of getting drunk and . . . will get drunk in defiance of . . . all the excise taxes which Congress might be wicked enough to impose."

But in the end, easterners dominated Congress; the whiskey tax passed easily in March 1791. The mob attacked Robert Johnson six months later, and over the next two years the resistance in western Pennsylvania only hardened. Citizens burned a tax collector in effigy. A throng broke into the home of a revenue agent and "swore that if he did not produce his commission...they would instantly put him to death." Most important, no taxes were paid. Congress amended the law repeatedly to make it less onerous on western distillers. But the defiance of federal authority continued.

Though easterners scorned frontier settlers, they had no objection to making money from investments in western land. Washington himself speculated avidly in western real estate. "What inducements have men to explore uninhabited wilds," he asked, "but the prospect of getting good lands?" By the time he became President he owned tens of thousands of acres on the frontier, including almost 5,000 in western Pennsylvania alone. But he constantly fought squatters there to retain his title. After the Revolutionary War he visited Washington County (named for him, of course) to meet with claimants to one of his tracts. When they would not agree to his proposed settlement of the dispute, he grew angry: "rising from his seat and holding a red silk handkerchief by one corner, he said, 'Gentlemen, I will have this land just as surely as I now have this handkerchief.'" When the squatters still wouldn't give in, Washington apparently swore at them; one squatter, who happened to be a justice of the peace, fined the general on the spot for profanity.

As unrest related to the whiskey tax continued, Washington appeared privately to despair that the frontier would never submit to a central government. Writing to his contacts in western Pennsylvania, he said that the lands he owned there had been more "plague than profit" and suggested he was ready to sell. Giving up on a personal investment was one thing; would the President decline to press the nation's claims as well?

In July 1794 the tension in western Pennsylvania finally boiled over. Hamilton, possibly trying to provoke an incident, dispatched U.S. Marshal David Lenox to serve warrants on 60 distillers in the area to appear in court. Lenox teamed up with John Neville, one of the wealthiest men in the district, who guided the marshal to the homes of the men he sought. Neville had been a Revolutionary War general, but he was now a federal revenue agent and, consequently, widely despised.

The two men arrived at William Miller's farm one hot day at about noon. Miller, in his own words, went "mad with passion" and refused to accept the summons. As Lenox argued with Miller, Neville noticed a crowd of 30 or 40 men coming down the lane. The men had been working in a nearby field and had heard that two federal officials were in the area. The mob carried pitchforks and muskets; they had also been drinking whiskey. They calmed down when they realized that Miller was not being arrested, but as Lenox and Neville were riding off, someone fired a gun. It was unclear whether the shot was fired into the air in frustration or was aimed at the two men. Hamilton would later claim the latter.

The mob spread word of Lenox's mission, and a militia that was gathering to fight Indians decided instead to march to Neville's house (where they mistakenly believed Lenox was staying) and capture the marshal. The next morning almost 40 men surrounded Neville's mansion. Neville fired a gun from inside the house, killing a man. The mob began shooting. At a signal Neville's slaves, to whom he had given guns, also began firing. The fight ended when the mob withdrew, but Neville knew they would return.

The next afternoon, a militia of 500 men marched up the hill toward Neville's house. The old general had persuaded 10 soldiers from a nearby fort to protect him. The soldiers snuck him away to safety, but they refused to surrender the house. An hour-long gun battle started between the militia outside and the soldiers in the house. When it was over, two militiamen lay dead. The soldiers surrendered the mansion, and the militia burned it to the ground. The Whiskey Rebellion had begun.

Washington very nearly avoided having to cope with the crisis. In 1792 the President had come close to refusing a second term in office. Now 60 years old, the once powerful body that had carried him through frontier wars and the Revolutionary War had started to break down. Doctors had removed a large tumor from his thigh (without, of course, anesthesia—one surgeon had cried "Cut away...deeper still....You see how well he bears it!"). Then a deadly case of pneumonia struck Washington. The President survived, but many of his friends thought he had never been the same since. He tired more easily, and he believed his memory had worsened.

And he dreaded the challenges a second term would bring. Washington had begun to sense that he could not overcome the factional tensions tearing at the country and at his own administration. The two principal figures of his own Cabinet, Hamilton and Secretary of State Thomas Jefferson, had emerged as the leaders of two nascent political parties, each bitterly opposed to the other. Hamilton's Federalists believed in a strong national government and a mercantile economy. Republicans envisioned an agrarian America of small farmers, with a government that intruded on the lives of its people as little as possible. Rancor between the two factions grew steadily during the President's first term. Both sides enlisted newspapers to trumpet their own point of view and to vilify the enemy. Federalists were branded as monarchists, Republicans as prophets of anarchy. Washington realized there was little he could do to stop any of it.

In addition to political differences, regional strains also tore at the nation's fabric. There was of course the troubled relationship between north and south. The President had to be careful to balance even his diplomatic appointments between northerners and southerners.

Now, however, Washington faced an even more severe threat: the possibility that the west would sever itself from the Union. British observers believed that the west's connection to the east depended on "a very precarious sort of tenure" and that a separation would occur shortly. The British and Spanish, as the President knew, were constantly looking for chances to exploit this tension to increase their influence on the frontier.

Washington took the threat of western secession seriously; he believed the frontier was critical for national unity. The opportunity it afforded might be the only thing that could cement the delicate bond between the North and the South. But he could not control the frontier. As Jefferson recognized, if the western territories determined to secede, "we are incapable of a single effort to retain them."

Washington might have relished the thought of retirement, but he was the only man with the stature to transcend partisan and regional differences and hold the nation together. Two years before, when the President had been near death from pneumonia, Jefferson had written to a friend, "You cannot conceive of the public alarm on this occasion. It proves how much depends on his life." Now Jefferson told the President that "North and South will hang together if they have you to hang on." In public rallies and newspapers, the public pleaded for him to stay.

Whether he ever really wanted to go home or not, Washington ultimately agreed to continue what he called "the extreme wretchedness of his existence" as President. Just as it had done four years before, the Electoral College voted for him unanimously.

The second term turned out to be every bit as difficult as he had feared. Jefferson left the Cabinet at the end of 1793, frustrated that Washington seemed more and more to favor Hamilton. Republican newspapers began to criticize the President openly. Political clubs called Democratic Societies formed across the country (including western Pennsylvania) to support Republican ideas. Washington, ever opposed to parties, considered them "incendiaries of public peace" that wished to "poison and discontent the minds of the people."

And there were new troubles in the west. On two occasions, Americans "of very decent manners and appearance" had contacted the British ambassador about an alliance between the frontier territories and Great Britain. Western Pennsylvanians had approached the Spanish ambassador. The administration found out about each of these meetings. A credible report reached Philadelphia that Kentuckians planned to attack New Orleans and secede from the Union.

When the Cabinet convened on August 2, 1794, to discuss the rebellion in western Pennsylvania, all of these developments weighed on the minds of those present. Hamilton, predictably, insisted that force should be used to capture the men responsible for the attacks on federal officials. Knowing Washington disapproved of the Democratic Societies, he referred to "formal public meetings" where speakers voiced their opposition to the tax. Pennsylvanian officials sitting in on the discussion argued that the state's judicial system was competent to find and punish the rioters. In the end, the President ordered the appointment of a three-man commission to travel west and negotiate with the rebels to obey the law.

But either before the Cabinet meeting or shortly thereafter, Washington concluded that Hamilton was right; circumstances had changed, and the attacks on Neville's house demanded a forceful response from the government. For years the President had steadfastly refused to use the military to enforce the whiskey tax, but resistance had turned into open, and violent, rebellion.

Washington had fought a long and difficult war to create an independent United States. He had been one of the first to push for a new constitution when anarchy might have engulfed the nation following Great Britain's defeat. He had devoted his entire public life to creating and strengthening a unified nation. Political parties, regional tensions, and the scheming of hostile countries now threatened to undo all his work. The time had come to send a message that the government would enforce the law, that the nation would defend its territory, and that the republican experiment set forth in the Constitution and ratified by the states would not be abandoned at the first challenge. The unrest in western Pennsylvania, Washington determined, would be put down by a federal army.

The decision carried enormous risks. The government had no standing army to send in, so Washington would have to ask the states to raise and send troops. The states would have to use a draft. Most conscripts would be poor and possibly reluctant to march against their fellow citizens. Marching these men, many if not most of whom would have no military experience, across the Appalachians into rough and unfamiliar territory would be a difficult task. And it all had to be done quickly; if the army did not make it across the mountains before winter set in then it would have to wait until the next spring. By then it could be too late.

And no one in the capital knew how formidable the enemy would be. As the days went by, discouraging reports came in. The events at Neville's house appeared to have radicalized more respectable members of the community; some now took active roles in drumming up resistance to federal authority. In early August, 7,000 rebels marched on Pittsburgh, at that time a settlement of only 1,000 people. The rebels threatened to plunder "Sodom," as they called it, but were placated when residents gave out large amounts of free whiskey. But Washington knew frontiersmen were tough; if they determined to resist the federal force in an organized fashion, then they would be a dangerous foe.

The rebels refused to agree to the terms offered by the President's peace commission. Even worse, violence associated with the events in Pennsylvania had spread to four other states. British agents, always watching closely, said it was the gravest crisis the young country had faced. With "the deepest regret for the occasion, but withal the most solemn conviction that the essential interests of the Union demand it," Washington formally requested the states to provide 12,000 soldiers to suppress the whiskey rebels.

But who would lead it? When he asked who had guided the young nation through its gravest tests, the President could only have one answer. At some point in August or early September, he decided to assume command of the army himself. It was the first and only time a sitting President would ever lead troops in the field. The reasons Washington chose to do so are not clear, but his presence with the troops served at least two purposes.

First, the President hoped to be a moderating influence. Support for the government could erode quickly if the army treated the citizens of western Pennsylvania more harshly than necessary. One observer said that in his time with the troops Washington "labored incessantly" to ensure that soldiers were "scrupulously regardful of the rights of their fellow citizens." Second, his presence on the scene would underscore, more effectively than anything else could, the government's determination that its laws would be obeyed.

In early October, the federal forces assembled at Carlisle, Pennsylvania. As Washington left Philadelphia to join his troops, he must have reflected on his days as a general. He had first led the Continental Army into battle against the British almost 20 years before. Now he would command an army against his fellow citizens, many of whom thought he and the government he led were just as oppressive as the British King had been. Some of the rebels may even have fought by Washington's side in the Revolution. It could not have been what he had hoped for.

And at 62, Washington was considerably older than he had been the last time he commanded troops in the field. Indicative of that, two months before, Washington had wrenched his back so hard while riding that for a while he couldn't sit upright—the accident was the first serious physical injury he had ever experienced.

But when the Commander in Chief put on his old Revolutionary War uniform, mounted his horse, and paraded before his assembled troops on October 4, he gave no sign of infirmity. Any veterans in the crowd must have felt a nostalgic swell of pride at the sight of their aged leader. One soldier, driven to hyperbole, wrote that "the man of the people, with a mien intrepid as that of Hector, yet graceful as that of Paris, moved slowly onward with his attending officers, nor once turned his eagle eye from the dazzling effulgence of the steel clad band." Newspapers across the country ran long descriptions of the spectacle. European ministers sent copies to their home countries. Word quickly spread west across the mountains.

As it turned out, the federal government had drastically overestimated the rebels' resolve. The unrest in western Pennsylvania never had a clear objective. As delegates from the western counties met together during August and September, it became clear that relatively few favored seceding from the Union or resisting the army. When the news arrived that the federal army, with Washington at its head, was marching west over the mountains, the movement's leaders either submitted or snuck off into the wilderness. After only two weeks with the troops, the President felt sure enough of the situation to return to the capital.

The army continued west but found little to do when it arrived on the scene. After a month of investigation, 20 suspects were sent to Philadelphia for trial. Just two of these men were convicted, and the President pardoned both. Jefferson caustically remarked that an "insurrection was announced and proclaimed and armed against, but could never be found."

By acting decisively to quell the threat, Washington had proven that the federal government would stand behind the law. Many continued to fear that the government would destroy their dearly purchased freedoms. But as President Washington noted in his farewell address, a strong government, not a weak one, was the "main Pillar . . . of your tranquility at home; your peace abroad; of your safety; of your prosperity; of that very Liberty which you so highly prize."

As for the whiskey tax, the government never successfully collected it on the frontier. When Jefferson was elected President in 1800, he and Congress quickly acted to repeal it.

Washington, meanwhile, received benefits besides the thanks of his countrymen. The restoration of stability in western Pennsylvania, combined with some long-awaited defeats of Indians on the frontier, made property on the frontier much more desirable. In the years following the rebellion, the value of Washington's western lands, the "cream of the country in which they lie," increased in value by 50 percent.

BY THE PRESIDENT OF
THE UNITED STATES OF AMERICA.
A PROCLAMATION.

Whereas from a hope that the combinations against the Constitution and laws of the United States in certain of the western counties of Pennsylvania would yield to time and reflection I thought it sufficient in the first instance rather to take measures for calling forth the militia than immediately to embody them, but the moment is now come when the overtures of forgiveness, with no other condition than a submission to law, have been only partially accepted; when every form of conciliation not inconsistent with the being of Government has been adopted without effect; when the well-disposed in those counties are unable by their influence and example to reclaim the wicked from their fury, and are compelled to associate in their own defense; when the proffered lenity has been perversely misinterpreted into an apprehension that the citizens will march with reluctance; when the opportunity of examining the serious consequences of a treasonable opposition has been employed in propagating principles of anarchy, endeavoring through emissaries to alienate the friends of order from its support, and inviting its enemies to perpetrate similar acts of insurrection; when it is manifest that violence would continue to be exercised upon every attempt to enforce the laws; when, therefore, Government is set at defiance, the contest being whether a small portion of the United States shall dictate to the whole Union, and, at the expense of those who desire peace, indulge a desperate ambition:

Now, therefore, I, George Washington, President of the United States, in obedience to that high and irresistible duty consigned to me by the Constitution "to take care that the laws be faithfully executed," deploring that the American name should be sullied by the outrages of citizens on their own Government, commiserating such as remain obstinate from delusion, but resolved, in perfect reliance on that gracious Providence which so signally displays its goodness towards this country, to reduce the refractory to a due subordination to the law, do hereby declare and make known that, with a satisfaction which can be equaled only by the merits of the militia summoned into service from the States of New Jersey, Pennsylvania, Maryland, and Virginia, I have received intelligence of their patriotic alacrity in obeying the call of the present, though painful, yet commanding necessity; that a force which, according to every reasonable expectation, is adequate to the exigency is already is motion to the scene of disaffection; that those who have confided or shall confide in the protection of Government shall meet full succor under the standard and from the arms of the United States; that those who, having offended against the laws, have since entitled themselves to indemnity will be treated with the most liberal good faith if they shall not have forfeited their claim by any subsequent conduct, arid that instructions are given accordingly.

And I do moreover exhort all individuals, officers, and bodies of men to contemplate with abhorrence the measures leading directly or indirectly to those crimes which produce this resort to military coercion; to check in their respective spheres the efforts of misguided or designing men to substitute their misrepresentation in the place of truth and their discontents in the place of stable government, and to call to mind that, as the people of the United States have been permitted, under the Divine favor, in perfect freedom, after solemn deliberation, and in an enlightened age, to elect their own government, so will their gratitude for this inestimable blessing be best distinguished by firm exertions to maintain the Constitution and the laws.

And, lastly, I again warn all persons whomsoever and wheresoever not to abet, aid, or comfort the insurgents aforesaid, as they will answer the contrary at their peril; and I do also require all officers and other citizens, according to their several duties, as far as may be in their power, to bring under the cognizance of the laws all offenders in the premises.

In testimony whereof I have caused the seal of the United States of America to be affixed to these presents, and signed the same with my hand. Done at the city of Philadelphia, the 25th day of September, 1794, and of the Independence of the United States of America the nineteenth.

GEORGE WASHINGTON.

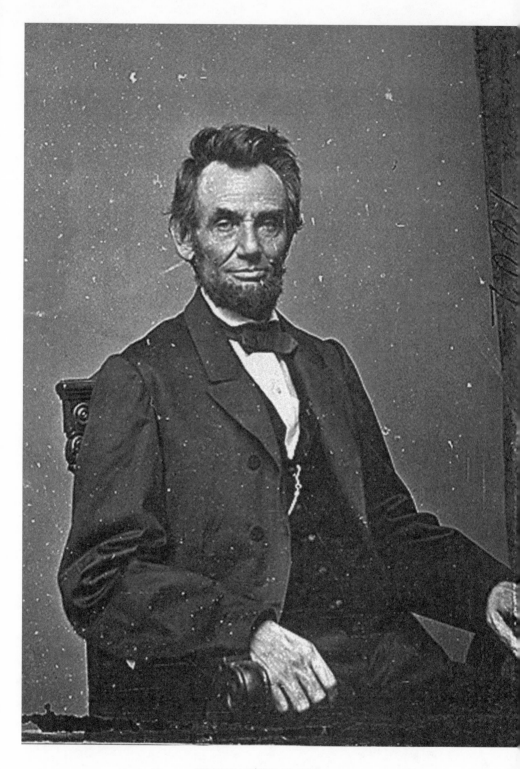

ABRAHAM LINCOLN, CA. 1860.

National Archives & Records Administration

CHAPTER 2

TO THINE OWN SELF BE TRUE

Abraham Lincoln and the Emancipation Proclamation

It was near midnight on Sunday, September 21, 1862, when eight slaves escaped from their master's Wilmington plantation into the North Carolina night. They waited exactly an hour after the watchman's final rounds before silently stealing away one by one. William Benjamin Gould, a small and soft-spoken 24-year-old, was among the band of fugitives. He slipped outside and crept toward the river. Indian summer rain fell on the group as they untied a docked rowboat and started the nightlong trip from Wilmington down Cape Fear River toward the Atlantic.

The men were well aware of the danger they faced as they traveled downstream. Though their tiny boat had to cover 28 nautical miles before daybreak, they could not risk hoisting the sail. There were sentries posted the length of the river between Wilmington and the ocean, and any one of them might soon be on the lookout for eight fugitive slaves. They quietly rowed through the night.

One of the busiest ports in the Confederacy, Wilmington was heavily fortified. Fort Caswell, the main source of protection for the city, stood at the mouth of Cape Fear River, where it empties into the Atlantic. Wilmington was under blockade by a Union naval patrol, and Caswell held it in check at the coast. To William Gould and his fellow fugitives, that meant there would be soldiers, and plenty of them, in between their stolen boat and freedom.

Gould was intelligent and well-read, and he knew that the timing of his escape was of key importance. Once caught, a fugitive slave had no chance of ever attempting such "bad behavior" again. Most were hanged on the spot to make an example. The Civil War quickly proved to be just the opportunity he was waiting for. As Gould later wrote in his journal, he decided just after the start of the war to "leave the land of chivalry and seek protection under the banner of the free."

The war started in April 1861. In September some of the female slaves, who worked in the home and were privy to the owner's conversations, heard news that the Union had started conscripting escaped slaves from the South into the war service of the North. Rumors spread quickly among the slaves that any who made it into a Union camp would be seized as enemy property. While many of the slave masters were away at war, whole families of slaves walked off their plantations and into Union camps, proclaiming "I'm contraband" at the gate. As contraband, a slave was not freed; he was merely accepted as confiscated Confederate property. But he would not be returned to his master, and that was close enough to freedom for William Gould and other runaways.

Just after dawn the boat slid under the nose of Fort Caswell and into the swells of the Atlantic. Lofting a sail high in the morning breeze, the eight men approached two ships flying the Union colors. The ship nearest the rowboat brought William and the others on board. Still within sight of Fort Caswell but safely on deck, the eight men excitedly declared themselves contraband. They were met with exclamations of "Welcome to the USS *Cambridge*, men!" Lookouts on the second Union vessel recorded this event in the ship's log for Monday, September 22, 1862:

"At 11:20 the Cambridge reported picking up a boat with eight contrabands on board, lying off Fort Caswell." William Gould had done it. He was not yet free, but he was no longer a slave.

On the very same day, barely more than half an hour after the eight contrabands were picked up by the *USS Cambridge*, President Abraham Lincoln walked into a meeting with the members of his Cabinet. It was a routine Monday meeting, during which Lincoln typically heard opinions and suggestions from his closest advisers about matters of utmost importance to the Union government. For the Lincoln administration, which had been in office less than a month when the Civil War erupted, matters of state consisted almost entirely of matters of war. The agenda for this meeting was no different. Though it was not immediately apparent to those in attendance, it would be recorded in the annals of American history as the moment of Lincoln's most politically ambitious and audacious act as President.

As was his habit, Lincoln rose early that day. Just after sunrise and before even eating breakfast, he walked the short distance down Pennsylvania Avenue to the War Department building. There, in a tiny annex room once used as a library, stood the central telegraph office. Though buried in stacks of paper, it pulsed with life as its many clerks shuffled between telegraph machine and filing cabinets. Even when the office stood empty, as it sometimes did during Lincoln's early morning visits, the telegraph machine filled the room with noisy chatter as it received messages from the front and tapped them out.

President Lincoln always started his day in this cramped office, where he could take a long look at the news coming in from the war front and, as he would say, give his "freshest face" to issues of military strategy. "Lincoln came over from the White House several times a day," recorded one telegraph room employee. To avoid being reached, he didn't keep a permanent desk or work space there, preferring instead to sit at the desk of the War Department's telegraph superintendent, Thomas Eckert. Lincoln relied on the telegraph room as a place to concentrate and to get away from the pressures surrounding him at the White House. "I come here to escape my persecutors," another telegraph operator quoted him as saying.

Some of Lincoln's "persecutors" were nothing more than the masses of citizens he welcomed into his White House. The son of small-town Illinois farmers, he stubbornly insisted on keeping an open-door policy at his offices. "There is nobody to bar our passage," a journalist wrote in the *Sacramento Union* of the President's meeting chambers, "and the multitude, washed or unwashed, always has free egress and ingress." Some visitors, according to the same journalist, came as "relic-hunting vandals, who actually clip off small bits" from the carpet and draperies in the White House as take-home souvenirs.

Most people, however, came to ask Lincoln for a pardon. He was known for granting these in cases where a Union soldier had been sentenced to death. "No man on earth hated blood as Lincoln did, and he seized eagerly upon any excuse to pardon a man when the charge could possibly justify it," another journalist wrote. "The generals always wanted an execution carried out before it could possibly be brought before the President."

Widows or mothers of dead soldiers always seemed to work their magic with Lincoln. "I haint got no pay as was cumin toe him and none of his bounty munney," wrote a destitute widow. "I no yo du what is rite and yu will see to me a pore wider wumman." Lincoln found her an appointment as a postmaster in Washington. Another woman who had already lost one son in battle and was about to lose another on charges of deserting the army wrote to Lincoln, pleading her son's case. He answered her, "If this man had more than one life, I think a little hanging would not hurt this one. But after he is once dead we cannot bring him back, no matter how sorry we may be; so the boy shall be pardoned."

However sensitive to the value of human life, President Lincoln could only be pushed so far. He could tell the difference between those who had been abused by the terrible circumstances of war and those who were simply abusing his time. One Congressman from Massachusetts pleaded for a convicted slave trader's release from jail. "You know my weakness is to be, if possible, easily moved by appeals for mercy," said Lincoln, "and if this man were guilty of the foulest murder that the arm of man could perpetrate, I might forgive him on such an appeal." Then came the indignation, "But the man who could go to Africa, and rob her of her children . . . is worse than the most depraved murderer. No! He may rot in jail before he shall have liberty by any act of mine."

When not worn down by the pressures of public office, Lincoln was worn out by his wife. Mary Todd Lincoln was difficult to handle and psychologically troubled. A notorious spendthrift, she opened accounts at the finest stores in Washington on her husband's credit. Lincoln was forced to borrow money his first months in the White House to cover himself financially because of Mary's spending habits. "Lincoln was economical in everything," a close friend and former legal associate wrote, "but his family was much given to entertainments, and saw and enjoyed many ways of spending money not observable by him."

To compound these problems, just after Lincoln was elected, their 12-year-old son Willie had died of typhoid fever. Lincoln was devastated, but Mary came undone. Her favorite entertainment became consulting expensive clairvoyants about little Willie. "Willie lives," she once told her half-sister. "He comes to me every night and stands at the foot of the bed with the same sweet adorable smile he always has had." Her grief lasted for months (if not years) and was so intense that Lincoln warned he would have no choice but to send her to an asylum if she couldn't control herself. (She never did, and 10 years after Lincoln's assassination, her oldest son, Robert, committed her to a sanitarium in Illinois.)

Reduced at home to parenting his manic wife, Lincoln—in his official responsibilities—was often forced to act as referee to quarrelsome Cabinet members. Two in particular, Secretary of State William Seward and Secretary of the Navy Gideon Welles, were notorious for feuding with each other. Seward especially grated on Lincoln's nerves. A Senator for more than a decade, Seward was the leading Republican candidate for President in 1860. He had lost the nomination to Lincoln by only a thin margin. Arrogant and outspoken, he accepted his Cabinet appointment with a condescending and critical attitude toward the President. When Seward first went to the White House to welcome Lincoln, he found the President polishing his boots. Seward instructed Lincoln that, "In Washington, we do not blacken our own boots." But Lincoln gave as good as he got, asking, "Indeed, then whose boots do you blacken, Mr. Secretary?" Even so, Seward wasn't Lincoln's biggest Cabinet headache.

Immediately after being selected to the Cabinet, Secretary of the Treasury Salmon P. Chase announced that he intended to run against Lincoln for the next Republican presidential nomination. He constantly dogged the President's decisions in an attempt to create dissatisfaction within the party. Lincoln likened Chase's ambitions to "a horsefly on an ox, keeping him up to his work." He further described that "Mr. Chase makes a good secretary, and I shall keep him where he is."

Though he could scoff at Seward's conceit and disregard Chase's nagging, what Lincoln could never afford to ignore was the war. After Virginia seceded from the Union in April 1861, only the Potomac River stood between Washington and the Confederacy. The capital was within easy firing range of Rebel cannons for months into the war.

On the northern Washington border, Maryland was neutral in the conflict but allowed slavery and harbored many supporters of the Confederacy. When Lincoln asked for volunteers in April, Rebels in Maryland burned bridges and ripped up railroad tracks to prevent recruits from reaching Washington. Only Fort Washington defended the Union capital as the war began, and it was virtually unmanned, lay almost 15 miles away, and had been built as a coastal lookout during the War of 1812.

The army itself was in no better shape. Lincoln's general-in-chief, George McClellan, had quit the military to work in the railroad industry by the time the Civil War began. Lincoln had high hopes when he invited McClellan out of retirement, and the press cheerfully dubbed him "Little Napoleon." However, McClellan didn't deliver on his military reputation. "Suppose a man whose profession it is to understand military matters is asked how long it will take him and what he requires to accomplish certain things," Lincoln complained, "and when he has had all he asked and the time comes, he does nothing." McClellan once fought within sight of the Confederate capital Richmond, only to stop inexplicably short of advancing on the city. "He is an admirable engineer," said Lincoln, "but he seems to have a special talent for a stationary engine." At that time, Lincoln didn't yet see in Ulysses Grant the leadership that he eventually employed to win the war, and McClellan appeared to be his only choice.

As Commander in Chief, Lincoln was in a fragile position. With only three months' military experience, and in the tiny Illinois militia at that, he found himself managing large-scale military operations for the first time in his life. Confederate President Jefferson Davis, on the other hand, had graduated from West Point and had served as Secretary of War for four years under President Pierce.

In addition, Lincoln lived under the constant threat that one of the four neutral border states—Maryland, Delaware, Kentucky, and Missouri—would secede and join the South over the issue of slavery, which all four allowed. If Maryland seceded, Washington would be left virtually surrounded by the enemy. And the military pressure on the President wasn't coming only from the Confederacy. England, the world's foremost superpower, threatened war against Lincoln because the Union's naval blockade of the South prevented delivery of cotton to Europe, hurting England's lucrative textile industry.

With advisers whom he couldn't trust, weak military leadership, and a horde of personal pressures at the White House, Lincoln was unsure where to turn or what to believe in. During his campaign, he had written, "I want every man to have the chance, and I believe a black man is entitled to it, in which he can better his condition." He spoke from experience. From simple and impoverished beginnings, Lincoln had made himself into an educated man, a successful lawyer, and an eloquent President. But once in office, Lincoln acted like a different man. When the Union General John Frémont ordered that all slaves in Missouri be emancipated, Lincoln, ignoring his personal beliefs and his campaign platform, wrote a letter revoking the order and relieving Frémont of his command. Hurt and outraged, the Northern black community demanded an explanation. "This letter of Abraham Lincoln," wrote the black journalist Robert Hamilton, "hurls back into the hell of slavery the thousands in Missouri rightfully set free by the proclamation of General Frémont." Furthermore, "it deprives the cause of the Union of its chiefest hold upon the heart of the public, and gives the rebels aid and comfort greater than they could have gained from any other earthly source."

Notwithstanding the criticisms, Lincoln simply could not risk alienating the border states while the Northern war effort sputtered. Though the North had plenty of soldiers and the industrial resources to ensure an easy victory, by June 1862 it looked like Lincoln would lose the war. During a series of conflicts known as the Seven Days' Battles, General McClellan led his regiment, the single largest in the Union army, to a humiliating defeat at the hands of the star Southern General Robert E. Lee. The defeat was demoralizing for the Union. "The feeling of despondency here is very great," wrote a New York diarist. "Things look disastrous," recorded another. South of the Mason-Dixon Line, the victory provoked sentiment that the war was already drawing to a close. As one Richmond civilian wrote, "The fatal blow has been dealt this 'grand army' of the North. General Lee has turned the tide."

The North was furious with Lincoln's leadership. Horace Greeley, an editor of the widely read *New York Tribune*, published an editorial criticizing Lincoln's direction and resolve. Greeley also called for Lincoln to make good on his promise to emancipate the nation's slaves. Lincoln wrote a response to Greeley, "My paramount object in this struggle is to save the Union, and is not either to save or destroy slavery. If I could save the Union without freeing any slaves I would do it, and if I could save it by freeing all the slaves I would do that.... I have here stated my purpose according to my view of official duty; and I intend no modification of my oft-expressed personal wish that all men everywhere could be free."

Already 30 pounds lighter since taking office, Lincoln desperately needed some relief. He found it in his passion for theater. The poet Walt Whitman called Lincoln "one of the best of the late commentators on Shakespeare," and the President often found consolation in the lines of the master. Particularly fond of *Hamlet*, he was excited to see Edwin Booth (one of the most famous actors of his day and brother of Lincoln's own assassin, John Wilkes Booth) perform in the play. Lincoln was also fond of performing Shakespeare himself in the solace of the telegraph office. "On one occasion," wrote a telegraph operator, "I was his only auditor and he recited several passages to me with as much interest apparently as if there had been a full house."

After the Seven Days' Battles, Lincoln made more practical use of his time at the telegraph office. He used it as a fortress, barricading himself inside. It was time to push General McClellan aside and wage the war on his own terms. Consulting only the telegraph operator Thomas Eckert, he devised a plan of battle. As Eckert recorded, "Upon his arrival early one morning in July, 1862, shortly after the Seven Day's Fight, he asked me for some paper, as he wanted to write something . . . . When ready to leave, he asked me to take charge of what he had written and not allow any one to see it." In his private sanctum, Lincoln worked several hours a day for days on end, writing slowly and methodically. "He did not write much at once. He would study between times and when he had made up his mind he would put down a line or two, and then sit quiet again."

Lincoln finished writing in the middle of July. Only a few days later, while traveling in a carriage with Secretaries Seward and Welles, he asked them what they would think if he freed the slaves. Both men were shocked. Naturally, Seward had a few critiques; after regaining his composure, he suggested that the act might seem desperate, coming so soon after the Union defeat in the Seven Days' Battles. He also mentioned that England, who wanted the war to end as soon as possible, might see the perfect opportunity to enter the conflict if it thought the Union was close to defeat. After several minutes passed, Welles still appeared too shaken to comment. Lincoln let the issue drop.

But the President mentioned his plan to free the slaves again at a Cabinet meeting nine days later, and this time he wasn't asking advice. Lincoln simply announced that his intentions were to eventually carry it out. The Cabinet was just as stunned by Lincoln's announcement as Seward and Welles had been. Edwin Stanton, the Secretary of War, spoke first, suggesting that the slaves should be freed immediately to boost morale of the troops. The other Cabinet members argued either in favor or against the plan based on their opinions of England's possible involvement in the war. Again Lincoln let the issue pass, but this time the course was set. The President had decided, much like the North Carolina slave William Gould, to wait for the right time to act.

Such a moment didn't present itself to Lincoln until the fall of that year. On September 17, the Union struck a huge blow against the Confederacy at the Battle of Antietam. It was the bloodiest battle of the war, but it culminated in General Lee's retreat and the first major Union victory since its defeat at the Seven Days' Battles. Finally. Lincoln immediately made plans to visit his troops at Antietam, knowing it would be a special opportunity. The victory at Antietam was sure to echo loudly in the Union press, but Lincoln wanted to push even harder against the morale of the South. Keeping his troops motivated to fight was the key to winning the war, and before Lincoln left Washington, he would send another, even more devastating jolt to the Rebels.

Lincoln walked into the Cabinet room on September 22 with a large stack of papers. The Cabinet members weren't sure what to expect, but they must have guessed that it was something very important. They quieted down and waited in expectation. Finally Lincoln spoke, or rather read aloud, "In the Faul of 1856, I showed my show in Utiky, a trooly grate sitty in the State of New York." The President was speaking in an uneducated, low-brow dialect. "The people gave me a cordual recepshun. The press was loud in her prases."

The Cabinet members were utterly flummoxed. But the President continued, "1 day as I was givin a descripshun of my

Beests and Snails in my usual flowry stile what was my skorn &
disgust to see a big burly feller walk up to the cage containin my
wax figgers of the Lord's Last Supper, and cease Judas Iscarrot by
the feet and drag him out on the ground. He then commenced fur
to pound him as hard as he cood.

"'What under the son are you abowt?' cried I." Lincoln was
giving a full-on performance and greatly enjoying himself.

"Sez he, 'What did you bring this pussylanermus cuss here
fur? & he hit the wax figger another tremenjis blow on the hed.'"

The Cabinet members looked at one another and back to
the President, who gave no indication of stopping anytime soon.
Lincoln continued to read, "Sez I, 'You egrejus ass, that air's a
wax figger—a representashun of the false 'Postle.'

"Sez he, 'That's all very well fur you to say; but I tell you,
old man, that Judas Iscarrot can't show hisself in Utiky with
impunerty by a darn site!' with which observashun he kaved in
Judassis hed. The young man belonged to 1 of the first famerlies
in Utiky. I sood him, and the joory brawt in a verdick of Arson
in the 3d degree."

The President was greatly amused—Cabinet members in
front of him were not. Lincoln had been reading "High-Handed
Outrage in Utiky" by one of his favorite humorists, Artemis
Ward. Secretary of War Stanton was incensed that the President
would read such a silly story in the midst of what was, for all
intents and purposes, a war council.

"Gentlemen," Lincoln chided them, "with the fearful strain
that is upon me night and day, if I did not laugh I should die, and
you need this medicine as much as I do." He paused. "Gentlemen,
I have, as you are aware, thought a great deal about the relation of

this war to slavery." The showman himself, Lincoln took a long pause. "I have, as you are aware, thought a great deal about the relation of this war to slavery."

With that, Lincoln officially announced his Emancipation Proclamation. Though it wasn't signed until January 1, the effect of the edict on the Union was immediate. The document proclaimed, "All persons held as slave within any State . . . in rebellion against the United States . . . as a fit and necessary war measure for suppressing said rebellion" would be "thenceforward and forever free." The black press that had criticized Lincoln's weak stance on slavery a year before was ecstatic. "We shout for joy that we live to record this righteous decree," wrote Frederick Douglass. "Oh! Lift up now your voices with joy and thanksgiving, for with freedom to the slave will come peace and safety to your country."

Though it would take two more years of brutal fighting to quell the rebellion, Lincoln had turned the tide in the Union's favor. The Emancipation Proclamation transformed the Union overnight from an oppressive regime withholding the right of sovereignty from the South into a moral army whose goal was the liberation of an oppressed people. It also made certain that England and its strongly abolitionist government would not enter the war in defense of the Confederacy. Lincoln had decisively set the course for a Northern victory and the preservation of the Union.

By only freeing slaves in the Confederacy, Lincoln avoided making a moral argument against slavery in favor of the harder-hitting sales pitch that it was a strategy of war. After all, every slave taken under the Union was a net gain of two: one for the Union's war effort and one taken from the Confederacy. Without making any statement about equality or civil rights, Lincoln was able to tack his goal of emancipation onto the larger, more pressing goal of ending the war—saving Union lives and saving the Union itself. He took a potentially dangerous and polarizing issue for the North and turned it into the perfect reason for the Union to unite in support of the war against the inhumane, slave-owning Confederates.

"I do the very best I know how—the very best I can," Lincoln wrote to a friend. "If the end brings me out all right, what's said against me won't amount to anything. If the end brings me out wrong, ten angels swearing I was right would make no difference." He might have quoted from his favorite play, *Hamlet*: "To thine own self be true." Lincoln indeed was brought out "all right" in the end. So were a great many others.

William Gould reached the *USS Cambridge* as an escaped slave the morning of Lincoln's proclamation. Gould presumed that he was now merely "contraband" property and that he might remain so for years to come. Though he had no way of yet knowing, by that afternoon, he would be free at last.

President Abraham Lincoln
The Emancipation Proclamation
January 1, 1863

By the President of the United States of America:

A Proclamation.

Whereas, on the twenty-second day of September, in the year of our Lord one thousand eight hundred and sixty-two, a proclamation was issued by the President of the United States, containing, among other things, the following, to wit:

That on the first day of January, in the year of our Lord one thousand eight hundred and sixty-three, all persons held as slaves within any State or designated part of a State, the people whereof shall then be in rebellion against the United States, shall be then, thenceforward, and forever free; and the Executive Government of the United States, including the military and naval authority thereof, will recognize and maintain the freedom of such persons, and will do no act or acts to repress such persons, or any of them, in any efforts they may make for their actual freedom.

That the Executive will, on the first day of January aforesaid, by proclamation, designate the States and parts of States, if any, in which the people thereof, respectively, shall then be in rebellion against the United States; and the fact that any State, or the people thereof, shall on that day be, in good faith, represented in the Congress of the United States by members chosen thereto at elections wherein a majority of the qualified voters of such State shall have participated, shall, in the absence of strong countervailing testimony, be deemed conclusive evidence that such State, and the people thereof, are not then in rebellion against the United States.

Now, therefore I, Abraham Lincoln, President of the United States, by virtue of the power in me vested as Commander-in-Chief, of the Army and Navy of the United States in time of actual armed rebellion against the authority and government of the United States, and as a fit and necessary war measure for suppressing said rebellion, do, on this first day of January, in the year of our Lord one thousand eight hundred and sixty-three, and in accordance with my purpose so to do publicly proclaimed for the full period of one hundred days, from the day first above mentioned, order and designate as the States and parts of States wherein the people thereof respectively, are this day in rebellion against the United States, the following, to wit:

Arkansas, Texas, Louisiana, (except the Parishes of St. Bernard, Plaquemines, Jefferson, St. John, St. Charles, St. James Ascension, Assumption, Terrebonne, Lafourche, St. Mary, St. Martin, and Orleans, including the City of New Orleans) Mississippi, Alabama, Florida, Georgia, South Carolina, North Carolina, and Virginia, (except the forty-eight counties designated as West Virginia, and also the counties of Berkley, Accomac, Northampton, Elizabeth City, York, Princess Ann, and Norfolk, including the cities of Norfolk and Portsmouth[)], and which excepted parts, are for the present, left precisely as if this proclamation were not issued.

And by virtue of the power, and for the purpose aforesaid, I do order and declare that all persons held as slaves within said designated States, and parts of States, are, and henceforward shall be free; and that the Executive Government of the United States, including the military and naval authorities thereof, will recognize and maintain the freedom of said persons.

And I hereby enjoin upon the people so declared to be free to abstain from all violence, unless in necessary self-defence; and I recommend to them that, in all cases when allowed, they labor faithfully for reasonable wages.

And I further declare and make known, that such persons of suitable condition, will be received into the armed service of the United States to garrison forts, positions, stations, and other places, and to man vessels of all sorts in said service.

And upon this act, sincerely believed to be an act of justice, warranted by the Constitution, upon military necessity, I invoke the considerate judgment of mankind, and the gracious favor of Almighty God.

In witness whereof, I have hereunto set my hand and caused the seal of the United States to be affixed.

Done at the City of Washington, this first day of January,

in the year of our Lord one thousand eight hundred and sixty
three, and of the Independence of the United States of America
the eighty-seventh.

By the President: ABRAHAM LINCOLN
WILLIAM H. SEWARD, Secretary of State.

GROVER CLEVELAND

The Granger Collection, New York.

CHAPTER 3

CONSTITUTION BE DAMNED

Grover Cleveland and the Pullman Strike

Grover Cleveland once killed a man. Two, actually. Of course, they'd already been sentenced to death. As sheriff of Erie County, New York, to avoid wasting government money on hiring a hangman, he simply hanged the men himself.

During a harrowing week in July two decades later, he saved more than enough lives to compensate. What few Americans today realize is that in 1896, from July 4 to July 8, Chicago, Illinois, became a war zone. Mobs of angry citizens destroyed property, blew up bridges, derailed trains, and lit the grounds of the World's Fair ablaze. *The Washington Post* wrote that the "preservation of civilization" was at stake.

Some at the time put the blame for the riots on the financial panic engulfing the world. With the country in the midst of a depression, many were unemployed and angry, and looking for a reason to revolt. 12 million visitors came to Chicago that year to see the World's Fair exhibitions, crowding the streets with potential dissidents. But the real spark was much more ordinary. It wasn't millions of the frustrated unemployed; rather it was a few thousand of the gainfully employed in a tiny town 15 miles from downtown Chicago. The town was called Pullman, and it got its name from the railroad cars its residents built.

In the 19th century, long before there were stretch limousines and first-class flights, a Pullman sleeper car was the ultimate luxury in travel. Pullman cars were anything but ordinary. Cherry wood seats, richly upholstered in red plush fabric, transformed into comfortable beds at night. Porters in each car turned down the sheets, helped with luggage, shined shoes, pressed clothes, and entertained children. Pipes brought steam from the locomotive to heat the cars in the winter, and the earliest forms of air-conditioning cooled the passengers when the weather turned warm. Gaslights illuminated ceiling chandeliers and silk-shaded table lamps. Passengers relaxed in the parlor car, enjoying a selection of contemporary books and magazines, and ate gourmet meals in the dining car, served on china worthy of the country's most expensive restaurants, and drank fine wine and liquor in extravagant crystal glassware. While the men and women who lived alongside the railroad tracks still washed in tin basins, Pullman passengers enjoyed hot showers in spacious bathrooms with marble countertops, as the trains rolled along at 35 miles per hour.

Pullman cars were used for President Lincoln's funeral procession. General Ulysses Grant rode in one on his return home from the Civil War. Each costing upwards of $150,000 in today's money to build, Pullman sleeper cars catered to some of the richest men and women in America.

And in Pullman, Illinois, the most expensive transportation for America's richest was being built by some of the country's poorest. George Pullman, a Chicago businessman who made his fortune moving buildings when the city installed a new sewer system, had bought 4,000 acres of land in the nearby suburbs to set up a company town. He wanted to replace the overcrowded and unsanitary working-class communities with a clean, safe, and "culturally enriching" environment that would improve productivity and inspire loyalty. It would be a place, Pullman said, where "many of the evils to which [laborers] are ordinarily exposed [were] made impossible." He hoped to lower his costs, increase profits, and introduce the world to a whole new way of running a business.

Workers in the town of Pullman lived on well-paved streets in identical brick homes, with perfectly manicured lawns and state-of-the-art amenities like indoor plumbing, gas, and garbage removal. Pullman ran his town as a model of financial efficiency. Not wanting to waste anything, the sewage was processed and used as fertilizer to grow crops that were then sold back to the residents. Excess carpentry shavings doubled as fuel for the boilers; runoff water was fed into the local lake. Visitors, who came from around the country to marvel at Pullman's model community, stayed in the Hotel Florence, named for Pullman's daughter.

But things in Pullman were not as idyllic as they appeared. George Pullman exercised tremendous control over the lives of his residents—he chose which stores could open, which books the library owned, and which performances could be staged in the theater. He built just one church, with one type of worship, preaching a nondenominational Puritan ethic, and he virtually prohibited alcohol (the Hotel Florence was the one exception, and it would serve only visitors, not residents). He hired "spotters" to watch over the town and report residents who behaved "undesirably." In addition, Pullman, in order to turn a profit, set prices in the town higher than they were in the surrounding communities, and he marked up the cost of utilities. Nevertheless, by 1893, 12,000 workers and family members were living in

Pullman. Many did so not entirely by choice—workers who did not live in the town found themselves the first to be cut from the workforce in hard times.

And hard times fell in 1893. Across the country, unemployment spread. Nationally, the rate approached 15 percent—and was higher in many states. In 1896, unemployment stood at 25 percent in Pennsylvania, 33 percent in New York, and 43 percent in Michigan. Banks foreclosed on farms across the West. In Kansas alone, between 1887 and 1893, 11,000 farms went under. The railroad industry was hit particularly hard. As the economy sputtered, railway companies, whose trains had previously carried the nation's goods from coast to coast, lost billions of dollars.

Demand for the luxury Pullman cars fell precipitously, as fewer and fewer could afford to pay the fares. George Pullman was forced to accept contracts at a loss, hoping business would turn around; when it didn't, layoffs began, and Pullman slashed wages.

But those who lived in Pullman and continued to hold their jobs found that while Pullman the boss had cut their salaries, Pullman the landlord did not adjust their rents accordingly. Since the company subtracted rent *before* paying out wages, employees found their checks growing smaller and smaller. Even worse, while salaries for the low-level workers fell, the managerial class found its pay unchanged, and Pullman continued to pay dividends to stockholders.

Jennie Curtis had been working in the plant for five years as a stitcher when she found her wages cut 35 percent, from 17 cents an hour to just 11, and she owed Pullman $15 in back rent. Another worker reported, "One man has a pay check in his possession of two cents after paying rent. He has never cashed it, preferring to

keep it as a memento. He has framed it." A third worker explained,
"We are born in a Pullman house, fed from the Pullman shops, taught in the Pullman school, catechized in the Pullman Church, and when we die we shall go to the Pullman Hell."

Angry and upset, a group of employees went to George Pullman himself to voice their concerns, begging him to lower the rents. They were assured that they would not be persecuted for speaking up. But the meeting brought no progress, and a few of those who voiced grievances found their jobs terminated, despite Pullman's promises. Others, afraid that their jobs would go next, turned to Eugene Debs and the newly formed American Railway Union for help. Debs was a former Indiana state legislator who believed in the power of labor unions to fight against unfair working conditions.

On May 11, 1894, 4,000 employees of the Pullman Palace Car Company—90 percent of the workforce—walked out on their jobs. They hoped their strike would gain the attention of the man in the White House. President Grover Cleveland, a proven friend of labor, would surely be their savior.

Grover Cleveland knew what it meant to work for a living. He grew up in Fayetteville, New York, a small farming community by the Erie Canal, where his father, a Presbyterian minister, raised nine children on a modest salary. The family's efforts to make ends meet instilled young Grover with the value of thrift, while his father's uncompromising character infused him with a strong sense of integrity.

Cleveland got his start in politics after a career in law. Despite no formal education beyond high school, he had passed the bar and had become a lawyer after studying under attorneys at a firm in Buffalo. His work as a lawyer pushed him into local politics, and he found himself a rising star. He served as Democratic supervisor of his local ward, then assistant district attorney of Erie County, and in 1870 he became the county's sheriff. After his three-year term ended, Cleveland opened a private law practice, claming he was done with politics for good.

But in 1881, desperate for a mayoral candidate with some local name recognition, Buffalo's Democratic leaders approached Cleveland. He won the election and, as mayor, continued to build on the scrupulous reputation he had earned as sheriff—contracts, for a change, went to the lowest bidder, not to the most politically powerful. The party leaders noticed his success, and just six months into office, they returned—now they wanted Cleveland to run for governor.

Agreeable to both of New York's warring political machines, Cleveland found himself elected as a compromise candidate. He called himself "ugly honest" and told a friend, "I have only one thing to do, and that is to do right, and that is easy." He went to work immediately, cutting projects he deemed inessential and erasing decades of corruption. The "veto mayor" of Buffalo quickly became New York's "veto governor," acting on principle regardless of political considerations.

For example, the state legislature passed a law forcing a New York City rail line to cut its fare from a dime to a nickel. Cutting fares was the ultimate in no-lose legislation: everyone wins but the owner of the rail line. But Cleveland consulted the contract that the city had signed with the transit company and found that the company was within its rights to charge a dime. So Cleveland vetoed the law, certain the veto would destroy his popularity. Instead, he found himself praised for his principles.

Meanwhile, as governor he proved over and over again that pragmatism could defeat partisanship. He reached across party lines to get things done, working, for instance, with a young Republican legislator named Theodore Roosevelt on more than one occasion.

Despite the powerful New York political machines working against him (because as governor he had undermined their influence), Cleveland found himself the Democratic nominee in the 1884 presidential election. His campaign slogan illustrated his core philosophy: "Public office is a public trust."

Once on the national stage, Cleveland found himself forced to defend his character. First came a paternity charge. Instead of refuting the accusation, he admitted the affair, emphasizing that he had seen his obligations through and provided for the child he had fathered. As if that were not enough, it was revealed that Cleveland had hired a substitute to fulfill his military obligation during the Civil War. He explained that he had done so only after his two brothers had agreed to enlist and had chosen him to stay at home to support their widowed mother.

Despite the scandals, Cleveland eked out a victory. He arrived at the White House as something of a reluctant President. "I look upon the four years next to come as a dreadful self-inflicted penance for the good of my country," Cleveland wrote to a friend. "I can see no pleasure in it and no satisfaction, only a hope that I may be of service to my people."

As the first Democratic President since before the Civil War, Cleveland took steps toward reconciliation and reform. He appointed a Confederate leader as Secretary of the Interior and later Supreme Court Justice. He chose his political appointees based on ability and effectiveness, not political party. He'd had practice turning away favor-seekers as governor—those petitioning him would be received with a confused look and the line, "I'm afraid I'm not certain what you mean."

Most critically for the workers in Pullman, Cleveland was the first President to address labor issues seriously: he pushed Congress to create a federal arbitration process; he argued against abuse of labor in his 1886 State of the Union address; and he signed legislation legalizing labor unions. "The capitalist can protect himself, but the wage earner is practically defenseless," said Cleveland.

Cleveland lost reelection to the White House to Benjamin Harrison in 1888, but while there, he had gained a wife. He wed Frances Folsom, the daughter of one of his deceased friends and a girl he had known almost since her birth. He was 49 and she was 21, fresh from college, and the press loved her. The wedding was the first to be conducted in the White House; the wedding band was led by John Philip Sousa himself. The couple barely had any peace on their honeymoon, with the reporters trailing right behind.

Upon leaving the White House after the first term, Frances told the butler to keep the furniture clean. She predicted they would return four years later.

Frances's prediction came true. Benjamin Harrison spent his time in the White House squandering the surplus of government cash Cleveland had generated, and four years after turning him away, the public brought Grover Cleveland back for a second tour of duty. He remains the only man to serve two non-consecutive terms as President. But when he returned to the White House in 1893, the financial state of the nation was troubling. When the economic panic of 1893 hit, the United States plunged toward crisis. Fortunately, Cleveland's progressive and prescient support of labor unions would protect countless workers and save innumerable jobs.

In his first term, Cleveland had successfully pushed for legislation to legalize labor unions. By this time, thousands of rail workers had united to form the American Railway Union (ARU). When the ARU prevailed in a strike against the Great Northern Railway, word spread and membership surged. Because 20 miles of tracks ran across Pullman property, employees there were eligible to join, and they did. When the Pullman employees struck, the first place they turned was the ARU and its leader, Eugene Debs.

Pullman's workers presented their plight to Debs at the next union meeting. "I believe a rich plunderer like Pullman is a greater felon than a poor thief," responded Debs. The ARU immediately contributed $2,000 to the strike fund. They also authorized a support strike, with a plan to stop attaching Pullman cars to their trains, and vowed not to operate any trains with Pullman cars. The discontent of the 4,000 Pullman employees exploded onto the national stage.

George Pullman's response to the strike was to close down shop and lock out all of the workers. Living in the town of Pullman, where else could they possibly go for work? He presumed the striking workers would quickly relent. While citizens groups, mayors, and city councils urged Pullman to arbitrate, he refused to budge. He found support in a nationwide union of rail-line managers called the General Managers Association (GMA). When the ARU employees refused to handle the Pullman cars, the GMA would fire them.

Quickly, the same series of events spread from coast to coast: a switchman would refuse to hitch a Pullman car, he would be fired, and the rest of the crew would walk out in support. On the first day of the ARU support strike, 5,000 employees walked out. The next day, the number rose to 40,000; the day after, 100,000. The strike was about to spin out of control. The Knights of Labor offered to join the ARU by calling a general strike of all workers in the city of Chicago. Debs appreciated the support but, for the time being, declined the offer. In the meantime, George Pullman, seemingly oblivious to the circumstances, headed off to vacation on the Jersey shore.

Debs' reluctance to accept the Knights' offer stemmed from concerns over the country's economic climate. Given the massive unemployment rates, sympathy for striking workers would be low. In addition, Debs feared that the contentious nature of the workers-versus-managers relationship might lead to violence; he did not want to risk pushing it over the edge. Debs knew that any further escalation of the strike might encourage government interference. The government, Debs realized, would have an excuse to move in and protest if the strike disrupted the U.S. mail. As long as the mail stayed safe and the strike did not lead to violence, Debs thought it could be maintained until Pullman capitulated.

But Debs' hopes soon faded. The built-up discontent led to a minor outbreak of rioting near Chicago. Illinois Governor John Altgeld dispatched state militia, and quelled the disorder—for the moment. However, Altgeld made a decision not to call on the federal government for help, knowing that once the government showed up, the strike would be put down—Altgeld didn't want that. His sympathies lay with the workers.

Back in Washington, President Cleveland and Attorney General Richard Olney became concerned. One of their worries stemmed from the recent World's Fair in Chicago, which had brought 12 million people to the city, many without jobs who had nowhere to go. Now Cleveland worried they might turn into a rampaging mob.

Still occupied with the tariff legislation that had lost him the previous election, Cleveland delegated much of the authority to deal with the strike to Olney. A meticulous chief executive, Cleveland read every bill that passed his desk and spent much of his days engaged in the nitty-gritty of legislation, researching and devising provisions himself. Because Cleveland cared so much about the tariff issue—he wanted to give as much money back to the people as he could, especially during tough economic times—Olney served as Cleveland's filter for information and his point man. However, Olney had his own agenda.

Before becoming Attorney General, Olney had generated a small fortune serving the railways as a lawyer, specializing in mergers and acquisitions, and not being particularly sympathetic to labor. Olney had in fact agreed to become Attorney General only after being assured that he could continue to have connections with his firm and several railway companies. In office, he continued to receive retainers from several rail lines. As the labor strife got worse, Pullman's friends at the GMA asked Olney to appoint former railroad counsel Edwin Walker as the Special Federal Attorney for the strike. Knowing where Walker's sympathies lay, Olney made the appointment in less than two hours.

For Cleveland's part, his past priorities had demonstrated a sympathy for the workers—he hated Pullman and his fellow robber barons. But Cleveland was concerned that the growing mob of striking workers would lead to something terrible. With the Civil War only 30 years in the past, it seemed all too possible that the country could again split in two, only this time along class lines. Revolutions had been triggered over less. Cleveland couldn't risk the situation further deteriorating without doing something to stop it. Despite his support of the workers, Cleveland knew the best thing for the country was to contain the violence sooner rather than later. He wanted to find a way to end the conflict, but legally, and with as few casualties as possible.

Like Debs, Cleveland saw the linchpin to government involvement as the interference with the delivery of the U.S. mail. "If it takes every dollar in the Treasury and every soldier in the United States Army to deliver a postal card in Chicago," Cleveland said, "that postal card shall be delivered."

On July 1, 1894, the dam started to buckle. Two thousand people blocked the tracks at Blue Island, just outside Chicago, and stopped several trains. The U.S. Marshal on the scene wired Olney to ask for help. Olney couldn't send in federal troops quite yet, but he started to plan for it. He had Federal Attorney Walker draft an injunction against any activities that encouraged the disruption of the mail—the next time there was violence, reinforcements would arrive. Olney hoped the mere threat of federal involvement would be enough to stop the disorder.

Within hours, Walker's injunction was granted. The next evening a Deputy Marshal read it aloud at the site of the previous day's violence. The crowd responded angrily. Between 2,000 and 3,000 people rioted, rocking a U.S. mail train back and forth until it rolled off the tracks and plunged into a ditch. They then proceeded to light the railcar on fire and rampage through the train yard. Walker wired Olney: "It is the opinion of all that the orders of the court cannot be enforced except by the aid of the Regular Army."

As the situation spiraled out of control, President Cleveland decided he had to step in himself to monitor the predicament. He pored over telegrams from the marshals on the scene. Advisers showed him newspapers depicting mail trains on fire and rioting mobs of enraged workers. Cleveland's big decision now was whether or not to send in the Army. The choice seemed straightforward—except that under the Constitution, the President does not have the authority to dispatch troops to a state without the request or consent of the state's governor. In this case, Governor Altgeld pointedly did *not* want federal help. To make his position doubly clear, Altgeld sent a fiery telegraph to the President. "The State of Illinois is not only able to take care of itself," he wrote, "but it stands ready to furnish the Federal Government any assistance it may need elsewhere."

At 3:00 that afternoon, Cleveland received a telegram directly from Walker that read, "No force less than the regular troops of the United States can procure the passage of the mail trains or enforce the orders of the court." Cleveland, firmly believing that the fate of the country was at stake, immediately authorized the War Department to dispatch troops, Governor Altgeld and the Constitution be damned.

This was the first time since the Civil War that the federal government had ordered soldiers into action against American citizens. To Cleveland it came down to the preservation of order, no matter the legal ramifications. The sheriff in him won out over the lawyer.

Eugene Debs reacted with strong words to the news that federal troops would soon be arriving: "The first shots fired by regular soldiers at the mobs here will be a signal for civil war. I believe this as firmly as I believe in the ultimate success of our course. Bloodshed will follow, and ninety percent of the people of the United States will be arrayed against the other ten percent. And I would not care to be arrayed against the laboring people in the contest, or find myself out of the ranks of labor when the struggle ended."

Cleveland also feared the worst, and responded accordingly. Federal troops arrived to quell the riots, ironically, on July 4. While patriotic citizens set off fireworks, in the city of Chicago they set fires. Thousands of angry protestors lay waste to the city. At the Chicago rail yards more freight trains were flipped over and cars set ablaze. A huge fire that night destroyed the expositions on the grounds of the World's Fair. Chicago degenerated into lawlessness and chaos.

It continued for four days. On July 6, a rail deputy shot two men, inciting the largest riot of all—6,000 rail workers destroyed over $340,000 worth of railroad property on a single day as over 700 railroad cars were torched. The next day, a mob attacked the state militia. The soldiers fired back, killing 4 rioters and wounding 20 others. Reinforcements for the federal troops were called up from surrounding states. No American city had ever experienced such anarchy in peacetime.

On July 10, Debs was arrested for disrupting the mail. Without Debs at the helm coordinating the efforts of the strikers and providing encouragement, the situation stabilized. Workers feared they too would be arrested, and the violence subsided.

By July 20, the railroads were running as before and President Cleveland called off the federal troops.

But by the time the riots ended, rail service throughout the country had been disrupted, and the effects had been felt far beyond the epicenter in Chicago. In Indiana, union members as well as unaffiliated men attacked scabs, derailed trains, and cut telegraph lines. Bridges were blown up in the Oklahoma Territory; men in Utah fired on rail yards; in New Mexico, trains were derailed. Across the country, over 16,000 federal soldiers were eventually dispatched to put down the rioting. By the time it was over, 40 men had died in seven states, at least 11 in Chicago itself.

Although his heart was still with the laborers, Cleveland believed he had made the right choice for the country. But he hated what he had done and fully expected to be vilified by the people. To his surprise, the public overwhelmingly supported his actions. A rhyme circulated in the country's newspapers. The President read it with relief and satisfaction:

> *The railroad strike played merry hob;*
> *The land was set aflame*
> *Could Grover order out the troops*
> *To block the striker's game?*
> *One Altgeld yelled excitedly*
> *"Such tactics I forbid;*
> *You can't trot out these soldiers" yet*
> *That's just what Grover did.*
> *In after years when people talk*
> *Of present stirring times,*
> *And of the action needful to*
> *Sit down on public crimes,*

They'll all of them acknowledge then
(The fact cannot be hid)
That whatever was the best to do
Is just what Grover did.

For his part, Debs was sentenced to six months in prison; the other leaders of the ARU were sentenced to three. Debs' conviction was appealed, and the U.S. Supreme Court upheld the judgment that Cleveland's actions were lawful to protect the mail.

In the aftermath of the Pullman strike, Debs' politics would later grow more radical. He would run for President five times on the American Socialist Party ticket. Years later, he would say that the Pullman incident "baptized [him] in Socialism in the roar of the conflict."

Though contrary to the U.S. Constitution, Cleveland's decision to send in the troops held up in court too, much to Governor Altgeld's dismay. (Altgeld, whose stand against the government action made him few friends among the politically powerful, lost his reelection campaign for governor in 1896.)

After the strike, most of Pullman's workers returned to their jobs on the condition they never engage in union activity again—but George Pullman became a reviled figure throughout the country. He died just three years later, in 1897. Paranoid that his body would be desecrated after his death, Pullman left detailed instructions that atop his burial site should be placed layers of rail ties, concrete, and asphalt to protect his remains.

The following year, the Illinois Supreme Court issued a ruling requiring the Pullman Palace Car Company to sell its nonindustrial property—virtually the entire town of Pullman. The City of Chicago annexed the town and took over control of the parks, streets, and the school system. Pullman, with its well-paved streets and identical brick homes, is now just another Chicago neighborhood.

President Cleveland, despite the public's support of his decision to send in troops, felt he had betrayed the workers. He tried to make amends—later in 1894 he instituted the annual celebration of Labor Day.

In 1896, tired of fighting battles, he retired to Princeton, New Jersey, where he spent his retirement lecturing to the public, advising Princeton University President Woodrow Wilson, and watching his legacy grow as a respected elder statesman.

On his death in 1908, newspapers domestic and abroad lauded Cleveland's integrity. The *London Morning Post* wrote that "Cleveland was one of the great men of his time. . . . As President he did not lift a finger for the Democratic Party, but merely served the United States. He was the strongest man that has lived in the White House since the death of Washington." They also reported on Cleveland's dying words: "I have tried so hard to do right."

President Grover Cleveland

Excerpt from his book, The Government in the Chicago Strike of 1894

A painful emergency is created when public duty forces the necessity of placing trained soldiers face to face with riotous opposition to the general Government, and all acute and determined defiance to law and order. This course, once entered upon, admits of no backward step; and an appreciation of the consequences that may ensue cannot fail to oppress those responsible for its adoption with sadly disturbing reflections. Nevertheless, it was perfectly plain that, whatever the outcome might be, the situation positively demanded such precaution and preparation as would insure readiness and promptness in case the presence of a military force should finally be found necessary. . . .

I hope I have been successful thus far in my effort satisfactorily to exhibit the extensive reach and perilous tendency to the convulsion under consideration, the careful promptness which characterized the interference of the Government, the constant desire of the national administration to avoid extreme measures, the scrupulous limitation of its interference to purposes which were clearly within its constitutional competency and duty, and the gratifying and important results of its conservative but stern activity.

I must not fail to mention here as part of the history of this perplexing affair, a contribution made by the governor of Illinois to its annoyances. This official not only refused to regard the riotous disturbances within the borders of his State as a sufficient cause for an application to the Federal Government for its protection "against domestic violence" under the mandate of the Constitution, but he actually protested against the presence of Federal troops sent into the State upon the general Government's own initiative and for the purpose of defending itself in the exercise of its well-defined legitimate functions.

EXECUTIVE ACTION

ANDREW JACKSON

U.S. Senate Collection

CHAPTER 4

BREAKING THE BANK

·

Andrew Jackson and the Second National Bank

On Friday, May 30, 1806, as the sun peeked over the trees at a wooded clearing along the Red River in Harrison Mills, Kentucky, two men arrived. They stood 24 feet apart and readied their matching .70-caliber pistols. For them, this was the culmination of a day and a night of travel from Tennessee, where dueling was illegal. One of the men, Charles Dickinson, 27 years old, had already killed 26 people in duels. Dickinson spent the ride to Kentucky shooting at cards, apples, and any other target he could find. Back in Nashville, he'd been eager to wager that he would kill his opponent on the first shot. That opponent, now standing just across the field, gun in hand, was tall and slender and experienced in the art of dueling but no marksman. He had once fired at an Indian rushing toward him, missed repeatedly, and instead ended up simply hitting him on the head with his gun.

General John Overton "called the shot" and Dickinson raised his pistol. Dickinson fired, aiming for the large brass coat button over his opponent's heart. Dickinson saw a puff of dust fly from the man's clothes and could see him clutching at his chest—but the man remained standing. "My God! Have I missed him?" asked Dickinson. His opponent raised his gun and slowly and deliberately squeezed the trigger. No explosion. The pistol stopped half-cock. According to the rules of the duel, not a shot. The man raised his gun again, took extra careful aim, and fired. Dickinson, receiving a wound that tore through his middle, fell to the ground.

Dickinson's doctor attended to the injury in a vain effort to save him. He would be dead by late that evening. Meanwhile, his opponent noticed that his own left boot was filling with blood, and his brass overcoat button was gone. Dickinson's bullet hadn't missed at all—it shattered two ribs and landed just inches from the man's heart. The loose fit of the overcoat had saved him. Or, perhaps, the rumor was true that the man had spent the previous evening removing the buttons from his coat and re-sewing them three inches lower so that a bullet aimed for the heart (the upper brass button) would strike only a rib.

"I don't see how you stayed on your feet after that wound," the doctor said.

"I would have stood up long enough to kill him if he had put a bullet in my brain," answered the duel's victor.

Two decades later, that bullet, still inside the man's chest, made it to the White House, along with so many others that it was said Andrew Jackson rattled like a bag of marbles. Jackson suffered abdominal pain all his life from bullets he had taken fighting 103 duels before becoming President. As it turned out, Dickinson's was the only duel in which Jackson killed his adversary. Ironically, most parties expected Jackson to be killed that day. Only no duelist had ever felled "Old Hickory."

Duels in the early years of America were often expedient ways to resolve political fights and get rid of unwanted opponents (recall Aaron Burr and Alexander Hamilton). The Dickinson duel had been set up to do just that. Jackson's opponents convinced Dickinson (at that time the single most famous duelist in the country) to insult Jackson's wife to his face, knowing that Jackson would then challenge him to a duel. Jackson's opponents assumed that Dickinson would dispose of this former Senator and future President without much trouble.

The Dickinson duel—like most of Jackson's—was fought to defend the honor of his wife, Rachel. She and Andrew met in a Nashville boardinghouse while Rachel was unhappily married to another man. Her first husband had left her to get a divorce. Andrew and Rachel fell madly in love and quickly married. Two years later, Rachel's first husband returned—having never actually gotten the divorce—and discovered his wife "living in sin." The divorce finally went through and the Jacksons remarried. But for the rest of her life, the "adulteress" label followed Rachel Jackson. Prepared to defend his wife's honor at every turn, Andrew kept 37 pistols in duel-ready condition.

As Jackson had expected, Rachel's past became an issue in his successful campaign for the presidency in 1828. When he discovered a pamphlet circulating about Rachel's adultery and bigamy from decades before, Rachel became hysterical. Mere months after his election victory, but before his inauguration, Rachel suffered a heart attack and died. Jackson was inconsolable; he had once written a note to her: "[to] spend my time with you alone in sweet retirement [is] my only ambition and ultimate wish." After defending her honor throughout their marriage, as President he channeled that energy into defending the honor of his country.

During his presidency, Jackson's greatest challenge was another sort of duel. This opponent wore different clothes and wielded a different weapon than Charles Dickinson and, to Jackson's mind, posed a much greater danger. Nicholas Biddle, the wealthy president of the Second Bank of the United States, held in his hands the power to control the financial future of virtually every American—to let them prosper, or to make them fall. All it took to kill Dickinson was a pistol and a steady hand; to kill Biddle's bank, Jackson would need an entirely different set of weapons and skills.

It is quite extraordinary to consider today how much power the Second Bank of the United States held in Jackson's time. The bank was an enormously wealthy institution. In 1830, it controlled $13 million in notes (paper currency)—accounting for 20 percent of the total money in circulation—and its capital (paper currency plus outstanding loans) of $35 million was more than double the annual expenditures of the U.S. government. In comparison, no bank today is even one-fifth as wealthy.

Although the bank handled much of the country's money, it was privately owned, and through a sweetheart deal with the government, the bank's wealthy shareholders earned unusually high profits of 8 to 10 percent virtually risk-free. These shareholders were profiting from the deposits of ordinary Americans. Even more disturbing, many of the bank's shareholders were not Americans themselves. More than a quarter of the bank's stock (over $7 million) belonged to 383 well-connected foreigners (the rest belonged to fewer than a thousand rich Americans). These foreigners effectively had the power to control the nation's money supply. In the event of a war, this could prove especially disastrous—the enemy could potentially cripple the American economy through its power and influence over its monies and currency. To the millions of Americans who did not own stock in the bank—including President Jackson himself—this seemed at best obscene, and at worst dangerous for America. Because the bank was privately held, the government had effectively ceded control of the money supply to a select group of wealthy aristocrats, many of whom were not even American citizens.

At the head of the bank was perhaps the wealthiest of them all: Nicholas Biddle, from a family that could best be described as the Rockefellers of its time. Growing up, Nicholas was a young prodigy. He enrolled at the University of Pennsylvania at the age of 10 and eventually transferred and earned a degree at Princeton at 15.

Biddle's life proceeded typically for a bright young man from one of the nation's richest families. He spent most of his teenage years traveling around Europe, becoming an authority on Greek culture, learning about international finance in Paris, and spending time with the U.S. Minister to Great Britain (and future President), James Monroe, in London. When Biddle returned to Philadelphia, President Jefferson asked if he would prepare the journals of Lewis and Clark (after their Western expedition) for publication. Biddle turned down the assignment (imagine saying "no" to President Jefferson) due to his election to the Pennsylvania House of Representatives.

Needing a place to live while serving his state, Biddle found one of the few remaining plots of forest bordering the Delaware River and bought it at an astronomical price. He built an enormous manor house on 100 acres, including stables filled with the country's finest racehorses. Biddle enlisted an architect to construct glorious stone walls on the property to create giant hothouses in which he could grow the country's finest table grapes. The grapes actually became quite popular, and Biddle's descendants profited from them through the 1870s.

After Biddle's time in the Pennsylvania House, the bank's board of 20 directors appointed him to run the Second Bank, after mismanagement by previous bank presidents. Biddle ran it quite well. In the wake of a financial panic in 1819, he helped the country avoid financial chaos, and in the years that followed he worked to create the most stable currency the nation had ever had. This currency allowed citizens to have access to money relatively easily—the reason the bank had been chartered in the first place. Although the potential for corruption was obvious due to the sheer size of the bank, many people overlooked it because the bank served a crucial purpose—it made money available to those who needed it, addressing one of the country's biggest problems.

Today, it is hard to imagine living in a world without a standard currency—without the ability to rely on a store accepting your dollars, or even the ability of the store to exchange the money from customers for new merchandise to sell the next day. At its founding, America built its economy on metallic currency—gold and silver. As industrialization took hold in the early 1800s, the economy expanded prodigiously to a point where the need for currency outgrew the gold and silver supply. Paper money became an obvious substitute. But without a national paper currency, anyone could issue paper money. As long as you could find somebody who trusted the issuer—a large bank, a small bank, or the man down the street—to redeem the note for its value in gold or silver, it worked. The problem? Even among banks, it was hard to know whom to trust. In 1828, for example, the 17 banks in Mississippi circulated notes with a face value of $6 million based on metal worth just $303,000. The banks simply hoped that by the time the notes were brought for redemption, new deposits would have increased their supply sufficiently. If not, those who held the bills would find them worth, literally, no more than the paper they were printed on.

With thousands of different types of bills, issued by hundreds of banks (or sometimes by no bank at all), guidebooks emerged with detailed descriptions of genuine bank notes and lists of common forgeries and counterfeits. One book carried 5,400 descriptions of unique notes in great detail: "mechanic and sailor standing, two females seated, harbor and mountains in distance." Counterfeiters developed tricks to stay one step ahead—some would chemically erase the name of a defunct bank from a set of bills and replace it with the name of a solvent bank; others would create generic notes meant to closely resemble genuine ones; yet others would steal the printing plates from a legitimate bank and simply print notes of their own.

The act of redeeming even a legitimate note issued by a bank could be difficult—if you couldn't find the bank. Some banks would issue money and then literally disappear into the woods so people couldn't find them, especially in the West, where there was vast land in which to hide. These were called "wildcat banks" because they would have to be hunted down in the trees among the wildcats.

Inspectors charged with ensuring that a particular bank could stand behind its notes would find barrels of coins that were actually kegs of glass or broken nails with just a thin layer of coins on top. These barrels would sometimes be secretly taken from bank to bank to repeatedly pose as "money" to fool the inspectors. Given the rampant cheating, banks would refuse to accept currency printed by any institution they were unfamiliar with, creating confusion, uncertainty, and tremendous anxiety regarding the money supply.

The public was justifiably convinced that banking existed only to swindle people—with gold and silver, despite their scarcity, this had never been a problem. This was the result, argued a growing number of "hard money" advocates, when banks assigned monetary value to something that didn't have any intrinsic worth.

Despite the difficulties associated with paper money, the truth remained that there just wasn't enough silver and gold in the system. Given a choice between risky money and no money at all, most people preferred the former.

Andrew Jackson was not "most people." Jackson grew up in radically different circumstances from the wealthy Biddle. The first President to grow up in a log cabin (as opposed to an estate), Jackson left school at the age of 13 to fight with the South Carolina militia in the Revolutionary War. Throughout his public life, many considered him an unsophisticated man. In some ways this held true. "[I]t's a damn poor mind that can only think of one way to spell a word" is one of Jackson's more rustic points. However, before being elected President, Jackson had served as a lawyer, a general, a U.S. Representative, a U.S. Senator, a justice of the Tennessee Supreme Court, and the governor of Florida. While the "unsophisticated outsider" label might have helped him win the presidential election, Jackson enjoyed an impressive political résumé.

Jackson's beliefs on money and banking dated back to 1797 (during George Washington's presidency), when the 30-year-old Jackson bought land in Tennessee, hoping to sell it for a profit. He found a buyer. But the buyer paid in promissory notes and eventually went bankrupt. This left Jackson, who had endorsed the notes and used them, responsible for the debt. It took Jackson 10 years to pay off this obligation, and he narrowly escaped debtor's prison. The experience led him to a visceral distrust of paper money and banking—he had been hurt badly, and it made him uncomfortable to think the same fate might befall others. Banks, to Jackson, represented the opposite of hard work and honorable wealth creation. Bankers made their money on interest from loans, in effect benefiting from the industry of others. Jackson also believed that by making loans relatively easy, banks enticed the common man to pursue unnecessary extravagance and luxury and to accumulate debt he could not afford.

"I do not dislike your Bank any more than all banks," Jackson once told Nicholas Biddle regarding the Second Bank. To James Polk he wrote, "I hate ragg, tagg banks and empty pockets" and "every one that knows me, does know that I have been always opposed to the U. States Bank, nay all Banks."

Jackson's belief that banking caused more harm than good became more rigid following the Panic of 1819. In that year, numerous banks failed, and investigations uncovered massive corruption. Banks stopped payments on notes, and while the banks foreclosed on the property of common debtors, they treated insiders differently. Even while account-holders suffered, the banks paid dividends to their stockholders, gave allowances to political allies who owed the banks money, and the bankers themselves profited handsomely by buying up their own notes at a discount. The rich and powerful escaped with the money, while the rest had worthless paper.

Understandably, Jackson took office skeptical of the Second Bank and the unchecked power it held over the American economy. On its face, the bank's purpose seemed proper—to end the chaos of uncontrolled paper currency and to provide some stability and oversight to America's banking system. The bank did this by ensuring that individual state banks had sufficient gold and silver to back up their notes and by serving as a lender of last resort. The problem was that tension resulted because the bank existed as a private institution but served as a storehouse of public funds. The bank controlled the government's money, but the government did not control the bank. This unchecked power insulated the bank's appointed board of directors from any accountability and made it especially susceptible to corruption. Critics sounded warnings, and Jackson listened.

For all the good it may have been doing, the bank, led by Biddle, was indisputably corrupt. It bribed political candidates and occupants in office; it even bought newspapers in order to campaign for those allied to its interests. Senator Daniel Webster, chairman of the Senate Committee on Finance, wrote to Biddle at one point, saying that his yearly "retainer" had not been "renewed or refreshed as usual. If it be wished that my relations to the Bank should be continued, it may be well to send me the usual retainers." The bank in fact spent over a million dollars in unaccounted-for funds and loaned an astonishing $30 million (approximately $600 million in today's money) to members of Congress, editors of newspapers, and other politicians, mostly without security.

Jackson's options when he entered office were limited. Besides the political hurdles (his wealthy, and in many cases, corrupt, political colleagues loved the bank for obvious reasons, and seeking to curtail its power would not win the new President many friends), Jackson had practical considerations. The bank's charter did not expire for eight more years, and even if he could somehow kill the bank, it held much of the country's money— where would that money go?

Jackson began slowly. He launched an investigation into one branch of the bank for electioneering because it had based its loan decisions during the previous election cycle on the political affiliation of the borrower. Jackson asked Biddle to appoint a new bipartisan set of directors for the branch. Biddle refused. Jackson investigated another branch for similar activities. Biddle refused to admit any wrongdoing. The President of the United States was getting nowhere. So he fired a warning shot.

In front of Congress, Jackson denounced the bank, hoping to rally support against the corruption. His effort failed. Biddle's friends on Capitol Hill formed a committee that published a report describing the bank in glowing terms. Now, Biddle decided to go on the offensive. He printed hundreds of copies of the report and distributed them to influential people throughout the country with demands: not only did he want Jackson to stop the investigations, he wanted to get the bank's charter renewed early so that Jackson would have no hope of ending the bank's reign over the economy. Although the charter was due to expire in 1836, Biddle feared that if Jackson won the 1832 election the charter would never be renewed.

Biddle's actions only further incensed the President, fueling his distrust of the bank. But the growing support for re-charter worried the President. If Biddle made the bank an issue, Jackson might lose reelection in 1832. He responded that if Biddle did not turn it into a campaign issue, Jackson would allow it to apply for re-charter and simply let the Congress decide. Jackson hoped that by the time of the re-charter vote, enough corruption would be uncovered that the bank would lose its mandate. Biddle, however, worried that after the election Jackson would renege on his promise and, with nothing to lose politically, would resume his fight against the bank.

Biddle strategized with Henry Clay, Jackson's upcoming opponent in the 1832 election. The two men chose to make an aggressive move they believed would box in Jackson and ensure the bank's survival. Instead of just making the bank a campaign issue, they would race to bring the re-charter bill to a vote *before* the election—with a Congress they knew would pass it easily. Jackson would then be faced with two choices: cave to political pressure and allow the bill to go through (ensuring the bank's survival regardless of the outcome of the election) or veto the bill and lose the election to Clay, who, in his first act as President, would renew the charter. If Jackson vetoed the bill, the election would become a referendum on the bank. Biddle and Clay thought they had trapped the President.

For Jackson, here was a decision that pitted his honor against political realities. If he did what he believed was right, he would not only likely sacrifice his political career, but in the end, the outcome might be the same regardless. This would prove the ultimate test of Jackson's integrity and savvy. "The Bank," he told Martin Van Buren, an adviser at that time, "is trying to kill me, but I will kill it." The duelist then added, "I will prove to them that I never flinch."

The shot was called. The bank bill passed easily in both houses. Jackson had to make his choice. Party leaders pleaded with the President not to veto the bill. When that failed, they begged him to issue what they called a "milk and water half-way veto," measuring his language and leaving open the possibility of renewing the charter after the election. Not only did Jackson's reelection concern them, but their own political fates were on the line.

Jackson decided that if he were to lose this final duel, he would go down with the same stand on principle with which he had lived his life. He set out to craft the most stinging veto message ever issued by a sitting President. He would fight with any and every weapon, taking his position directly to the people. On July 10, he addressed the Senate. Henry Clay listened in shock to Jackson's words: "It is to be regretted that the rich and powerful too often bend the acts of government to their selfish purposes . . . many of our rich men have not been content with equal protection and equal benefits, but have besought us to make them richer by act of Congress . . . . [I am] against any prostitution of our Government to the advancement of the few at the expense of the many."

Jackson announced, loud and clear, that he championed the people, not the powerful, and that he would not allow the rich to trample over the rights of the common man. It was classic Populist rhetoric, 50 years before the Populist movement. For the first time, the President used the veto as a political tool, appealing directly to America's citizens.

Reactions to the veto—largely from the bank-funded press— ranged from indignation to contempt. Newspaper editorials condemned the speech for promoting class warfare. Senator Daniel Webster told the Senate that the veto message "effects alarm for the public freedom, when nothing endangers that freedom." He failed to mention the conflict of interest on his own part.

Three days later, by just three votes, the Senate failed to achieve the two-thirds majority necessary to override the veto. Biddle and Clay hoped for as much. An override would be anticlimactic. These two men wanted to take this to the streets; they wanted to watch the American public humiliate Jackson by voting him out of office. Biddle loved that Jackson had left no room to turn back. "As to the veto message, I am delighted with it . . . . It is really a manifesto of anarchy such as Marat or Robespierre might have issued to the mob . . . and my hope is, that it will contribute to relieve the country from the dominion of these miserable people."

Biddle put his plan into motion. He spent over $100,000 (the equivalent of more than $2 million today) of the bank's money to paper the nation with copies of Jackson's veto message. Biddle believed that if people read the message and saw that Jackson aimed to kill the bank, they would rally in support of Clay. It turned out to be a terrible miscalculation.

Jackson won the election of 1832 in a landslide. Just as crushing to Biddle—of the 240 new members elected to the House of Representatives, almost 60 percent supported Jackson, killing any hope that the new Congress would override the veto. "The veto works well," wrote Jackson. "Instead of crushing me as was expected [and] intended, it will crush the Bank."

Crowned the victor by the American people, Jackson had fired what he thought would be the final shot. Gradually he withdrew the government's deposits from the Second Bank and placed them in state banks. The benefits of life without the bank exceeded even Jackson's wildest expectations. The government began to run a surplus, and for the first time in the nation's young history, Jackson paid off the entire federal debt.

But Biddle would not yield, and still had one last weapon. Even as Jackson stripped the bank of its funds, it still held enough money that Biddle could manipulate the nation's economy to cause real financial panic. As a last-ditch effort to convince the public that his bank was necessary for economic stability, Biddle began a scorched-earth "contraction" policy to disrupt the nation's prosperity. All at once, he called in loans and demanded immediate payment of outstanding bills in a concerted effort to destroy the American economy. Banks were left gasping for air: "we have never seen or felt anything like the present pressure, and it is becoming every day worse and worse," reported one banking journal. At some point, Biddle "lost his grip on reality," and it took the House of Representatives stepping in to stop Biddle's baffling scheme to push the United States into a depression. His actions alienated all remaining bank supporters and served mostly to validate Jackson's initial concerns that the bank enjoyed too much unchecked power.

Broke and disgraced, the Second Bank limped along until its charter expired in 1836. Biddle tried reopening it as a small Pennsylvania state bank, but several years later it went insolvent and disappeared for good. Jackson had won an unambiguous victory for the American people. Indeed, he had crushed the bank.

"To you, everyone placed in authority is ultimately responsible," Jackson told the nation in his farewell message. He took that mandate seriously and stood up to defend what he believed in, political pressures be damned. He not only won this final duel, he triumphed mightily over the richest and most powerful people in his young country. In the end, Nicholas Biddle learned what duelist Charles Dickinson had discovered long before: "Old Hickory" could not be felled.

President Andrew Jackson
Excerpts from Veto Message
Regarding the Bank of the United States
July 10, 1832

To the Senate

The bill "to modify and continue" the act entitled "An act to incorporate the subscribers to the Bank of the United States" was presented to me on the 4th July instant. Having considered it with that solemn regard to the principles of the Constitution which the day was calculated to inspire, and come to the conclusion that it ought not to become a law, I herewith return it to the Senate, in which it originated, with my objections.

A bank of the United States is in many respects convenient for the Government and useful to the people. Entertaining this opinion, and deeply impressed with the belief that some of the powers and privileges possessed by the existing bank are unauthorized by the Constitution, subversive of the rights of the States, and dangerous to the liberties of the people, I felt it my duty at an early period of my Administration to call the attention of Congress to the practicability of organizing an institution combining all its advantages and obviating these objections. I sincerely regret that in the act before me I can perceive none of those modifications of the bank charter which are necessary, in my opinion, to make it compatible with justice, with sound policy, or with the Constitution of our country.

The present corporate body, denominated the president, directors, and company of the Bank of the United States, will have existed at the time this act is intended to take effect twenty years. It enjoys an exclusive privilege of banking under the authority of the General Government, a monopoly of its favor and support, and, as a necessary consequence, almost a monopoly of the foreign and domestic exchange. The powers, privileges, and favors bestowed upon it in the original charter, by increasing the value of the stock far above its par value, operated as a gratuity of many millions to the stockholders.

An apology may be found for the failure to guard against this result in the consideration that the effect of the original act of incorporation could not be certainly foreseen at the time of its passage. The act before me proposes another gratuity to the holders of the same stock, and in many cases to the same men, of at least seven millions more. This donation finds no apology in any uncertainty as to the effect of the act. On all hands it is conceded that its passage will increase at least so or 30 percent more the market price of the stock, subject to the payment of the annuity of $200,000 per year secured by the act, thus adding in a moment one-fourth to its par value. It is not our own citizens only who are to receive the bounty of our Government. More than eight millions of the stock of this bank are held by foreigners. By this act the American Republic proposes virtually to make them a present of some millions of dollars. For these gratuities to foreigners and to some of our own opulent citizens the act secures no equivalent whatever. They are the certain gains of the present stockholders under the operation of this act, after making full allowance for the payment of the bonus.

Every monopoly and all exclusive privileges are granted at the expense of the public, which ought to receive a fair equivalent. The many millions which this act proposes to bestow on the stockholders of the existing bank must come directly or indirectly out of the earnings of the American people. It is due to them, therefore, if their Government sell monopolies and exclusive privileges, that they should at least exact for them as much as they are worth in open market. The value of the monopoly in this case may be correctly ascertained. The twenty-eight millions of stock would probably be at an advance of 50 percent, and command in market at least $42,000,000, subject to the payment of the present bonus. The present value of the monopoly, therefore, is $17,000,000, and this the act proposes to sell for three millions, payable in fifteen annual installments of $200,000 each.

It is not conceivable how the present stockholders can have any claim to the special favor of the Government. The present corporation has enjoyed its monopoly during the period stipulated in the original contract. If we must have such a corporation, why should not the Government sell out the whole stock and thus secure to the people the full market value of the privileges granted? Why should not Congress create and sell twenty-eight millions of stock, incorporating the purchasers with all the powers and privileges secured in this act and putting the premium upon the sales into the Treasury?

But this act does not permit competition in the purchase of this monopoly. It seems to be predicated on the erroneous idea that the present stockholders have a prescriptive right not only to the favor but to the bounty of Government. It appears that more than a fourth part of the stock is held by foreigners and the residue is held by a few hundred of our own citizens, chiefly of the richest class. For their benefit does this act exclude the whole American people from competition in the purchase of this monopoly and dispose of it for many millions less than it is worth. This seems the less excusable because some of our citizens not now stockholders petitioned that the door of competition might be opened, and offered to take a charter on terms much more favorable to the Government and country.

But this proposition, although made by men whose aggregate wealth is believed to be equal to all the private stock in the existing bank, has been set aside, and the bounty of our Government is proposed to be again bestowed on the few who have been fortunate enough to secure the stock and at this moment wield the power of the existing institution. I can not perceive the justice or policy of this course. If our Government must sell monopolies, it would seem to be its duty to take nothing less than their full value, and if gratuities must be made once in fifteen or twenty years let them not be bestowed on the subjects of a foreign government nor upon a designated and favored class of men in our own country. It is but justice and good policy, as far as the nature of the case will admit, to confine our favors to our own fellow-citizens, and let each in his turn enjoy an opportunity to profit by our bounty. In the bearings of the act before me upon these points I find ample reasons why it should not become a law.

It has been urged as an argument in favor of rechartering the present bank that the calling in its loans will produce great embarrassment and distress. The time allowed to close its concerns is ample, and if it has been well managed its pressure will be light, and heavy only in case its management has been bad. If, therefore, it shall produce distress, the fault will be its own, and it would furnish a reason against renewing a power which has been so obviously abused. But will there ever be a time when this reason will be less powerful? To acknowledge its force is to admit that the bank ought to be perpetual, and as a consequence the present stockholders and those inheriting their rights as successors be established a privileged order, clothed both with great political power and enjoying immense pecuniary advantages from their connection with the Government.

The modifications of the existing charter proposed by this act are not such, in my view, as make it consistent with the rights of the States or the liberties of the people. The qualification of the right of the bank to hold real estate, the limitation of its power to establish branches, and the power reserved to Congress to forbid the circulation of small notes are restrictions comparatively of little value or importance. All the objectionable principles of the existing corporation, and most of its odious features, are retained without alleviation . . .

Is there no danger to our liberty and independence in a bank that in its nature has so little to bind it to our country? The president of the bank has told us that most of the State banks exist by its forbearance. Should its influence become concentered, as it may under the operation of such an act as this, in the hands of a self-elected directory whose interests are identified with those of the foreign stockholders, will there not be cause to tremble for the purity of our elections in peace and for the independence of our country in war? Their power would be great whenever they might choose to exert it; but if this monopoly were regularly renewed every fifteen or twenty years on terms proposed by themselves, they might seldom in peace put forth their strength to influence elections or control the affairs of the nation. But if any private citizen or public functionary should interpose to curtail its powers or prevent a renewal of its privileges, it can not be doubted that he would be made to feel its influence.

Should the stock of the bank principally pass into the hands of the subjects of a foreign country, and we should unfortunately become involved in a war with that country, what would be our condition? Of the course which would be pursued by a bank almost wholly owned by the subjects of a foreign power, and managed by those whose interests, if not affections, would run in the same direction there can be no doubt. All its operations within would be in aid of the hostile fleets and armies without. Controlling our currency, receiving our public moneys, and holding thousands of our citizens in dependence, it would be more formidable and dangerous than the naval and military power of the enemy.

If we must have a bank with private stockholders, every consideration of sound policy and every impulse of American feeling admonishes that it should be purely American. Its stockholders should be composed exclusively of our own citizens, who at least ought to be friendly to our Government and willing to support it in times of difficulty and danger. So abundant is domestic capital that competition in subscribing for the stock of local banks has recently led almost to riots. To a bank exclusively of American stockholders, possessing the powers and privileges granted by this act, subscriptions for $200,000,000 could be readily obtained. Instead of sending abroad the stock of the bank in which the Government must deposit its funds and on which it must rely to sustain its credit in times of emergency, it would rather seem to be expedient to prohibit its sale to aliens under penalty of absolute forfeiture . . . .

This act authorizes and encourages transfers of its stock to foreigners and grants them an exemption from all State and national taxation. So far from being "necessary and proper" that the bank should possess this power to make it a safe and efficient agent of the Government in its fiscal operations, it is calculated to convert the Bank of the United States into a foreign bank, to impoverish our people in time of peace, to disseminate a foreign influence through every section of the Republic, and in war to endanger our independence.

The several States reserved the power at the formation of the Constitution to regulate and control titles and transfers of real property, and most, if not all, of them have laws disqualifying aliens from acquiring or holding lands within their limits. But this act, in disregard of the undoubted right of the States to prescribe such disqualifications, gives to aliens stockholders in this bank an interest and title, as members of the corporation, to all the real property it may acquire within any of the States of this Union.

This privilege granted to aliens is not "necessary" to enable the bank to perform its public duties, nor in any sense "proper," because it is vitally subversive of the rights of the States.

The Government of the United States have no constitutional power to purchase lands within the States except "for the erection of forts, magazines, arsenals, dockyards, and other needful buildings," and even for these objects only "by the consent of the legislature of the State in which the same shall be." By making themselves stockholders in the bank and granting to the corporation the power to purchase lands for other purposes they assume a power not granted in the Constitution and grant to others what they do not themselves possess. It is not necessary to the receiving, safe-keeping, or transmission of the funds of the Government that the bank should possess this power, and it is not proper that Congress should thus enlarge the powers delegated to them in the Constitution.

The old Bank of the United States possessed a capital of only $11,000,000, which was found fully sufficient to enable it with dispatch and safety to perform all the functions required of it by the Government. The capital of the present bank is $35,000,000— at least twenty-four more than experience has proved to be necessary to enable a bank to perform its public functions. The public debt which existed during the period of the old bank and on the establishment of the new has been nearly paid off, and our revenue will soon be reduced. This increase of capital is therefore not for public but for private purposes.

The Government is the only "proper" judge where its agents should reside and keep their offices, because it best knows where their presence will be "necessary." It can not, therefore, be "necessary" or "proper" to authorize the bank to locate branches where it pleases to perform the public service, without consulting the Government, and contrary to its will. The principle laid down by the Supreme Court concedes that Congress can not establish a bank for purposes of private speculation and gain, but only as a means of executing the delegated powers of the General Government. By the same principle a branch bank can not constitutionally be established for other than public purposes. The power which this act gives to establish two branches in any State, without the injunction or request of the Government and for other than public purposes, is not "necessary" to the due execution of the powers delegated to Congress . . . .

It is to be regretted that the rich and powerful too often bend the acts of government to their selfish purposes. Distinctions in society will always exist under every just government. Equality of talents, of education, or of wealth can not be produced by human institutions. In the full enjoyment of the gifts of Heaven and the fruits of superior industry, economy, and virtue, every man is equally entitled to protection by law; but when the laws undertake to add to these natural and just advantages artificial distinctions, to grant titles, gratuities, and exclusive privileges, to make the rich richer and the potent more powerful, the humble members of society—the farmers, mechanics, and laborers— who have neither the time nor the means of securing like favors to themselves, have a right to complain of the injustice of their

Government. There are no necessary evils in government. Its
evils exist only in its abuses. If it would confine itself to equal
protection, and, as Heaven does its rains, shower its favors alike
on the high and the low, the rich and the poor, it would be an
unqualified blessing. In the act before me there seems to be a wide
and unnecessary departure from these just principles.

Nor is our Government to be maintained or our Union
preserved by invasions of the rights and powers of the several
States. In thus attempting to make our General Government strong
we make it weak. Its true strength consists in leaving individuals
and States as much as possible to themselves—in making itself
felt, not in its power, but in its beneficence; not in its control, but in
its protection; not in binding the States more closely to the center,
but leaving each to move unobstructed in its proper orbit.

Experience should teach us wisdom. Most of the difficulties
our Government now encounters and most of the dangers which
impend over our Union have sprung from an abandonment of the
legitimate objects of Government by our national legislation, and
the adoption of such principles as are embodied in this act. Many
of our rich men have not been content with equal protection and
equal benefits, but have besought us to make them richer by act
of Congress. By attempting to gratify their desires we have in the
results of our legislation arrayed section against section, interest
against interest, and man against man, in a fearful commotion
which threatens to shake the foundations of our Union. It is time
to pause in our career to review our principles, and if possible
revive that devoted patriotism and spirit of compromise which

distinguished the sages of the Revolution and the fathers of our Union. If we can not at once, in justice to interests vested under improvident legislation, make our Government what it ought to be, we can at least take a stand against all new grants of monopolies and exclusive privileges, against any prostitution of our Government to the advancement of the few at the expense of the many, and in favor of compromise and gradual reform in our code of laws and system of political economy.

I have now done my duty to my country. If sustained by my fellow citizens, I shall be grateful and happy; if not, I shall find in the motives which impel me ample grounds for contentment and peace. In the difficulties which surround us and the dangers which threaten our institutions there is cause for neither dismay nor alarm. For relief and deliverance let us firmly rely on that kind Providence which I am sure watches with peculiar care over the destinies of our Republic, and on the intelligence and wisdom of our countrymen. Through His abundant goodness and heir patriotic devotion our liberty and Union will be preserved.

ANDREW JOHNSON, CA. 1865.

National Archives & Records Administration.

CHAPTER 5

MR. JOHNSON GOES TO WASHINGTON

Andrew Johnson and His Secretary of War

Throughout the Lincoln–Johnson campaign, Andrew Johnson, the vice presidential candidate, traveled the country to deliver the rough-and-tumble stump speeches for which he was famous. Immediately following Lincoln's landslide victory, Johnson went back to Tennessee to finish his tenure as military governor, anxious for his home state to rejoin the Union after its participation on the Confederate side of the Civil War. But as the day of the inauguration drew nearer, Johnson began to procrastinate about his departure for Washington.

Johnson telegrammed Lincoln and asked if it would be all right for him to skip the inauguration—he had previous commitments in Tennessee. Self-confidence or self-doubt, who knew? Stunned, President Lincoln instructed the Vice President elect that his attendance at the Capitol for his own inauguration was very much required.

Still, Johnson persisted. He next wrote to his friend John Forney for help in changing the President's mind. Forney was even more horrified and ordered his friend to get to Washington immediately.

Johnson finally conceded that he had no choice. However, complaining of illness, he did not arrive in the capital until the eve of the inauguration.

The next morning, Johnson awoke to gloomy rain and a bad hangover. The night before, he and Forney had celebrated at a supper overflowing with whiskey. The gray morning at hand left him without further time or excuses. Nerves jangling, he stuffed his tired body into his inaugural finery: a black formal frock coat, a silk vest, and doeskin pants. A former tailor, he always dressed impeccably. His preparations complete, Andrew Johnson set out from his boardinghouse to be sworn in as Vice President of the United States.

Along the way to the noontime ceremonies, he stopped off at the Vice President's office in the Capitol, where Hannibal Hamlin, whom he was replacing, and Hamlin's son Charles waited for him. Still feeling the effects of the night before, Johnson asked for some whiskey, which was promptly sent in. The conversation was cordial and relaxed, so he did not hesitate to fill his glass full and drink it straight. Then, he had another. Perhaps, if Johnson had been kinder to Hamlin at the convention, the departing Vice President might have gently dissuaded him. But he did not. Nor did he stop Johnson when, as they made their way to the Senate chamber, he rushed back to hurriedly gulp down a third whiskey.

With President Lincoln, Mrs. Lincoln, members of the Cabinet, Senators, Congressmen, the Supreme Court Justices, foreign dignitaries, military and naval officials, and throngs of spectators and journalists assembled before them, Hamlin and a tottering Johnson entered the Senate chamber arm in arm. Adrenaline kicked the alcohol into full effect. The outgoing Vice President introduced his successor, who took the floor and, in his first official act of office, embarked upon a prodigiously drunken rant.

Slurring his words, Johnson subjected his distinguished audience to a rambling account of his rags-to-riches success. An entirely self-made man who had never attended school, he regaled them with how, with little more than a rucksack on his shoulder, he had escaped near slave-status as a tailor's apprentice in North Carolina and literally walked most of the way to Tennessee, where he became a successful businessman and property owner, and then climbed the political rungs as alderman, mayor, state legislator, congressman, governor, and senator.

He continued with effusive praise and gratitude for "the people," who had engineered this spectacular rise in status. Then, ignoring all protocol, he began to harangue the Cabinet members—"I will say to you, Mr. Secretary Seward, and to you, Mr. Secretary Stanton, and to you Mr. Secretary . . . "

Mortified, they watched him lean over to Forney and snort, "Who is the Secretary of the Navy?"

"Mr. Welles," came the painfully whispered reply.

"And to you, Mr. Secretary Welles, I would say, you all derive your power from the people." Johnson might have continued indefinitely if Hamlin hadn't elbowed him aside.

Those who didn't witness it firsthand read about it afterward. The *New York World* remarked that in comparison with Johnson "even Caligula's horse was respectable."

Thoroughly humiliated, Johnson fled the capital and hid at a friend's farm for two full weeks. Many assumed that he had vanished to continue on his drinking binge, which was not true. Only Lincoln defended him. "I have known Andy Johnson for many years," the President said. "He made a bad slip the other day, but you need not be scared; Andy ain't no drunk." In truth, the inauguration was the first and last occasion at which Johnson appeared intoxicated. Unfortunately, he could not have chosen a worse moment for this singular lapse of self-control. When he finally skulked back into Washington, the President avoided him.

It had seemed like such a good idea at the time of Lincoln's reelection campaign to nominate Johnson as his running mate. Johnson had become a Northern hero and political star when he remained the sole Southerner in the Senate as others opted for secession. His fierce, fire-and-brimstone speeches against any threat to the Union made front-page news. Bands serenaded him and speaking engagements poured in. Then, as military governor of Tennessee, Johnson had bravely defended Nashville against the Rebels firsthand and severely punished captured Confederates.

A few had voiced objections. The curmudgeonly House Leader Thaddeus Stevens growled, "Can't you find a candidate for Vice President, without going down to one of those damned rebel provinces to pick one up?" But the majority of Union party leaders had chosen Johnson, albeit as the dancing monkey, not the ringmaster. His disastrous performance at the inauguration made them wonder if they had made a grave mistake.

Grumbled misgivings erupted into full-fledged shock when, only six weeks later, on April 14, 1865, Abraham Lincoln was assassinated at the Ford Theater by John Wilkes Booth. Johnson, who disdained theatrical "frivolities," lay sleeping peacefully when the deadly attack took place. His fellow boarder Leonard Farwell, former governor of Wisconsin, witnessed the deed firsthand and rushed back to waken the Vice President with the news.

Panic ensued when they learned that Secretary of State Seward had also been stabbed. Guards promptly arrived to protect Johnson, since the extent of the plot was unknown. They did not yet realize that Booth's co-conspirator, George Atzerodt, had that morning taken the room above Johnson's with the intention of killing him as well. The would-be murderer had grilled the hotel's bartender for information about the Vice President all evening, but at the appointed hour, 10:15 p.m., as his lawyer later explained, "Atzerodt was guzzling like a Falstaff."

As Johnson struggled in those first, shocking moments to comprehend what had happened, his private secretary, William Browning, revealed that he had found a startling note in his message box:

Don't wish to disturb you. Are you at home?

J. Wilkes Booth

Bellboys reported that Booth had written it that afternoon after inquiring whether the Vice President and his assistant were in. Before the shooting, Browning had mistakenly thought that the actor-turned-assassin, whom he had met in Nashville, had intended the note for him. The haunting message underlined how narrowly the Vice President had escaped death even as it poisonously insinuated that Booth and Johnson were acquainted. But the ambitious politician spared no time for morbid introspection. He rushed to the dying President's side across the street from the theater at the Peterson House, where Lincoln had been moved, and, with equal discretion, Johnson took care not to linger too long or to appear to be coveting the tragedy that might elevate him.

At 7:22 the next morning, Lincoln passed away. The Cabinet immediately notified Johnson, who had himself somberly sworn-in at his hotel a few hours later. In a speech rare for both its brevity and its modesty, he declared himself "almost overwhelmed by the announcement of the sad event which has so recently occurred."

He continued, "I feel incompetent to perform duties so important and responsible as those which have been unexpectedly thrust upon me." The words lacked inspiration but observers were comforted by their new chief executive's resolve to tackle the presidency as best as he fumblingly could.

Tactfully permitting Mrs. Lincoln to take her time vacating the White House, Johnson gathered the members of Lincoln's Cabinet at the Treasury at noon that same day. This disparate group, an odd marriage of powerful War Democrats and Republicans, had frequently bridled under Lincoln's command. Now, the novice President who had drunkenly berated them would have to control them. Without his ally Seward, who lay at home recuperating, Johnson faced the arrogant, needle-tongued Secretary of War, Edwin M. Stanton, who had been known to call even Lincoln, a man he greatly respected, "the original gorilla," or more simply, "a damned fool."

Johnson vowed to continue the late President's policies, informed the group that they would all keep their posts, and appointed a temporary replacement for Seward. That afternoon, divisive matters could wait; there were assassins to apprehend. Stanton, whom many blamed for leaving Lincoln unprotected at the theater, begged Johnson to allow him to take charge of the investigation. Profoundly grieved and outraged, Johnson unhesitatingly agreed. His hot-tempered war secretary quickly caught all but one of the conspirators. Booth was shot and killed in the attempt to capture him. At Stanton's suggestion, Johnson ordered the collaborators tried under the harsh auspices of a military court. All things considered, Johnson and his administration got off to a good start.

With the assassination crisis behind him, Johnson got down to White House business. He issued a proclamation appointing a provisional governor for Virginia and granted general amnesty to former Confederates. Nothing was mentioned about the prickly issue of whether the freed slaves should be given the vote. Johnson's Cabinet, split in two bitterly entrenched camps, had failed to reach any consensus on the subject. The President had listened to them all. Then, without further discussion, he acted upon the dictates of his own conscience. Congress was never consulted. He decided to leave that decision to the discretion of the individual states.

Johnson was not a great man. Unable to shed the racism of his upbringing and his belief that only a few aristocratic plantation owners had led the South astray, and unable to comprehend the depth of animosity on both sides of the Mason-Dixon Line, he was incapable of forging a new era. He was, as Lincoln credited him, a well-meaning man, however limited. With mulish obstinacy, Johnson fixated on restoring the South as quickly as possible, critics be damned.

Emboldened by his first exercise of executive power, Johnson soon issued proclamations for the other Southern states and liberally invoked his right to grant pardons. Reports swirled through the papers of unsightly throngs of former Confederates crowding the White House lobby in the hope of obtaining one. Some contended that the President was collaborating with an unsavory but enterprising widow who set up a business brokering the introductions. Rumors suggested that the chief executive might, with his Southern leniency, go so far as to pardon Jefferson Davis, the incarcerated president of the former Confederate States.

With each passing day, Johnson's wartime heroism and bold anti-secession stance receded further into the past. His former Confederate enemies revered him as a savior. His Northern friends dropped him as quickly as they had picked him up.

With their own, far more punitive ideas about how to treat the Rebel provinces, congressional radicals, then on summer recess, were aghast. The cantankerous Stevens complained to Senator Charles Sumner, "Is there no way to arrest the insane course of the President in Washington?" He was certain that Johnson would be "crowned king" before Congress met again. Sumner visited the White House to plead for full enfranchisement of the freed slaves. But Johnson refused to make any concessions because voting rights had always been determined by the states. Worse still, the President mistakenly used the Senator's hat as a spittoon. Attempts to reason with him were abandoned. When Congress reconvened that autumn, the anti-Johnson faction focused on how to thwart him by passing its own Reconstruction plan.

Johnson had no intention of handing the matter over to Congress without a fight. He vetoed their Freedman's Bureau Bill, which expanded the authority and functions of the organization protecting freed slaves, and then the Civil Rights Act, which granted citizenship to Southern blacks, determined to see Southern representatives participate in all national decisions. In the first instance, Johnson's objections were sustained, but at the second check to their powers, congressional members banded together and overturned the presidential veto. Only four Republicans stood by the administration. Johnson's defeat was monumental.

Led by Stanton, several Cabinet members began to openly disavow their chief executive. In addition to publicly disagreeing with Johnson's policies, Stanton tried to oversee his own brand of Reconstruction rather than carry out the orders of his commander. The war secretary held secret discussions with his congressional allies on how best to curb the President's powers. His treachery did not stop there. On the eve of the New Orleans convention called to enfranchise blacks in Louisiana in July 1866, Stanton withheld from the President an urgent telegram that warned of the dangerous riots threatened by vengeful Confederates. The result was that Johnson did nothing to prevent the uprising that left 40 people dead and more than 140 wounded. In fact, he inadvertently encouraged it by questioning the legality of the delegates and ordering the state attorney general to suppress all illegal assemblies, and was blamed for the tragedy.

The public grew increasingly alarmed. Johnson had so thoroughly alienated the nation that many believed he had plotted Lincoln's murder. Writing to a friend, Mary Todd Lincoln fumed:

> [T]hat miserable inebriate Johnson, had cognizance of my husband's death—Why, was that card of Booth's, found in his box, some acquaintance certainly existed—I have been deeply impressed, with the harrowing thought, that he, had an understanding with the conspirators & they knew their man. . . .As sure, as you & I live, Johnson had some hand in all this.

Misjudging public sentiment, the President decided to appeal directly to the people for support. Dragging Seward and Welles in tow, he embarked on a multi-city tour, crassly denouncing his opponents and praising his own policies in stump speeches wherever he went. General Ulysses Grant, who had also been forced along, hid in his railway car and drank heavily. Crowds cheered the triumphant general expectantly but found themselves stuck with an apologetic Johnson, whom they loudly heckled. The distasteful and ill-conceived campaign backfired.

Midterm elections returned a Congress heavily stacked against the President. He continued to veto their motions in lengthy and venomous messages (he would do so an extraordinary 29 times), but he was powerless to stop them. As the *New York World* put it, "The President can outreason Congress but Congress can outvote him." They frequently overturned him within the course of the day, sometimes in the space of half an hour.

Congress's vehement dislike for the President grew by leaps and bounds. The possibility of impeachment, that last-ditch constitutional recourse permitting Congress to rid itself of a President guilty of "treason, bribery, or other high crimes or misdemeanors," began to circulate as an idea. Such a drastic step had never before been taken. But these were drastic times. In January 1867 the more zealous of Johnson's detractors formed a commission headed up by Representative Ben Butler of Massachusetts to investigate the President's actions. They looked at his drinking and at his bankbooks. Johnson's ties to Jefferson Davis were reexamined, as were possible connections between the President and Booth.

Secret Service Chief Lafayette C. Baker revealed that 18 pages had been ripped out of the diary recovered with Booth's body. "Who spoliated that book?" Butler thundered. "Who suppressed that evidence? Who caused an innocent woman to be hung when he had in his pocket the diary which had stated at least what was the idea and the purpose of the main conspirators in the case?" Johnson was curious enough about the missing pages to launch his own investigation. Stanton reported that they had never been in the government's possession.

Still, the situation was frightening. What if Congress suspended the President until the impeachment trial? Some Johnson supporters offered to raise troops for an armed resistance. Although the President had no intention of taking any such action, gossip that he might spread wildly.

Unwilling to take their chances solely on impeachment, and worried that Johnson might dismiss their Cabinet spy, Stanton's congressional friends passed the Office of Tenure Act, which decreed that the President could not fire any Cabinet members without House approval. However, the motion protected Cabinet members only "for and during the term of the President by whom they may have been appointed, and for one month thereafter." Since Johnson had retained Stanton from Lincoln's Cabinet, many (but not all) argued that he was exempt from the law.

Johnson set about writing another acidic veto. During the Cabinet discussion, even Stanton opposed this threat to executive powers, as he was later reminded. And when the President, complaining of rheumatism in his arm, asked his war secretary to write the veto message, Stanton passed the job to Secretary of State Seward.

Of course, Stanton had no reason to dirty his hands since he knew that Congress would promptly override the veto, which it did. Stunned at the routine speed of the session, one observer was told, "We pay no attention anymore to what he [Johnson] says."

As spring turned into summer, Congress continued to postpone the impeachment hearing to search for hard evidence against Johnson. Representative James M. Ashley of Ohio repeatedly testified that he was sure that he could find it. So desperate were Johnson's enemies to incriminate him that they offered to pardon a convicted perjurer in return for damning testimony. No fool, the proposed witness knew where pardons could be easily had and marched straight to the White House with his sordid tale. Johnson publicized the story widely and won the round.

In the meantime, the President learned of the telegram that Stanton had withheld before the New Orleans riot and soon discovered that his war secretary had suppressed other critical communications. It was no secret that Stanton disagreed with Johnson's policies. Now there was proof that Stanton was actively manipulating the President's political demise. Johnson, quite reasonably, began to contemplate how best to rid himself of the traitor in his Cabinet.

Johnson acted while news of the bribed perjurer was still fresh. On August 5, 1867, he formally requested the war secretary's resignation. Stanton haughtily refused. The President left his war secretary "hanging on the hooks of uncertainty for a few days" and then "suspended" him and quietly approached General Grant to serve as ad interim secretary, pending approval. In all of this, the President conformed to the letter, if not the spirit, of the new law. Grant took over Stanton's position through the congressional recess.

Events and opinion seemed to be swinging in Johnson's favor. When Ashley finally presented his long-awaited impeachment report in late November, it seemed little more than the lunatic ranting of a conspiracy fanatic. Although he avowed that he was certain that Presidents who died in office, including Lincoln, were poisoned by their successors, he admitted that he had not found the kind of concrete proof that would satisfy most. *Harper's Weekly* dismissively sniffed, "We can not but think that Mr. Ashley was unduly excited." The motion to impeach was defeated.

But the victory was hollow and short-lived. On January 13, 1868, the House ordered Grant to turn his office back over to Stanton, which he happily did. Johnson was livid and minced no words letting the general know how he felt.

Stymied at every turn, the President confronted the issue head-on. Unlike his previous attempt, on February 21, 1868, he entirely ignored the Office of Tenure Act and simply appointed Adjutant General Lorenzo Thomas as his new Secretary of War. He wanted to goad Congress into taking him to court because he was fairly certain that the new law would be deemed unconstitutional. Even if it wasn't, he was done jockeying with his enemies, whatever the consequences. He was, after all, the legally appointed President of the United States and he thought it was high time for both his Cabinet and Congress to start treating him that way.

Following Johnson's instructions, Thomas showed up at the War Department and summarily delivered to Stanton the official letter relieving him of his duties. "Do you wish me to vacate at once," Stanton hissed from his sofa, "or am I to be permitted to stay long enough to remove my property?" Thomas relented, agreeing to return later.

Then Stanton, with Grant's help, holed himself up in his office and swore to defend it against all intruders. As the news spread, Senators and Congressmen rushed over to aid Stanton at the War Department. Others sent messages of support. The most memorable was Charles Sumner's one-word telegram: "Stick."

Anti-Johnson hysteria crescendoed when the story of his latest "misdeed" reached the House. "Didn't I tell you so," Stevens roared. "If you don't kill the beast, it will kill you." This time they thought they had him. In their eyes he had clearly broken the law. Not that they had any intention of letting the Supreme Court decide this; impeachment, once again, was the word spread across Washington.

That night Thomas, attending a ball, boasted that he would take the War Department by morning. Instead, Stanton sent the police to arrest Thomas before he was properly out of bed. The President was thrilled. "Very well, that is the place I want it in— the courts," he told Thomas before sending him to the Attorney General, who advised him to obey the summons and post the $5,000 bond.

Thomas lost hours following up on this advice. By the time he arrived at the War Department, Stanton was firmly positioned and ordered him out. Thomas refused to go. A tense standoff ensued until Thomas complained, "The next time you have me arrested, please don't do it before I get something to eat." Stanton put his arm around his colleague's neck...then called for whiskey. The two men sat and drank together, waiting to see what would happen next.

Congress convinced Stanton to drop his case against Thomas and, with breakneck speed (a mere three days), pushed through the impeachment motion and a list of charges. Thaddeus Stevens, nearing death and determined to take out "the beast" before he expired, feared these "charges" were a bit thin, so, at his suggestion, they tacked on two more for good measure.

The President took the news with perfect equanimity. As handsomely dressed as ever, the tailor-president continued to preside over White House banquets, even inviting congressional members to a reception, lest they think he was quaking in his boots. Visitors observed no anxiety on his face. Privately, Johnson cursed his enemies and proudly declared, "I am right and I intend to stand by. I do not want this Government to relapse into despotism."

Spectators clamored for tickets to the President's trial, the show of the century. The police struggled to keep back throngs of women and blacks, who protested being barred admission. On March 30, 1868, the proceedings opened with Massachusetts Representative Ben Butler, who had led the first impeachment commission and who was famous for his wild courtroom antics. He commenced with droning testimony about the nature of impeachable crimes and then continued with a numbing speech about the legality of denying Johnson the right to test the constitutionality of the new law. Finally, he gave the crowd what they wanted.

"By murder most foul," Butler raged, "did he succeed to the Presidency and is the elect of an assassin to that high office, and not of the people." There it was, the old accusation of Johnson conspiring with Booth. However, in all the months that the anti-Johnson hotheads had been searching for solid proof, nothing had ever turned up.

Political sentiment began to turn. The charges seemed trumped up; the congressional radicals seemed to have overreached. Prosecution witnesses added little to Butler's opening tirade except the bizarre suggestion that Johnson should be "banished to the black hole in the Southern sky." The President's defense team argued with calm logic that he had every right to differ from the congressional majority.

When the vote was finally taken on May 16, Johnson received enough, barely enough, support to finish his presidency in good standing. With 35 for and 19 against, only one vote short of the two-thirds majority necessary to convict, the impeachment motion failed. Most senators towed the party line. All conservatives and Democrats voted "not guilty"; radical Republicans voted "guilty." However, seven moderate Republicans, after receiving private assurances that Johnson would do nothing further to impede congressional Reconstruction, decided that there was not enough evidence to convict him. "How does it happen," one radical journalist bemoaned, "that just enough and no more Senators are convinced of the President's innocence?" Butler, with equal disbelief, initiated an investigation of the seven suspect Republican senators who had voted "not guilty."

Johnson had won the day. He immediately fired Secretary of War Stanton, who now beat a hasty retreat from his office lest officers arrive to arrest him. Johnson's victory strengthened the presidency.

Incredibly enough, on the heels of the impeachment scandal, Johnson was shocked, angry, and hurt not to receive his party's presidential nomination for another term. He never did realize that national opinions and needs differed from those of the white, working-class constituents of East Tennessee who had carried him from one political victory to the next. When his term ended, ignoring precedent, he refused to ceremonially hand over the presidency to Grant because of the general's betrayal. The

stomach-turning recollection of his first inaugural performance
may have added to his distaste for the event. Instead, Johnson
delivered an embittered farewell address to "the people," which
the *New York Herald* deemed more appropriate for "some political
gathering in Tennessee."

Johnson's home state remained loyal to the very end and
finally accorded him the "triumphal vindication over enemies"
that he longed for. In 1875, Tennessee returned him to the U.S.
Senate, where he became the only President to serve as Senator
after serving as Chief Executive. Hardly back in his old Senate
seat, the former President rose to his feet and viciously denounced
the Senate's right to even discuss Grant's Reconstruction policies.
Stanton, Stevens, and Sumner had already passed on.

Johnson got the last word. Appeased, he died quietly a few
months later.

President Andrew Johnson
Excerpts from his Address to the Senate of the United States
December 12, 1867

Mr. Stanton refers generally to the Constitution and laws of the "United States," and says that a sense of public duty "under" these compels him to deny the right of the President to suspend him from office. As to his sense of duty under the Constitution, that will be considered in the sequel. As to his sense of duty under "the laws of the United States," he certainly can not refer to the law which creates the War Department, for that expressly confers upon the President the unlimited right to remove the head of the Department. The only other law bearing upon the question is the tenure-of-office act, passed by Congress over the Presidential veto March 2, 1867. This is the law which, under a sense of public duty, Mr. Stanton volunteers to defend.

There is no provision in this law which compels any officer coming within its provisions to remain in office. It forbids removals—not resignations. Mr. Stanton was perfectly free to resign at any moment, either upon his own motion or in compliance with a request or an order. It was a matter of choice or taste. There was nothing compulsory in the nature of legal obligation. Nor does he put his action upon that imperative ground. He says he acts under a "sense of public duty," not of legal obligation, compelling him to hold on and leaving him with no choice. The public duty which is upon him arises from the respect which he owes to the Constitution and the laws, violated in his own case. He is therefore compelled by this sense of public duty to vindicate violated law and to stand as its champion.

This was not the first occasion in which Mr. Stanton, in discharge of a public duty, was called upon to consider the provisions of that law. That tenure-of-office law did not pass without notice. Like other acts, it was sent to the President for approval. As is my custom, I submitted its consideration to my Cabinet for their advice upon the question whether I should approve it or not. It was a grave question of constitutional law, in which I would, of course, rely upon the opinion of the Attorney-General and of Mr. Stanton, who had once been Attorney-General.

Every member of my Cabinet advised me that the proposed law was unconstitutional. All spoke without doubt or reservation, but Mr. Stanton's condemnation of the law was the most elaborate and emphatic. He referred to the constitutional provisions, the debates in Congress, especially to the speech of Mr. Buchanan when a Senator, to the decisions of the Supreme Court, and to the usage from the beginning of the Government through every successive Administration, all concurring to establish the right of removal as vested by the Constitution in the President. To all these he added the weight of his own deliberate judgment, and advised me that it was my duty to defend the power of the President from usurpation and to veto the law.

I do not know when a sense of public duty is more imperative upon a head of Department than upon such an occasion as this. He acts then under the gravest obligations of the law, for when he is called upon by the President for advice it is the Constitution which speaks to him. All his other duties are left by the Constitution to be regulated by statute, but this duty was deemed so momentous that it is imposed by the Constitution itself.

After all this I was not prepared for the ground taken by Mr. Stanton in his note of August 12. I was not prepared to find him compelled by a new and indefinite sense of public duty, under "the Constitution," to assume the vindication of a law, which, under the solemn obligations of public duty imposed by the Constitution itself, he advised me was a violation of that Constitution. I make great allowance for a change of opinion, but such a change as this hardly falls within the limits of greatest indulgence.

Where our opinions take the shape of advice, and influence the action of others, the utmost stretch of charity will scarcely justify us in repudiating them when they come to be applied to ourselves.

But to proceed with the narrative. I was so much struck with the full mastery of the question manifested by Mr. Stanton, and was at the time so fully occupied with the preparation of another veto upon the pending reconstruction act, that I requested him to prepare the veto upon this tenure-of-office bill. This he declined, on the ground of physical disability to undergo at the time the labor of writing, but stated his readiness to furnish what aid might be required in the preparation of materials for the paper.

At the time this subject was before the Cabinet it seemed to be taken for granted that as to those members of the Cabinet who had been appointed by Mr. Lincoln their tenure of office was not fixed by the provisions of the act. I do not remember that the point was distinctly decided, but I well recollect that it was suggested by one member of the Cabinet who was appointed by Mr. Lincoln, and that no dissent was expressed.

Whether the point was well taken or not did not seem to me of any consequence, for the unanimous expression of opinion against the constitutionality and policy of the act was so decided that I felt no concern, so far as the act had reference to the gentlemen then present, that I would be embarrassed in the future. The bill had not then become a law. The limitation upon the power of removal was not yet imposed, and there was yet time to make any changes. If any one of these gentlemen had then said to me that he would avail himself of the provisions of that bill in case it became a law, I should not have hesitated a moment as to his removal. No pledge was then expressly given or required. But there are circumstances when to give an expressed pledge is not necessary, and when to require it is an imputation of bad faith. I felt that if these gentlemen came within the purview of the bill it was as to them a dead letter, and that none of them would ever take refuge under its provisions.

**PRESIDENT LYNDON JOHNSON AND DEFENSE SECRETARY ROBERT MCNAMARA
DURING A MEETING AT THE LBJ RANCH.**

LBJ Library Photo by Yoichi Okamoto.

CHAPTER 6

GUNS AND BUTTER

———◆———

Lyndon Johnson, the Vietnam War, and the Great Society

The six-foot, three-inch frame of Lyndon Johnson lay in the middle of an open space the size of a Texan pasture. His oversized ears rang with the sound of voices. He tried to get up and greet the speakers, but his hands and feet were tied to the ground. He lifted his head and saw thousands running toward him, taunting, "Coward! Traitor! Weakling!" They were holding stones.

"There would be Robert Kennedy out in front," Johnson remembered, "telling everyone that I had betrayed John Kennedy's commitment to South Vietnam. That I had let a democracy fall into the hands of the Communists. That I was a coward. An unmanly man. *A man without a spine*." Johnson braced for the blows as the stones flew toward him. Then he would wake up. It was the President's recurring nightmare.

Over 100 F-105 Thunderchiefs, F-100 Super Sabers, and B-57 Canberras accelerated across the demilitarized zone into enemy territory. One hundred and twenty seconds lay between the target—an ammunitions dump in Xom Bang—and the delivery of over 400 tons of bombs courtesy of the U.S. Air Force. On March 2, 1965, by order of President Lyndon B. Johnson, Operation Rolling Thunder commenced. America's war against North Vietnam had begun.

President Johnson was not caught up in this massive display of U.S. airpower. "I do not find it impressive at all," Johnson said.

"The guns and bombs, the rockets and warships, are all symbols
of human failure." But the only thing that stood in the way of plans
that *did* impress Johnson—giving minorities their right to vote,
boosting America's schools with federal funding, and providing
free medical care to the poor and elderly—was the "damn little
piss-ant country" of Vietnam.

Vietnam had cursed Johnson's plans on the home front once
before. When a "sonny boy" who needed "a little gray in his hair"
ordered him to leave for Saigon, Johnson had no right to refuse. After
all, LBJ hadn't won at the 1960 Democratic Convention, JFK had.

Serving as Kennedy's second in command tortured the
competitive Johnson. He soaked his misery in Cutty Sark. Often
too depressed to get out of bed, aides had to lift him up and
move his arms about to get him circulating. But when President
Kennedy launched his New Frontier, Vice President Johnson
found his reason to wake up in the morning.

Kennedy's fight in Congress against the issues of racism and
poverty thrilled Johnson. The rough-hewn Vice President yearned
to wipe America clean of these scourges; he had seen plenty of both
growing up in dirt-poor Texas. And LBJ was certain Kennedy
would want his support. Both men knew Johnson could be an
enormous help in passing the New Frontier through Congress.

But the President didn't care that his VP was formerly a
master of the Senate. He did care that Lyndon Johnson hovered
about like a gloomy vulture. "I cannot stand Johnson's damn long
face," complained Kennedy. "He just comes in, sits at the Cabinet
meetings with his face all screwed up." Kennedy searched for any
means possible to keep the coarse Texan far away from him. A trip
to Southeast Asia would be a perfect assignment for Johnson.

On the flight to South Vietnam, LBJ was livid. He knew he could be doing better things in Congress. The Vice President vented his irritation at anyone in his path and even ordered a loyal aide off the plane. "We're over the ocean," the aide explained. "I don't give a fucking damn!" Johnson shouted back.

Johnson was dour as his motorcade rolled from the Tan Son Nhut Airport. But when he saw admirers along the road to Saigon, he turned giddy. Emerging from his car with outstretched arms, Johnson grabbed the hands of the locals. He gave out U.S. Senate passes to the children and told them to get their "mamma and daddy to bring [them] to the Senate and Congress and see how the government works!"

His entourage lurching toward Saigon (he made his motorcade stop several times), the Vice President handed out cigarette lighters to the masses and distributed pencils inscribed with his message— "Compliments of your Senator—Lyndon B. Johnson—the greatest good for the greatest number." Johnson only wished that he were working for the greatest good within his *own* country.

Though Kennedy clearly wanted LBJ out of his hair, he did have a serious mission for the Vice President. At that time 692 American military "advisers" were stationed in South Vietnam. Eisenhower had sent them over because he feared the country would fall to the Communists in North Vietnam. Kennedy had written Prime Minister Ngo Dinh Diem a letter promising to send more American manpower. He wanted Johnson to personally deliver it.

By the time Diem was assassinated in November 1963, Kennedy had sent over 15,000 American military advisers to Vietnam. When Kennedy was assassinated three weeks later, Johnson became President. The last thing Johnson wanted to deal with was the military mess that two dead men had left in Vietnam.

Ignoring Southeast Asia, Johnson immediately turned to Congress. Free to flex his legislative muscle, LBJ blew past the filibuster of Southern Senators and signed a civil rights law far tougher than JFK could have passed. After passing the legislative goals of Kennedy's New Frontier, Johnson designed and orchestrated his own agenda to take to Capitol Hill.

The plan was pure Johnson—big and bold. It was the largest legislative reform plan in U.S. history. The goal was nothing less than to purify the cities, beautify the countryside, and free the nation of racism and poverty.

With over 100 bills in his plan, LBJ plotted how each one would move through Congress. Masterminding this grand scheme was an awesome task that only Franklin Roosevelt could rival. But even FDR didn't have LBJ's cachet in Congress. After three decades of congressional experience, Johnson had plenty of favors waiting to be returned on Capitol Hill. He planned to cash in on the Great Society.

But at the beginning of 1965, right at the time he launched his legislative flood to Congress, the curse of Vietnam threatened to suck it dry. Since taking office, Johnson had simply hoped that the South Vietnamese would "get off their butts and get out in those jungles and whip hell out of some Communists."

Only the South Vietnamese hadn't whipped hell out of anyone. The Vietcong was winning. And every adviser responsible for America's national security insisted that if the President kept ignoring the conflict, South Vietnam would fall to the Communists.

When these advisers offered Operation Rolling Thunder, the gradual and massive carpet-bombing of North Vietnam, Johnson reluctantly agreed. But when adviser McGeorge Bundy informed the President that his decision should "be known and understood by enough people to permit its orderly execution" (i.e., Congress), Johnson threw the suggestion back in his face.

Global conflict was Bundy's ballgame, but Congress was Johnson's court. Johnson was unsure how Rolling Thunder would play out in Vietnam, but like a Grand Master, he foresaw its endgame in Congress. And that was the destruction of his Great Society at the hands of hawks.

The Cold War was at its height, and hawks in Congress could still whip up Communist paranoia. Once they found out America had started a war in Vietnam, their cries could drown out the Great Society. "First we had to beat those Godless Communists," Johnson believed they would say, "and *then* we could worry about the homeless Americans."

The hawks were eager to sink their talons into Lyndon Johnson. He had beaten them on civil rights and routed one of their own in the presidential election. Killing the President's baby—the Great Society—would be a sweet revenge. Johnson would not take that risk. He saw only one way to keep the hawks at bay. He would simply pretend the war hadn't started. The launch of Rolling Thunder was kept a secret.

One day later, *The New York Times* reported that America had "decided to launch an undeclared and unexplained war in Vietnam." Johnson was incensed. Never was Johnson angrier than when information leaked—it compromised his control. "In total secrecy, absolutely no leaks!" were words that staff heard every day.

"I don't know how in the world that came out," defense chief McNamara told a furious Johnson. "I thought that was a very bad story."

"Somebody ought to be removed, Bob," demanded the President. "We want some heads to fall."

With the story out and the bombing campaign underway, enemies of the Great Society were ready to pounce. Johnson held them back with a lie. When LBJ told congressional leaders that he hadn't escalated the conflict at all, even the hawks thought twice to question the President: the "old bull" of the Senate still had the power to wreck their future in Congress.

Despite some grumbling on Capitol Hill over the alleged escalation in Vietnam, Johnson's damage control worked. Scores of Great Society bills advanced: air, water, and noise pollution laws; food stamps and housing bills; affirmative action plans; land preservation measures; new Cabinet posts; fairer immigration laws; a National Endowment for the Arts, a Kennedy Center for the Performing Arts, and a Corporation for Public Broadcasting.

As Johnson's dreams for America grew closer to reality, so did his nightmare of Vietnam. Johnson hoped that the air war would perform like a filibuster—"enormous resistance at first, then a steady whittling away, then Ho hurrying to get it over with." But as each wave of Rolling Thunder obliterated more countryside, the Vietcong was more emboldened to fight.

Johnson found it necessary once again to put on a hat he didn't care for—Commander in Chief. If he were going change all of America with his Great Society, he could certainly keep Vietnam from falling to the Communists.

"I'd like to have a scotch and water right now," he told a friend after an exhausting day dealing with Capitol Hill. "But I can't. I've got planes out tonight." Johnson wanted total clarity when he went down to the Situation Room. Inside this small, windowless

sanctum in the White House basement, Johnson traced his finger
over a wall map of Vietnam.

"How many tons of bombs will it take to destroy this?" he asked about a bridge north of Danang. "How important is that to the North Vietnamese?" The questions continued—the President didn't want so much as an outhouse bombed without his explicit permission.

Obsessed with masterminding the bombings, Johnson woke up at 3:30 every morning to check how his "boys" in Vietnam were doing. But his boys were losing, and no matter how hard the President tried to control Vietnam, the war kept slipping out of his reach. Needing something to hang on to, Johnson tightened his grip on the Great Society.

"Never has there been such a Hundred Days!" proclaimed Johnson. Though his Great Society was not yet complete, the first hundred days of the 89th Congress had brought a wealth of victories. The House had approved his plan to give "the wonders of modern medicine" to the elderly and the poor. Medicare and Medicaid was now on its way to the Senate. His voting rights bill had made it past committee, and Johnson believed his plan to give African-Americans a voice at the voting booth would go the distance.

Johnson celebrated with a well-earned trip to his Texas ranch. Looking out the window of his JetStar, a private plane he called "Air Force One-Half," Johnson knew the highway below would be lined with bluebonnet flowers from his legislative gift to Lady Bird—the Highway Beautification Act. But no success excited Johnson more than the reunion awaiting his landing.

Thirty-six years before, when the 20-year-old Johnson

arrived in the dilapidated cow town of Cotulla, Texas, he realized he hadn't been given a choice assignment for his first teaching job. Sweat soaked his new suit. The shanties had been baked dry by the 110-degree heat. The dirt-covered playground of the red brick schoolhouse didn't even have any equipment for the children. Segregation had left this school for Mexican children a state-ignored dump.

But the new teacher for the fifth, sixth, and seventh grades was determined to give his students a chance to reach for something better. The odds were against these children of migrant workers. They came to school without any breakfast and had an expression on their faces that asked, as Johnson remembered, "Why don't people like me? Why do they hate me because I'm brown?"

Every morning he would walk down the row and ask the students if they did their homework. If the girls answered no, he yelled at them and made them stay after school. The boys would get their ears yanked. "It hurt like the dickens," remembered one student. He forced all his kids to speak English. If any of the children said "buenos dias," he turned them over his knee and lashed them with stems from palm trees.

But the kids adored Mr. Johnson from Johnson City. He started a debate society, organized spelling bees, began baseball and track teams, coached the basketball league, and conducted the school band. He even tutored the janitor in English. "A lot of us felt he was too good for us," one student recalled. "We wanted to take advantage of his being here. It was like a blessing from the clear sky."

When the JetStar landed, Johnson was reunited with his former students. "I never thought then, in 1928, that I would be standing here in 1965," said Johnson. In the company of his students, Johnson signed the first major law of the Great Society. Now federal funding for every level of education would be doubled. Johnson believed the sons and daughters of his students would reap the benefits.

"This was a week to put a golden circle around," Lady Bird recorded in her diary. "So let us remember it, because there will be many ringed in black." The weeks to follow brought their share of black circles for Johnson. He spent his days fighting for a Great Society and his nights fighting the Vietcong. Unfortunately for Johnson, America stopped paying attention to his victories on the home front.

Columnists hammered the President for waging a covert war. Protests spread across college campuses. Demonstrations gathered around the Washington Monument. Joan Baez sang for peace, and speeches pleaded for an "immediate cessation" of the bombing. America's support for Lyndon Johnson—he had been elected in the largest popular landslide in American history the year before—began turning to determined opposition.

Johnson had worried about the hawks in Congress, but now the doves turned on him. As Senator William Fulbright spoke out against the President's secret air war, Johnson opted for sweet talk. "It's bad for you to take out after me," he told the liberal Senator. "Now you tell your wife I love her and I *am* sorry you're so damned cranky and grouchy all the time."

Handling Robert Kennedy was not so easy. The dogged brother of JFK was immune to LBJ's legendary powers of persuasion. On the Senate floor, RFK warned that the President risked sending "hundreds of thousands of American troops" to a conflict that "might easily lead to nuclear warfare."

Johnson was scared to death that a war debate would soon explode on Capitol Hill. Once that happened, Johnson knew Congress would abandon his war on poverty for the war overseas. His dream for a great society would die only halfway to completion.

"Oh, I could see it coming all right," predicted Johnson. "History provided too many cases where the sound of the bugle put an immediate end to the hopes and dreams of the best reformers." When LBJ was only five years old, his grandfather put him on his knee and told stories of how the Spanish-American War destroyed the reforms of Populism. World War I ended Woodrow Wilson's New Freedom when Johnson was a teenager. World War II derailed FDR's New Deal when Johnson served in Congress. And now the Vietnam War threatened to kill the Great Society.

The only things separating Johnson from the fate of his predecessors were his lies. And after a lifetime of politics, no one could lie better than LBJ. "In every conversation I have with him he lies," complained Robert Kennedy. "He lies even when he doesn't have to."

Johnson knew his "covert" bombing of the Vietcong was hardly a secret. By this time more bombs had been dropped on North Vietnam than in all of Europe in World War II. Refusing to acknowledge the truth about Rolling Thunder was only destroying the President's reputation. "When you run around saving your face all day," said Johnson, "you end up losing your ass at night."

Yet the lies worked in Congress. No one in Congress was naive enough to completely believe LBJ's denials over the war. But by downplaying Vietnam, Johnson offered Congress little reason to debate what he was doing in Southeast Asia. To call the President out on Vietnam would be to call him a liar. And with few exceptions, neither hawks nor doves were willing to go so far.

By that summer, LBJ was on the home stretch of finishing his

Great Society. The odds looked good. Johnson's "youthful dream of improving life for more people than any other political leader" seemed in reach. He believed the Great Society would redeem him. "Deep down I knew—I simply knew—that the American people loved me," believed Johnson. "After all that I'd done for them and given to them, how could they help but love me?"

Johnson even believed the North Vietnamese might one day love him as much as his Mexican schoolchildren did. He envisioned bringing quality medical care and education programs to North Vietnam. He supported a billion-dollar investment in development of the Mekong River, bringing power, food, and water to impoverished villagers via dams. "We're going to turn the Mekong into a Tennessee Valley," Johnson predicted.

Though Johnson believed North Vietnam could be turned into a Great Society, Ho Chi Minh had other plans. At the start of summer monsoon season, the Vietcong launched a deadly attack. The planes of Rolling Thunder could not aim their bombs through heavy rains. The South Vietnamese army collapsed. The Secretary of Defense told the President, "We're in a hell of a mess."

McNamara recommended that Johnson go in front of Congress and request a call up of 235,000 reserves and an increase in the regular armed forces by approximately 375,000 men. If Johnson took this course of action, McNamara concluded there stood "a good chance of achieving an acceptable outcome within a reasonable time in Vietnam."

Johnson knew he had to send over more American troops. He could not pull out of Vietnam. America had never lost a war before, and LBJ wasn't about to lose the first. But deceiving Congress on this escalation was going to be harder than it was during Rolling Thunder. It all came down to dollars.

McNamara recommended that Johnson ask Congress for a massive appropriation to cover costs of the escalation. Wars cost money, and American tax dollars had to come from coffers Congress ultimately controlled. Johnson knew Congress would hand over the money for Vietnam—but at the expense of his Great Society.

The choice was "guns" or "butter." There simply was not enough federal money available to wage a social war at home and a military war overseas. Even if Congress passed Medicare (which was still stuck in the Senate), the program would have no money to fund it. And the bulk of other Great Society programs wouldn't get enough money for a jump start.

Faced with the imminent death of his dreams, Johnson sank into depression. "He was a tormented man," aide Bill Moyers recalled. "He would just go within himself, just disappear." Once again Johnson retreated to his bed. Moyers found him with the covers pulled almost over his head. Johnson told him he felt as if a Louisiana swamp were pulling him down.

At 5:30 one morning, Johnson thrashed his towering frame under the covers. "I've got to call up 600,000 boys, make them leave their homes and their families!" Lady Bird awoke as her husband's terrifying cries filled the bedroom. "It was as though he were talking out loud, not especially to me," she recorded in her diary.

The First Lady knew her husband agonized at the announcement he soon had to make. "He had no stomach for it," she confided in her diary. "It wasn't the war he wanted. The one he wanted was on poverty and ignorance and disease and that was worth putting your life into."

As President Johnson reached the lectern of the White House East Room on July 28, 1965, he knew his words were better suited for a Joint Session of Congress than for this press conference. "I do not find it easy to send the flower of our youth, our fine young men, into battle," he told the press. Johnson knew the cost of war first-hand. During World War II, he was the first Congressman to leave the comfort of the House of Representatives to go fight in the South Pacific. "I think I know, too, how their mothers weep and how their families sorrow."

When his speech turned to numbers, LBJ kept them low. He told the press that he was only increasing troop commitments by 50,000. Johnson insisted this routine deployment was no change in current policy. He lied.

"There is something else, too," Johnson continued. "It is now my opportunity to help every child get an education, to help every Negro and every American citizen have an equal opportunity, to have every family get a decent home, and to help bring healing to the sick and dignity to the old. That is what I have lived for, that is what I have wanted all my life since I was a little boy, and I do not want to see all those hopes and all those dreams . . . drowned in the wasteful ravages of cruel wars. I am going to do all I can do to see that that never happens."

That afternoon Medicare passed the Senate by a vote of 70 to 24. For now Congress would wage the war *he* wanted to fight. Johnson had chosen both guns *and* butter. "After all," believed Johnson, "our country was built by pioneers who had a rifle in one hand to kill their enemies and an ax in the other to build their homes and provide for their families."

But guns and butter would come at an extraordinary cost for

LBJ. Inevitably the bill for Vietnam would have to be paid and Congress would have to write the checks. And once Congress found out they were paying for both the Great Society war and the Vietnam War, Johnson would be pilloried. If a President had tried to do this when he was majority leader, "by God," LBJ said, "Lyndon Johnson would have torn his balls off."

On August 27, 1965, Lyndon Johnson celebrated his 57th birthday. At Lady Bird's request, the White House kitchen staff decorated the cake with symbols of the Great Society. But the words on top were iced with irony: "You can have your cake and eat it too." As Johnson blew out the candles perhaps he made that wish. The tragedy and pinnacle of his presidency was that it came true.

The next month historian William Leuchtenburg interviewed President Johnson on the 89th Congress, only weeks before it closed. "Mr. President, this has been a remarkable Congress."

Johnson looked intently into his eyes.

"It is even arguable whether this isn't the most significant Congress ever."

"No it isn't," Johnson snapped. "It's not arguable. Not if you can read it isn't. Never before have the three independent branches been so productive. Never has the American system worked so efficiently in producing quality legislation—and at a time when our system is under attack all over the world." By the end of the 89th Congress, 90 out of 115 Great Society proposals had been passed.

"The first year or two in the White House was wine and roses," Lady Bird remembered. "But by the end, it was pure hell." As war protesters screamed "Hey, Hey, LBJ! How many kids did you kill today?" the country became overtaken by the war debate. By the end of his presidency, Johnson became a pariah in Congress and had lost the power to enact the full extent of his legislative dreams. But by then the greatest efforts of his Great Society had enough funding to take on a life of their own.

After Johnson chose not to run for reelection in 1968, he retired to his Texas ranch, a better fit for his outsize cowboy character. He drove his white Lincoln around the fields for hours, giving his four ranch hands ultimatums with the same tone he gave to his advisers. He micromanaged his ranch like he did Congress, noting with exact detail the number of eggs his chickens laid. Johnson had shut himself off to a hermit's existence. At least this isolated world was one he could control.

Though the Vietnam War raged on, Johnson rarely remarked on the conflict. The death of over 50,000 Americans was too great to acknowledge. Occasionally he kept tabs on the progress of his Great Society. He had once believed that his "baby" would grow into a beautiful woman. "I figured she'd be so big and beautiful that the American people couldn't help but fall in love with her," Johnson recalled from his ranch.

But President Richard Nixon had set his sights on slashing the programs with budget cuts. "She's getting thinner and thinner and uglier and uglier all the time," said Johnson. "The American people will refuse to look at her; they'll stick her in a closet to hide her away and there she'll die. And when she dies, I, too, will die."

On January 21, 1973, the day after his inauguration to a second term, President Nixon declared a cease-fire in Vietnam. Later that day, he announced his plan to dismantle the Great Society.

The day after that, Lyndon Johnson was dead.

President Lyndon Johnson
Presidential News Conference on Vietnam
July 28, 1965

My fellow Americans:

Not long ago I received a letter from a woman in the Midwest. She wrote:

Dear Mr. President:

In my humble way I am writing to you about the crisis in Viet-Nam. I have a son who is now in Viet-Nam. My husband served in World War II. Our country was at war, but now, this time, it is just something that I don't understand. Why?

Well, I have tried to answer that question dozens of times and more in practically every State in this Union. I have discussed it fully in Baltimore in April, in Washington in May, in San Francisco in June. Let me again, now, discuss it here in the East Room of the White House.

Why must young Americans, born into a land exultant with hope and with golden promise, toil and suffer and sometimes die in such a remote and distant place?

The answer, like the war itself, is not an easy one, but it echoes clearly from the painful lessons of half a century. Three times in my lifetime, in two World Wars and in Korea, Americans

have gone to far lands to fight for freedom. We have learned at a
terrible and a brutal cost that retreat does not bring safety and
weakness does not bring peace.

It is this lesson that has brought us to Viet-Nam. This is a
different kind of war. There are no marching armies or solemn
declarations. Some citizens of South Viet-Nam at times, with
understandable grievances, have joined in the attack on their own
government.

But we must not let this mask the central fact that this is really
war. It is guided by North Viet-Nam and it is spurred by Communist
China. Its goal is to conquer the South, to defeat American power,
and to extend the Asiatic dominion of communism.

There are great stakes in the balance.

Most of the non-Communist nations of Asia cannot, by
themselves and alone, resist the growing might and the grasping
ambition of Asian communism.

Our power, therefore, is a very vital shield. If we are driven
from the field in Viet-Nam, then no nation can ever again have
the same confidence in American promise, or in American
protection.

In each land the forces of independence would be considerably
weakened, and an Asia so threatened by Communist domination
would certainly imperil the security of the United States itself.

We did not choose to be the guardians at the gate, but there is no one else. Nor would surrender in Viet-Nam bring peace, because we learned from Hitler at Munich that success only feeds the appetite of aggression. The battle would be renewed in one country and then another country, bringing with it perhaps even larger and crueler conflict, as we have learned from the lessons of history.

Moreover, we are in Viet-Nam to fulfill one of the most solemn pledges of the American Nation. Three Presidents—President Eisenhower, President Kennedy, and your present President—over 11 years have committed themselves and have promised to help defend this small and valiant nation.

Strengthened by that promise, the people of South Viet-Nam have fought for many long years. Thousands of them have died. Thousands more have been crippled and scarred by war. We just cannot now dishonor our word, or abandon our commitment, or leave those who believed in us and who trusted us to the terror and repression and murder that would follow.

This, then, my fellow Americans, is why we are in Viet-Nam.

What are our goals in that war-strained land?

First, we intend to convince the Communists that we cannot be defeated by force of arms or by superior power. They are not easily convinced. In recent months they have greatly increased their fighting forces and their attacks and the number of incidents.

I have asked the Commanding General, General Westmoreland, what more he needs to meet this mounting aggression. He has told me. We will meet his needs.

I have today ordered to Viet-Nam the Air Mobile Division and certain other forces which will raise our fighting strength from 75,000 to 125,000 men almost immediately. Additional forces will be needed later, and they will be sent as requested.

This will make it necessary to increase our active fighting forces by raising the monthly draft call from 17,000 over a period of time to 35,000 per month, and for us to step up our campaign for voluntary enlistments.

After this past week of deliberations, I have concluded that it is not essential to order Reserve units into service now. If that necessity should later be indicated, I will give the matter most careful consideration and I will give the country—you—an adequate notice before taking such action, but only after full preparations.

We have also discussed with the Government of South Viet-Nam lately, the steps that we will take to substantially increase their own effort, both on the battlefield, and toward reform and progress in the villages. Ambassador Lodge is now formulating a new program to be tested upon his return to that area.

I have directed Secretary Rusk and Secretary McNamara to be available immediately to the Congress to review with these committees, the appropriate congressional committees, what we plan to do in these areas. I have asked them to be able to answer the questions of any member of Congress.

Secretary McNamara, in addition, will ask the Senate Appropriations Committee to add a limited amount to present legislation to help meet part of this new cost until a supplemental measure is ready and hearings can be held when the Congress assembles in January. In the meantime, we will use the authority contained in the present Defense appropriation bill under consideration to transfer funds in addition to the additional money that we will ask.

These steps, like our actions in the past, are carefully measured to do what must be done to bring an end to aggression and a peaceful settlement.

We do not want an expanding struggle with consequences that no one can perceive, nor will we bluster or bully or flaunt our power, but we will not surrender and we will not retreat.

For behind our American pledge lies the determination and resources, I believe, of all of the American Nation.

Second, once the Communists know, as we know, that a violent solution is impossible, then a peaceful solution is inevitable.

We are ready now, as we have always been, to move from the battlefield to the conference table. I have stated publicly and many times, again and again, America's willingness to begin unconditional discussions with any government, at any place, at any time. Fifteen efforts have been made to start these discussions with the help of 40 nations throughout the world, but there has been no answer.

But we are going to continue to persist, if persist we must, until death and desolation have led to the same conference table where others could now join us at a much smaller cost.

I have spoken many times of our objectives in Viet-Nam. So has the Government of South Viet-Nam. Hanoi has set forth its own proposals. We are ready to discuss their proposals and our proposals and any proposals of any government whose people may be affected, for we fear the meeting room no more than we fear the battlefield.

In this pursuit we welcome and we ask for the concern and the assistance of any nation and all nations. If the United Nations and its officials or any one of its 114 members can by deed or word, private initiative or public action, bring us nearer an honorable peace, then they will have the support and the gratitude of the United States of America.

I have directed Ambassador Goldberg to go to New York today and to present immediately to Secretary General U Thant a letter from me requesting that all the resource, energy, and immense prestige of the United Nations be employed to find ways to halt aggression and to bring peace in Viet-Nam.

I made a similar request at San Francisco a few weeks ago, because we do not seek the destruction of any government, nor do we covet a foot of any territory. But we insist and we will always insist that the people of South Viet-Nam shall have the right of choice, the right to shape their own destiny in free elections in the South or throughout all Viet-Nam under international supervision, and they shall not have any government imposed upon them by force and terror so long as we can prevent it.

This was the purpose of the 1954 agreements which the Communists have now cruelly shattered. If the machinery of those agreements was tragically weak, its purposes shall guide our action. As battle rages, we will continue as best we can to help the good people of South Viet-Nam enrich the condition of their life, to feed the hungry and to tend the sick, and teach the young, and shelter the homeless, and to help the farmer to increase his crops, and the worker to find a job.

It is an ancient but still terrible irony that while many leaders of men create division in pursuit of grand ambitions, the children of man are really united in the simple, elusive desire for a life of fruitful and rewarding toil.

As I said at Johns Hopkins in Baltimore, I hope that one day we can help all the people of Asia toward that desire. Eugene Black has made great progress since my appearance in Baltimore in that direction—not as the price of peace, for we are ready always to bear a more painful cost, but rather as a part of our obligations of justice toward our fellow man.

Let me also add now a personal note. I do not find it easy to send the flower of our youth, our fine young men, into battle. I have spoken to you today of the divisions and the forces and the battalions and the units, but I know them all, every one. I have seen them in a thousand streets, of a hundred towns, in every State in this Union—working and laughing and building, and filled with hope and life. I think I know, too, how their mothers weep and how their families sorrow.

This is the most agonizing and the most painful duty of your President. There is something else, too. When I was young, poverty was so common that we didn't know it had a name. An education was something that you had to fight for, and water was really life itself. I have now been in public life 35 years, more than three decades, and in each of those 35 years I have seen good men, and wise leaders, struggle to bring the blessings of this land to all of our people.

And now I am the President. It is now my opportunity to help every child get an education, to help every Negro and every American citizen have an equal opportunity, to have every family get a decent home, and to help bring healing to the sick and dignity to the old.

As I have said before, that is what I have lived for, that is what I have wanted all my life since I was a little boy, and I do not want to see all those hopes and all those dreams of so many people for so many years now drowned in the wasteful ravages of cruel wars. I am going to do all I can do to see that that never happens.

But I also know, as a realistic public servant, that as long as there are men who hate and destroy, we must have the courage to resist, or we will see it all, all that we have built, all that we hope to build, all of our dreams for freedom—all, all will be swept away on the flood of conquest.

So, too, this shall not happen. We will stand in Viet-Nam . . .

THE MAP
FOR PEACE

LT. GENERAL ULYSSES GRANT, COLD HARBOR, VIRGINIA, 1864.

National Archives & Records Administration.

CHAPTER 7

A GENERAL SKIRTS WAR

Ulysses Grant and Cuba

On a clear spring day in late April 1869, the schooner *Grapeshot* sailed from New York harbor. On board were two passengers, Charles Speakman of Indiana and Albert Wyeth of Pennsylvania. Both were headed for a peaceful sojourn in Jamaica. Wyeth, who was only 20, hoped the Caribbean's tropical air would improve his poor health. Each expected an uneventful voyage south.

But only hours after leaving port, the *Grapeshot* pulled up alongside another boat on the open water of New York Bay. Speakman and Wyeth saw a large number of armed men come aboard, apparently with the consent of the crew. The two Americans were alarmed. Why hadn't these fighters boarded the ship when it was in port? Speakman asked to be taken ashore. He had a wife and child and wanted to see them again. The crew assured him there was nothing to worry about, and the ship sailed on down the coast.

As the ship proceeded, the two Americans listened closely to the new arrivals for clues. Both suspected the same thing. The papers in New York were full of news about the rebellion in Cuba against the Spanish. Groups of wealthy Cuban exiles in the United States were organizing expeditions, sending arms and soldiers to the rebels. These expeditions violated American law, which would explain why the fighters on board the *Grapeshot* had boarded the ship only after it left port.

Most Americans supported the Cuban rebellion, but from a comfortable distance. From the safety of one's drawing room, it was easy to picture a noble band of freedom fighters battling the hated Spanish on palm-shaded beaches under the light of a tropical moon. Speakman and Wyeth, far from their drawing rooms, might have read enough in the papers to know better. Cuba was a nightmare.

Many of the rebels were liberated slaves—half a million Africans were enslaved on the island's sugar plantations—and had only their own machetes with which to fight. Some Congolese fought with poison-tipped daggers. Unable to match Spanish firepower, the rebels had retreated to the island's wild, forested interior, emerging mainly to burn fields and houses and to terrorize Spanish loyalists. They were known to string up captured Spanish soldiers head down over a slow fire.

The Spanish had responded to the insurgency with characteristic brutality. They gave rebels the "usual four shots in the back" or the garrote—an iron collar tightened around a victim's neck with a screw until he was strangled to death. They decreed that any male caught off his plantation without an excuse would be shot. Any house not flying a white flag would be burned. Spanish sympathizers heard that a play being performed in Havana included a rebel song and responded by massacring the play's audience during a performance.

As the *Grapeshot* continued on its way south, Speakman and Wyeth stared out over the Atlantic. The undeniable fact was this: vacationers heading for Jamaican beaches didn't bring 4,000 guns and two cannons along for the trip.

The Americans' fears, unfortunately, were entirely justified. When the *Grapeshot* reached the Caribbean in late June, the

fighters, who were indeed Cubans, took control of the ship and ran
her aground on a beach near Guantánamo. They forced Speakman
and Wyeth to disembark with them. The two men resolved to save
themselves. At the first opportunity, they escaped from the rebels
and surrendered to the Spanish authorities, hoping for safe passage
back to the mainland. The Spanish authorities promptly shot both
men. The executions, which took place over the vehement objections
of the American consul, violated the terms of a U.S.-Spanish treaty.
Speakman's death left his wife and child penniless.

Far to the north, in the White House, President Ulysses
Grant read of his countrymen's death with disgust. The behavior
of the Spanish was intolerable. They had already been audacious
enough to seize American ships on the open sea. U.S. citizens in
Cuba had been arrested without cause. If Spain was now going
to wantonly murder innocent Americans without trial, then the
United States would have to respond.

Since his inauguration four months before, Grant had been
under constant pressure to do something to help the rebels,
whose struggle attracted the attention of the American public for
a number of reasons. Americans instinctively opposed European
influence in the New World. And only four years after the Civil
War, they were also acutely aware of the injustice of slavery, which
the Cuban rebels had pledged to end. Finally, the rebels' draft
constitution endorsed the annexation of Cuba by the United States,
appealing to a growing sense of American Manifest Destiny—of
seeing, in the words of Grant's Secretary of War, John Rawlins,
"the aegis of our power spread over this continent."

It was a potent combination. "Something must be done
for Cuba," wailed the *New York Tribune*, echoing most other

newspapers. In the early months of Grant's term, the "something" people had in mind was for the President to officially recognize the rebels as combatants. Recognition was a diplomatic technicality, but enormous practical consequences followed from it. It would allow American aid—like the *Grapeshot* expedition—to flow to the rebels and could make a decisive difference in the war. And it would cost the government nothing.

Congress had joined the public in calling for the President to take this step. In April, the House of Representatives had passed a resolution expressing support for the rebels' "patriotic efforts to secure their independence" and promising to support the President if he should "recognize the independence and sovereignty of such government." Large majorities in both parties voted for the resolution.

But throughout the first months of his term, Grant did nothing. No one could quite figure out why. There was no doubt that the President personally sympathized with the rebel cause. And the former Union commander also felt that recognizing the rebels would repay the Spanish for their conduct during the Civil War. Spain had recognized the Confederacy early in that conflict, and Grant had not forgotten. He asked Charles Sumner, the chairman of the Senate's Foreign Relations Committee, "How would it do to issue a proclamation with regard to Cuba identical with that issued by Spain in regard to us?" Doing so was Grant's prerogative— why did he continue to delay?

By the summer of 1869, when Speakman and Wyeth were murdered, the pressure on Grant had grown intense. The Cuban exiles organized mass meetings in New York and elsewhere that drew thousands. Ladies sold their jewels to give money to the Cuban cause. Rawlins and other members of Grant's Cabinet urged "more speedy action." Editorials calling for the President to recognize the rebels blanketed the newspapers. Before, Grant could argue that he was merely continuing the policy of the last administration, but public pressure and continuing Spanish provocations were forcing him to confront the issue directly.

Despite public feeling and the President's own sympathies, Secretary of State Hamilton Fish pressed Grant not to recognize the rebels. A battle for the President's support quickly became a contest between Fish, whom Grant considered the ablest member of his Cabinet, and John Rawlins, an old friend and fellow soldier. After hearing of the murder of Speakman and Wyeth, Fish redoubled his efforts to persuade the President not to intervene.

Fish believed that recognition might be the first step leading the United States into war. Spain was sure to see recognition of the rebels as an act of hostility and would not shrink from a potential conflict— cartoons of war in Havana newspapers were already depicting the Spanish lion tearing apart the American eagle. Recognition might provoke the Spanish into even more egregious crimes against American citizens or interests, and then the public clamor in the United States for a war against Spain might become irresistible.

Spain had long since passed its peak as a world power, which only added to its resolve to hold on to Cuba. Spain had a large number of men to commit to any conflict, and a well-equipped navy guarded Cuban ports. The American army, meanwhile, was a mere skeleton force compared with its size at the end of the Civil War. Plus, the U.S. Army was already occupied with Reconstruction in the South and clashes between white settlers and Native Americans in the West. Besides, little more than four years had passed since Appomattox. Did the President want to lead his country into another war so soon—a war it didn't have to fight?

Furthermore, Fish, an attorney, did not believe that international law sanctioned recognition of the rebels. Foreign powers traditionally recognized only insurgencies with functioning governments. But the Cuban rebels ruled no territory. Some argued they were more a loose network of bandits than a unified movement. Notwithstanding their just cause, it was not enough to merit recognition.

Fish took into account another agenda. He was still pursuing substantial American claims against the British dating from the Civil War, when Confederate ships built in English shipyards had done major damage to Union shipping. The basis of these claims was that Britain should never have recognized the Confederacy during the Civil War. The U.S. government could hardly argue that British actions were improper if the President, at the same time, recognized the Cuban rebels, who were unquestionably less worthy of such legal approval than the Confederacy had been.

Finally, the Secretary of State argued, recognition might be unnecessary in any event—the Spanish had expressed a willingness to negotiate an end to the conflict. On July 1, Fish had sent American envoys to Madrid for this purpose. The murders of Speakman and Wyeth were outrageous, but the Spanish would leave the table if America recognized the rebels. Despite the murder of the two Americans, Grant agreed that the envoys should be given a chance. He would not, however, wait forever—particularly if the Spanish tried to use the talks as cover for further outrages.

Fish had succeeded in buying more time, but he knew that the prospects for a settlement with the Spanish were dim. They valued Cuba too highly. He just wanted time to whittle away at Grant, convincing him that America should not get involved.

As Fish carried out his plan, he had no indication of what the President thought. No one ever did. During the Civil War, Grant shouldered the ultimate responsibility for the success of the Union's armies. To do this, he enlisted a very capable staff of subordinates. But when the time came for a crucial decision, Grant did not call war councils. Instead, he would take his maps and cigars (he loaded his pockets with two dozen every morning) and withdraw, alone, to his tent. Curious officers, looking in, could see nothing through the thick haze of smoke but the burning tip of the general's cigar as he brooded in silence through the night.

The plans that emerged from the smoke were invariably risky. Many other Army officers considered them rash or even foolhardy. Early in the war, Grant's superiors responded to his penchant for taking chances by frantically searching for someone to replace him. "I fear Grant has made a fatal mistake," said Army Chief of Staff Henry Halleck, following yet another daring stroke late in the war. By then Halleck should have known that Grant's stratagems usually worked.

Halleck was not alone in underestimating Grant—most people did. Grant rarely impressed anyone. One man called him an "ordinary, scrubby-looking man, with a slightly seedy look, as if he was out of office on half-pay." Another thought him "plain as an old shoe." Add to this a habitual silence and you have what one historian described as a man with "the odd quality of unintentionally vanishing from view in any crowd."

But the men who served under Grant knew his haggard exterior concealed "natural qualities of a high order." Not the least of these, self-reliance. This quality had immediately endeared Grant to his Commander in Chief. Lincoln had been frustrated by a series of hesitant Union commanders: "You know how it's been with all the rest. As soon as I put a man in command of the army he'd come to me with a plan of campaign and about as much as say, 'Now, I don't believe I can do it, but if you say so I'll try it on,' and so put the responsibility of success or failure on me. . . . It isn't so with Grant. He hasn't told me what his plans are. . . . I'm glad to find a man who can go ahead without me."

Back in his office at the State Department, Hamilton Fish felt sympathy for those officers who had peeked into Grant's tent. He couldn't read the President's thoughts either, but unlike Lincoln, he desperately wanted to know. Fish decided to do the only thing he could—try to make Grant's choice an easy one.

For the next two months, the Secretary of State worked frantically to conclude a settlement with the Spanish. But a series of transatlantic cables between Madrid and Washington accomplished nothing. And the situation in Cuba only worsened. Hard-line Spanish sympathizers massacred rebels and suspects daily.

The President, meanwhile, appeared to lean more and more toward recognition. He reinforced naval forces in the Caribbean. In August, he appeared to lose patience altogether. While traveling, the President instructed Fish to issue a proclamation that would recognize the rebels if America did not receive a satisfactory reply to its latest settlement offer. Fish feared Secretary of War Rawlins' influence. Once again the Secretary of State convinced Grant to delay. But, unless the situation improved, it appeared to be only a matter of time before the President ordered recognition.

Through late summer, the Congress, the media, and American citizens became riled over the Cuba issue. On August 30, the *New York Sun* called it the government's duty "at once to

interfere in Cuba.... But this is a duty which we cannot hope to
see performed by an Administration so barren of great ideas, and
so deficient in character."

Grant returned to Washington. A Cabinet meeting was
scheduled for the next day. Cuba was at the top of the agenda.
The stage was set for a showdown between Secretary of State
Hamilton Fish and Secretary of War John Rawlins.

Fish dreaded a climactic fight with Rawlins for two reasons.
The first was the President's sheer unpredictability, amply
evidenced by Grant's Civil War record. The English poet
Matthew Arnold, who saw Grant when the former President
visited Britain in 1877, summed up the attitude of many toward
Grant's generalship. He thought Grant a "business-like man, who
by possession of unlimited resources in men and money, and by
the unsparing use of them, had been enabled to wear down and
exhaust the strength of the South, this was what I supposed Grant
to be, this and little more." In fact, casualties suffered by soldiers
under Grant were usually lower, proportionately, than those of
the Southern forces he faced. But Arnold's judgment also missed
entirely what made Grant different from other Union generals—
his determination to force the enemy to fight and, if necessary, to
take enormous risks in doing so. To the oft-frustrated Lincoln,
this was welcome: "The only evidence you have that he's any
place is that he makes things git! Wherever he is things move."

Though recognition of the Cuban rebels could set the nation
on a path leading to war, Fish was afraid this might not deter the
man who had been so unpredictable, risk-taking, and bold as to
have seized Vicksburg. That, Fish knew, was the real Grant.

Vicksburg, on the eastern bank of the Mississippi, had been the key to Union victory in the West. But in 1862 and 1863, Grant's army was stymied north of the city. Vicksburg's defenses were weaker on its southern side, but there was no easy way for the Union army to get there. Confederate artillery defended the river along a 14-mile line gauntlet. After six months, General Grant took his cigars and maps and retreated to the former ladies' salon of the *Magnolia*, his headquarters ship during the campaign. His officers, as usual, waited anxiously outside the door.

Grant emerged with perhaps the boldest plan of the war. The Union army (over 20,000 men) would board transports and drift down the river along its western bank, slipping by the Confederate guns under cover of darkness. Once below Vicksburg, the army would land on the east bank of the river and march north through Mississippi. The Union army would be outnumbered and without hope of resupply. So what? In Grant's own words, "[u]p to this time it had been regarded as an axiom in war that large bodies of troops must operate from a base of supplies which they always covered and guarded in all forward movements." Grant proposed that his army live off the land.

Like the rest of Grant's subordinates at the time, William Tecumseh Sherman was horrified. He openly objected to Grant: "Sherman then expressed his alarm at the plan I had ordered, saying that I was putting myself in a position voluntarily which an enemy would be glad to manoeuvre a year—or a long time—to get me in. I was going into the enemy's country, with a large river behind me and the enemy holding points strongly fortified above and below."

But Grant had decided his course, and the plan was set in motion. At first, he appeared to have made a horrible blunder.

When Union ships tried to sneak past the Rebel guns, the Confederates lit huge blazes on both sides of the river to light up their targets. Grant watched from the deck of the *Magnolia* as his ships took continuous fire for over 90 minutes.

Miraculously, the army sustained only minor losses. It successfully landed on the east bank of the river and moved through Mississippi easily without a supply chain. Ten weeks later, Vicksburg surrendered. The next year, the once-skeptical Sherman, commanding an army twice as large as Grant's had been, marched across Georgia utterly without a base of supply. Grant, meanwhile, headed east to take on Robert E. Lee. "Grant is my man," said Lincoln, "and I am his the rest of the war."

If Grant's unpredictability was one concern, Fish also feared a clash with Rawlins over Cuba because of the President's close relationship with the Secretary of War. Fish, a patrician New Yorker and a dozen years older than the President, had little in common with him (Grant was the son of an Ohio tanner), whereas Rawlins, a few years younger than Grant, had been a crucial presence in his life for years. The President would be sure to listen to anything Rawlins said with a strong sense of trust.

To understand the important relationship of John Rawlins to Ulysses Grant, one must appreciate Grant's severe drinking problem. As a young man, Grant graduated from West Point and became a career Army officer. In 1853 he was sent to Fort Humboldt, a remote outpost on the Pacific coast 250 miles north of San Francisco. Missing his wife and children, he took refuge in liquor. One day, his wife received an unexpected letter announcing his resignation from the Army. Her husband gave no explanation, but most now believe that his commanding officer found him drunk while on duty and demanded his resignation. He came East, penniless and with no idea how he would support his family.

Grant found himself to be unsuited for civilian life. For four years, he and his aptly named wife, Hardscrabble, struggled to farm a property in Missouri. He couldn't make it work. At one point, he pawned his watch so his family could celebrate Christmas. Then, to make ends meet, he sold firewood on street corners in St. Louis.

Finally, in his late 30s, Grant swallowed his pride and asked his father for a job in Illinois as a clerk. It was there that he met the tall, dark-eyed, and rigidly moral Rawlins. When the Southern states seceded, both men volunteered to fight for the Union. Grant initially had trouble securing appointment as an officer (rumors of his drinking had traveled east from Fort Humboldt), but a commission as colonel came in June 1861 and he quickly moved up the ranks. Rawlins served as Grant's adjutant for much of the war.

Despite the misery that the bottle had previously caused him, Grant drank as hard as ever during the war. But Rawlins kept him in check, scolding the general and threatening to resign if Grant did not immediately curb his habit. As a result, though Grant was drunk on occasions, there was never a serious charge during the war that liquor impaired Grant's performance. A journalist said this was due entirely to "Rawlins' uncompromising attitude, and Grant's acquiescence in what he knew to be for his own good."

Lincoln, for his part, was unconcerned with General Grant's habit. The now hoary anecdote is true: A group of congressmen came to the White House and pressed him to relieve Grant because he drank too much. Described Lincoln, "I then began to ask them if they knew what he drank, what brand of whiskey he used, telling them seriously that I wished they could find out . . . for if it made fighting generals like Grant, I should like to get some of it for distribution."

When Grant was elected President, he wanted to appoint his friend to command U.S. troops in Arizona, hoping that the desert air would help Rawlins' tuberculosis. But Rawlins objected; he wanted to be the Secretary of War. Though Grant had misgivings (Washington's swampy climate was the last thing Rawlins needed), he could not deny his friend.

The new young Secretary became what newspapers called the "aggressive spirit in the Cabinet," promoting the cause of the Cuban rebels. However, only a few months into Grant's presidency, by August of 1869, Rawlins had suffered a hemorrhage of the lungs—possibly on account of his insistence on remaining in the capital—and was near death.

The President and other members of the Cabinet gathered in the White House at noon on August 31. A hush fell as Rawlins, weak and clearly near the end, struggled through the door. Grant was appalled at his friend's decline. Trembling with weakness and emotion, the Secretary of War made a long and impassioned argument for supporting the rebels. He spoke of the tyranny of the Spanish, the brutality of their response to the rebellion, their offenses to American sovereignty, and their crimes against American citizens, including Speakman and Wyeth.

Rawlins then angrily attacked Fish for trying to delay action by the President. Finally, exhausted, he turned to Grant: "I have been your adjutant, and I think you will excuse me for being earnest." Restraining his emotions with difficulty, the President simply replied, "Certainly, and you are still my adjutant."

It was then Fish's turn to speak. He calmly reviewed why Grant should not recognize the rebels. We will never know if Grant had made up his mind before the meeting or if the arguments of that day convinced him. But as the discussion continued he began to write. When he finished he gave what he had written to Fish, who read the decision aloud:

> *The United States are willing to mediate between Spain and Cuba, in following terms: Immediate armistice. Cuba to recompense Spain for public property, etc. All Spaniards to be protected in their persons and property if they wish to remain on the island, or to withdraw from it, at their option . . . . These conditions to be accepted by September 25 (or October 1), or the United States to be regarded as having withdrawn all offer to mediate.*

Resisting the pressure from the public and Congress, his own sympathy for the Cubans, and, perhaps most of all, his respect and feeling for his dying friend, Grant had effectively chosen not to intervene in Cuba.

The motives for Grant's decision are a mystery. Fish had emphasized throughout 1869 that recognition was not justified in the legal sense, but it seems likely that the President had different concerns. Little more than four years before, Grant had walked through fields covered with wounded and dying men. More than anyone else in the room that day, he could appreciate what he called the "fearful lesson" of the Civil War, which, he said, "should teach us the necessity of avoiding wars in the future."

His refusal to recognize the Cuban rebels showed that he, at least, had learned the lesson.

Six days after that fateful Cabinet meeting, Rawlins died. In his final moments, he pleaded with a fellow Cabinet member, John Creswell, to "stand by the Cubans. Cuba must be free. Her tyrannical enemy must be crushed. . . . The Republic is responsible for its liberty." Grant cut short a visit to New York to be by Rawlins' side, arriving one hour too late.

The President later learned with surprise that a group of Cuban exiles had given the destitute Rawlins $28,000 in Cuban bonds. These were worthless, but they would have been honored at face value if the rebels had prevailed. Rawlins had no doubt been concerned for the welfare of his family following his death. And Grant did not doubt that Rawlins' belief in the justice of the rebels' cause had been genuine. Still, it provided a curious insight for Grant.

The Cuba issue did not die with Rawlins. The rebellion raged on, the Spanish committed more atrocities, and the American public continued to press for action. In early 1870, Congress again took up the question of the "atrocious and satanic barbarism" of the Spanish. John Sherman, the brother of Grant's fellow general, introduced a resolution recognizing the Cuban rebels. The measure, though probably unconstitutional (since the power of recognition was vested only in the President), would deal a serious political blow to Grant if it passed. The *New York Tribune* exulted that action was near: "Speak at last! Speak out, we entreat the representatives of the people, and speak at once!"

This time Grant wavered. He worried openly that opposing Congress would threaten the rest of his foreign policy. Throughout the spring, he tried to distance himself from what newspapers were calling Hamilton Fish's "do-nothing" policy. At one point, Fish threatened to resign unless he received more support from the President.

On Friday, June 10, two congressmen came to see Fish. They told him that the legislature was about to vote on recognition and that the vote would be close. Fish desperately wanted to prevent Congress from forcing a change in policy. He believed the only way to do so was for the President to send a special message to the Capitol.

Fish drafted the message over the weekend. It stated that recognition was a legal issue "not to be decided by sympathies for or prejudices against either party." The Cuban rebellion simply did not have a de facto government that justified recognition. Fish put the paper in front of the President before breakfast on Monday—but would Grant agree to send it to the Hill?

Grant reviewed the message and held another Cabinet debate. Grant made a few objections—he thought the message should condemn Spanish cruelty. But by now, most Cabinet members had fallen into line behind Fish. That afternoon, Grant agreed to send the message to Congress.

A courier bounded up the Capitol steps at four o'clock, just before debate on the resolution began. A cry of indignation arose from rebel supporters as the President's statement was read aloud. It was "the most impudent message ever sent" to Congress. Some asserted that it must have been drafted by a person in the pay of Spain. The debate was tumultuous. Speeches by supporters of recognition met with loud applause from the Cuban sympathizers packing the galleries. A fight nearly broke out in the House cloakroom. The next day the *Sun* declared: "under the demoralizing teachings of Hamilton Fish [Grant] has become another man—almost no man at all."

But the President's decision to state his position firmly had turned the tide. On June 16, the House voted 100 to 70 to reject the resolution. The Cuban rebels would not be recognized. Attorney General Rockwood Hoar called the vote the "greatest triumph the Administration has yet achieved." With characteristic simplicity, the President said only that he liked the vote "very much."

The Cuban rebellion dragged on for the remainder of Grant's two terms as President. Spain finally defeated the rebels, but over 250,000 people were killed in the conflict.

Grant had shown that he was not afraid to bear the burden of responsibility. Matthew Arnold, at least, agreed. The man who initially had such a low opinion of the general and President later revised his judgment. He might have been speaking of the Cuban crisis when he wrote admiringly that "[p]ublic opinion seemed in favour of a hard and insolent course, the authorities seemed putting pressure upon Grant to make him follow it. He resisted with firmness and dignity."

When Grant accepted his party's nomination for President, he concluded his speech with the words "Let us have peace." Most historians regard Grant's presidency as an abysmal failure. But Presidents are often judged on how they respond to disaster, not whether they avert it. Grant's decisions during the Cuban crisis prevented America from being drawn into yet another bloody war. One of the century's greatest generals preserved the peace he wanted so much.

President Ulysses Grant
Letter to Congress regarding Cuba
June 13, 1870

Soon after the opening of the present session of Congress, all that was officially known by the government of the condition of affairs in Cuba was communicated, and from time to time since all the correspondence that has taken place between Spain and the United States, relative to Cuban affairs, has been furnished for the information of that body. Previous to the meeting of Congress I adhered to the precedents of my predecessors in office in maintaining a strict neutrality in the affairs of Spain, with which government we were at peace. During the Session I have not felt myself justified in taking a step which might be attended with serious results without the advice of that body [the legislative branch of the government].

Three times since the beginning of the conflict in Cuba American vessels, protected by the United States flag, have been captured upon the high seas and carried into Spanish ports. In but one instance has there been any reparation made, and then tardily up to the present time, though repeatedly demanded and often promised, no copies even have been furnished this government of the evidence upon which the other two vessels were condemned. In view of these facts and the further fact that Spain, with all her Armies and Armament [the combined power of her army and navy], has not been able to suppress the rebellion which has now continued almost two years and in view of the failure of Spain to protect American citizens, or to give them time to prove their

innocence of complicity in conspiracy against Spanish authority,
as two American prisoners who were executed declared their
ability to do and the proximity to our own shores of the seat of
war, it becomes a question, how long we can permit this contest
without further noticing it and what our duty is to the unhappy
belligerents, to humanity and to ourselves.

I believe the time has come when a decided protest should be
entered, by the United States, against a further continuance of
the strife in Cuba, and against the summary manner of taking the
lives of prisoners, almost as soon as captured.

This grave question is submitted to Congress for its action.

COLONEL THEODORE ROOSEVELT, 1ST CAVALRY, U.S. VOLUNTEERS, 1898.

National Archives & Records Administration

CHAPTER 8

PEACE WARRIOR

———————◆———————

Theodore Roosevelt and the Russo-Japanese Peace Plan

On September 3, 1885, the Marquis de Morès, a distant relative of French kings, sat in a jail cell in the Dakota Territory and plotted his next move. Handsome, rich, and still in his late 20s, the Marquis had come to the West two years before intending to make a fortune in refrigerated beef, buy off the French army, and reclaim his country's throne. Buying up huge tracts of land, the "crazy Frenchman" had gotten himself into a boundary dispute with three frontiersmen. After one of the men threatened to shoot him "like a dog on sight," the Marquis, with some hired help, arranged an ambush. One of the men died in the fight, and de Morès now awaited trial for murder.

But today something else bothered him. A year before the Marquis had befriended a young New Yorker who had come west to hunt buffalo and start a ranch. The two had taken a trip to Montana together. Despite a couple of minor business disagreements, de Morès believed the man respected him. But now he saw an item in the newspaper that the two had quarreled—information not likely to improve his public image at this rather crucial time. How had the newspaper gotten the story? The Frenchman dashed off a letter:

> *My dear Roosevelt My principle is to take the bull by the horns.... The papers...published very stupid accounts of our quarreling.... Is this done by your order? I thought you my friend. If you are my enemy*

*I want to know it. I am always on hand as you know,
and between gentlemen it is easy to settle matters of
that sort directly.*

Theodore Roosevelt, also in his late 20s, recognized the challenge in the Marquis' words. But he had long since forgotten the smell of fear. When "Teedie" had been a sickly little boy in his family's New York City brownstone, his father had told him that "you have the mind but you have not the body." Teedie gritted his teeth and replied, "I'll make my body." The challenge of overcoming that obstacle had lit a spark in him, and ever since he had constantly looked for new ways to prove his mettle. The trait made him aggressive, even foolhardy.

Now, as the buckskinned young rancher sat on his Badlands property and peered through his spectacles at the Marquis' challenge, his first instinct was to accept. "I won't be bullied by a Frenchman.... What do you say if I make it rifles?"

But further reflection induced caution. Roosevelt knew that de Morès, a near legendary marksman, had killed at least two men in duels before. And Roosevelt did not consider himself a good shot (at least one Dakota resident disagreed: "Fer a crittur with a squint he were plumb handy with a gun"). Most important of all, he bore the Marquis no ill will. He drafted a careful response:

Most emphatically I am not your enemy; if I were you would know it, for I would be an open one ... however ... it is due to myself to say that the statement is not made through any fear of possible consequences to me; I too, as you know, am always on hand, and ever ready to hold myself accountable in any way for anything I have said or done.

The Marquis (acquitted but never crowned) backed down.
Roosevelt's reply had allowed both men to preserve their honor
and avoid a duel.

A mere 16 years later, "that dude Rosenfelder," the youngest
president ever, moved into the White House at a time when
international relations could be as dangerous as life on the Dakota
Badlands. The great imperial powers—Britain, France, Germany,
Russia, and, lately, America—raced to carve up the remainder
of the globe between themselves. Clashes inevitably occurred as
desirable territories became more scarce. The Germans challenged
the French in North Africa. America expelled the Spanish from
Cuba. Everyone fought for influence in China. At the same time,
nationalism ran rampant; patriots could not tolerate even the
slightest insult to their nation's honor.

An arms race had been underway for years. Nations aligned
and realigned themselves to maintain a delicate balance of power.
Europe had avoided a major war for 30 years, but the possibility
of world war weighed on everyone's mind.

To complicate matters, a new power arose in East Asia. Japan,
which in 1850 had been a completely isolated medieval shogunate,
had transformed itself in a mere 50 years into a modern industrial
power. Roosevelt admired Japanese determination and industry;
he too had made himself strong after being weak. To him the
Japanese were the world's "great new force."

The new President had nothing but contempt, however,
for czarist Russia. Vastly larger than Japan in territory and
population, Russia nevertheless seemed to be stuck in an earlier
century; of the major powers it was the only one still under the

rule of an absolute monarch. The regime struggled to keep the lid on dissent—outsiders believed a revolution was only a matter of time. "I do not believe in the future of any race," he said, "while it is under a crushing despotism."

Despite internal troubles, though, the Russian Bear continued to play the imperial game. Its push into Manchuria and Korea in the first years of Roosevelt's administration led directly to conflict with Japan, which now had territorial ambitions of its own. The two sides negotiated for months, but nothing would persuade the Russians to back down. In February 1904, the Japanese severed diplomatic relations and then launched a surprise attack on the main Russian naval base on the eastern coast of China. The Russo-Japanese War had begun. And many feared it would ignite the powder keg.

In any number of ways, war between Russia and Japan could lead directly to a general conflict among the other great nations. A weakened Russia, for example, might no longer be a sufficient counterweight to Germany and the aggressive Kaiser Wilhelm. If the Czar's army were destroyed, then Germany might feel free to misbehave in other parts of the globe. Or the victor in the Russo-Japanese conflict might attempt to take China, an action sure to provoke retaliation by the other powers, all of which wished to keep that enormous and chaotic country open to trade.

President Roosevelt watched the East Asian conflict with intense interest, keeping a huge map in the White House that he pinned with little flags to mark the combatants' positions. His interest was partly personal. Roosevelt loved war and wanted to see what would happen when the efficient Japanese went up against the somewhat backward Russians: "The Russians think only with half a mind. I think the Japanese will whip them handsomely."

Subsequent events proved him right. In battle after battle, the Japanese, who fought with suicidal courage, defeated the poorly led Russians. But casualties were heavy on both sides. Over 40,000 men died in an engagement in September 1904, and in another the next February there were 90,000 casualties.

Most people in the United States probably paid scant attention to the Russo-Japanese War. Isolated by two oceans, the nation traditionally had had little to fear from others. When Roosevelt assumed office, however, he knew this was no longer the case. America now had foreign territories; the Philippines and Hawaii might even be the next targets if, as Roosevelt feared, Japan got the "big head." More important, international stability was critical for the nation's economic well-being. At that time the United States produced more than half of the world's cotton, corn, and oil, and more than a third of its steel. It needed foreign markets for those goods. No matter what pacifist "flubdubs and flapdoodle mollycoddles" might say, the President knew that if there were a general war then America could well be drawn into it.

Roosevelt believed America's and the world's interests would be best served if the East Asian war would end "with Russia and Japan locked in a clinch, counterweighing one another." This meant bringing the conflict to an end before Russia collapsed or the Japanese overextended themselves and suffered defeat. But at least two problems stood in the way.

First, neither adversary wanted to stop fighting. The Japanese were winning every major engagement. And the Czar insisted, despite unremitting losses, on continuing to fight. The usually indecisive Nicholas, who Roosevelt thought a "preposterous little creature," appeared to be under the sway of his fiercely patriotic wife, Alexandra, who did not believe in peace without victory.

Second, even if the parties could be convinced that peace was in their interest, arranging negotiations would require uncommon delicacy. Patriotic pride dictated that neither side could appear to be the first to give in, and neither could seem to go more than halfway to obtain a settlement. Peace thus required a neutral party who would manage things so that both Russia and Japan preserved their dignity.

But Britain was an ally of Japan, and France backed Russia. Germany could not do it either; the Kaiser was a cousin of Nicholas and tended in any case to talk a little crazily about the "yellow peril." Everyone wanted the war to end, but the only power that both combatants felt they could trust was the United States. Hopes for peace thus rested squarely on the American President. To succeed he would need all of the tact and delicacy he had formerly employed to defuse the challenge of the Marquis de Morès.

Few people who knew him would have cast Theodore Roosevelt as a peacemaker. From an early age he displayed a marked belligerent streak. When arguments broke out at his Harvard "final club," he never hesitated to start throwing food. One unfortunate boy had an entire pumpkin thrown down on his head. When Roosevelt graduated and went out west, a drunk in a Badlands bar threatened him at gunpoint. He knocked the man down with three punches.

Roosevelt's political career had been a continuous series of battles, most of which he had started, against entrenched, powerful foes. In the New York legislature he sparred with the Tammany Hall political machine. He exposed massive corruption in the U.S. Postal Department as a civil service official. As President he took on J. P. Morgan and the trusts. Morgan, who could have wrecked the nation's economy if he wanted, came to the White House to see if he could "fix up" a competing company—Roosevelt bluntly refused him.

The President spent evenings in the White House engaged in various forms of personal combat. Sometimes he wrestled with a Japanese man in the library. On other nights he and an opponent played "singlesticks," putting on helmets and chest protectors and then beating each other with wooden rods. His usual partner, an old Rough Rider, said that in the heat of battle the President often forgot the rules. Mark Twain thought him "clearly insane."

But he was "insanest upon war and its supreme glories." Roosevelt spoiled for a fight with Spain even before the *Maine* blew up in Havana harbor. When McKinley did not push for war immediately following the explosion, Roosevelt, who was then an officer in the President's administration, fumed that "McKinley has no more backbone than a chocolate éclair."

When Congress did finally declare war, Roosevelt insisted on going, even though he was nearly 40 and had no military experience. "I would have turned from my wife's deathbed to answer that call." He led the Rough Riders' charge up Kettle Hill and shot a Spaniard himself; another soldier wrote Roosevelt's wife that "T. was just revelling in victory and gore."

To the consternation, no doubt, of many, the task of stopping the most destructive war in a generation now fell to this "madman."

As 1904 ended, Roosevelt moved pins around on his map and waited for his time to arrive. He promised a Japanese diplomat to send the Emperor a bearskin if the parties made peace. But the previous August, the Czar had refused his advice to deal with the Japanese. Instead, Nicholas ordered his Baltic Sea fleet to sail around the horn of Africa and mount a last-ditch effort to crush the enemy's navy.

When the fleet finally arrived in the western Pacific, in May 1905, the Japanese promptly, and completely, destroyed it. In a devastating battle, the Russians lost almost all of their 34 warships and managed to sink only three Japanese torpedo boats. Almost 5,000 Russians died in the engagement; Japanese deaths totaled 110.

The Czar could no longer ignore the truth that his county was beaten. Roosevelt sent the U.S. ambassador to Russia to meet secretly with Nicholas at his country retreat. The ambassador bore a blunt message from the President, calling Russia's situation "absolutely hopeless" and exhorting the Czar to avoid "inevitable disaster." At last Nicholas agreed that Russia would negotiate, but only if the Japanese consented to do so as well—and without knowing that the Czar had first given in. But unbeknownst to the Czar, the Japanese had already approached the President. Despite winning victory after victory, they had exhausted their resources and hoped to bring the war to a close.

A few days later, Roosevelt issued a public invitation to the adversaries to meet and negotiate a settlement. Both sides accepted. The first step had been taken; Roosevelt had successfully brought the adversaries to the table. A British newspaper hailed the President's "diplomatic abilities" and "finesse really extraordinary."

Roosevelt loved the compliment but he also knew that getting the parties to talk was one thing, concluding a successful treaty quite another. Numerous issues—influence in China and Korea, control over territory Japan had conquered during the war, the Russian payment of a war indemnity, to name a few—divided the two combatants.

The President initially suggested that the parties meet in Manchuria or Europe, perhaps hoping to avoid responsibility if the talks failed. But after weeks of wrangling, the parties would agree to meet only in America. In advance of the conference, both sides set out extreme positions and blustered that they wouldn't negotiate certain crucial points. And Roosevelt simply did not trust the Russians. He considered them "so corrupt, so treacherous and shifty, and so incompetent" that they could easily wreck everything.

If the talks failed for any reason, Roosevelt knew, he alone would suffer the blame. He looked for help from foreign powers. The British ambassador, whose intelligence the President estimated at "about eight guinea-pig power," said that the British would not agree to pressure Japan. France refused to take any action. "I know perfectly well that the whole world is watching me, and the condemnation that will come down on me, if the conference fails, will be world-wide too. But that's all right."

As the delegations made their way toward New York, many observers felt that only a successful peace conference could prevent global conflict. Henry Adams wrote to a friend: "I cannot stand to think about the Peace Conference. Literally I am trembling with terror . . . . The general debacle must now begin."

On August 5, 1905, yachts, cutters, and other boats filled Oyster Bay, just outside the President's home on Long Island. Occupying a prominent position was the presidential yacht, the *Mayflower*, where Roosevelt would formally open the peace conference. (Summer heat made Washington an undesirable location to conduct any sort of business.) A 21-gun salute greeted the President's arrival on board, and the guns kept firing almost continuously as diplomats, Cabinet members, and military officials also boarded the ship. Roosevelt had sent two identical cruisers to New York City to pick up the Japanese and Russian peace delegations. Much depended on this opening reception, where Roosevelt would introduce the delegates to one another for the first time and set the tone for the conference. One slip or perceived insult and the talks might be over before they began.

The Japanese arrived first, their boat approaching the *Mayflower* down a lane of water that had been left open for its passage. Foreign Minister Jutaro Komura stepped onto the boat at the head of the Japanese delegation. Komura, rail-thin, pale, and looking older than his 48 years, stood barely over five feet tall. Roosevelt had hoped Japan would send someone else; the Foreign Minister, he knew, favored rather harsh peace terms. Komura, for his part, feared he might actually be executed if he went home with a peace treaty unfavorable to his nation.

The chief Russian diplomat presented a stark contrast; some observers probably gasped as he walked up the *Mayflower*'s gangplank. Sergei Witte, bearded and standing nearly six and a half feet tall, seemed to personify Russia's vast size. Nicholas despised his lead delegate, who had opposed war with the Japanese from the start, and appointed him only after two preferred envoys pleaded ill health (Witte, for his part, thought Nicholas no better than a well-intentioned child).

Witte did not have high hopes for the conference. He had received hard-line instructions from the Czar. A few days earlier Witte had told Roosevelt that if the Japanese would not come to terms, Russia would gladly fight a defensive war "to the last extremity." He also believed Roosevelt lacked the skill to successfully conduct a diplomatic occasion of such importance. As his cruiser sailed to Oyster Bay, Witte worried that the President, a "typical American, inexperienced in and careless of formalities, would make a mess of the whole business . . . . I will not suffer a toast to our Emperor offered after one to the Mikado."

The Russian delegation proceeded below deck, where the President and the Japanese waited. After Roosevelt introduced each side to the other, everyone went in to lunch, watching closely for anything that might give offense. Seating the parties at tables would have created issues of precedence, so lunch was served buffet style, with seats arranged haphazardly in a corner. No one could argue that the other side was preferred.

Roosevelt was accustomed to dominating conversations, sometimes more than one at the same time, but in his youth he had spent enough time in New York City drawing rooms to learn to be politic when necessary. As the lunch continued he talked casually with the delegates, speaking French with the Russians and English with the Japanese. Neither side detected favoritism. After the meal, the President rose from his seat and proposed a toast. Witte's ears no doubt pricked up. The Japanese listened intently. Who would the President acknowledge first?

I drink to the welfare and prosperity of the sovereigns and to the peoples of the two great nations whose representatives have met one another on this ship. It is my most earnest hope and prayer, in the interest . . . of all civilized mankind, that a just and lasting peace may speedily be concluded between them.

Again neither side could complain. Roosevelt had successfully opened the conference. A Russian delegate said that the President handled the opening meeting with "admirable tact."

Roosevelt did not plan to take an active role at the conference; in fact, it would seem he wanted the negotiations to take place as far away from him as possible. So he remained at Oyster Bay and sent the delegates to Portsmouth, New Hampshire, to begin substantive talks. The two sides quickly came to agreement on a number of issues. Contention soon focused on only two major items: whether Russia would pay Japan an indemnity and who would own Sakhalin Island, a narrow strip of land off the eastern Siberian coast. Japan had seized the island from Russia as the peace delegations made their way to America.

The Czar's instructions to Witte clearly forbade the surrender of any Russian territory, but the Japanese insisted on keeping Sakhalin. As for an indemnity, defeated combatants in East Asia had traditionally paid a penalty. The Japanese believed they were entitled to at least 1 billion yen, but Russia flatly refused to pay anything. It had paid nothing to Napoleon, even when he had taken Moscow, and it would pay nothing now. Disagreement over the indemnity did not surprise Roosevelt; before talks even began he had asked the Japanese to drop any claim for money.

But the President grew increasingly frustrated with Russian intransigence and misbehavior. The Czar's stubbornness, if anything, worsened as the conference continued. And Witte had thoroughly annoyed the Japanese, who thought negotiations at the conference should be kept secret from the hordes of newspapermen crowding Portsmouth. The chief Russian diplomat had informally agreed to this arrangement, but almost immediately he started talking to every reporter he could find. The President vented his opinion: "The Russians are ten times worse than the Japs because they are so stupid and won't tell the truth." He wished to take the Czar and his underlings to a place on the coast and "run them violently down a steep place into the sea."

The talks were now two weeks old, the parties were deadlocked, and the Russians did not appear committed to negotiating in good faith. Roosevelt had told Komura that he would like the chance to step in if it appeared that the conference might break up. The Japanese envoy now dispatched a messenger to the President.

If anyone thought Roosevelt would stand idly by while the peace talks failed, they didn't know the President. Theodore Roosevelt thrived in the face of difficulty. As a young man he went to the West to prove that he could live outside the comfortable world of the New York aristocracy. On one hunting trip, he and his guide found themselves on an open prairie as darkness fell. They had had nothing to drink for nine hours but a couple of swallows from a slimy mud pool. The night grew cold, and the prairie offered no brush to start a fire. They feared Indian horse thieves, who might take their scalps as well as their mounts.

Before morning it rained. The guide awoke sopping in four inches of icy water only to hear Roosevelt muttering with pleasure: "By Godfrey, but this is fun!"

As a New York City police commissioner Roosevelt resolved to get truant officers back on their beat. So he prowled the streets at night looking as much for delinquent police as for delinquents, going without sleep for 40 hours at a stretch. Cops not on their watch received a rude shock when Roosevelt happened on them. The commissioner became a familiar sight at an all-night restaurant on the Bowery, where he would drop in at three in the morning for steaks, beer, and, sometimes, an impromptu press conference.

Seven years after the Portsmouth peace conference, in 1912, Roosevelt ran for President as a third-party candidate. As he left his hotel in Milwaukee to give a speech, a man walked up and shot him in the chest from only six feet away. His eyeglass case and the folded manuscript of his speech slowed the bullet, but it retained enough force to enter his right lung. Doctors insisted that he be taken to the hospital, but Roosevelt refused. "I will make this speech or die. It is one thing or the other." During the speech he unbuttoned his vest so the audience could see his bloodstained shirt, then thundered: "It takes more than that to kill a Bull Moose!"

When the Japanese messenger informed him of the imminent collapse of the talks, Roosevelt jumped into action. He sent a telegram to Witte at Portsmouth requesting that the Russian send someone down to Oyster Bay immediately. Witte read the telegram, which arrived after midnight, and ordered that his second in command, Baron Roman Rosen, make the trip. An

American diplomat woke Rosen up at 2:00 a.m., and the Baron
boarded a train five hours later.

Angry at being summoned as a mere go-between, Baron
Rosen's mood likely darkened when he arrived at Oyster Bay and
found Roosevelt clad in white flannels and playing tennis. The
President argued (according to some accounts, he continued to
play as he did so) that the Russians should cede Sakhalin to the
Japanese, who after all occupied the island already. Roosevelt also
advised submitting the indemnity question to an arbitrator, who,
he believed, would not force Russia to pay anything to Japan.

The Baron relayed this plan to Witte, who forwarded it to
the Czar along with another compromise plan that Witte had
formulated—Russia would cede the southern half of Sakhalin to
Japan and buy the northern half. The "purchase price," of course,
was just a disguised indemnity, but by calling the payment
something else Witte hoped to give the Japanese what they
wanted while maintaining Russian honor.

Perhaps not trusting Rosen, Roosevelt also sent the Czar
a direct appeal. The message stated baldly that Russia had no
ability to recover Sakhalin by force and would likely lose all of
eastern Siberia if the war continued. The President urged that in
the interest of Russia and of "broad humanity," the Czar should
agree to the compromise suggested by Witte.

Nicholas, meanwhile, had given Witte instructions to break
up the conference: "The Japanese desperately need money and we
will not give it to them . . . . It is useless to continue this undecided
situation." Witte used the President's message to the Czar as an
excuse to ignore these instructions; he could not break things off,
he said, until the Czar had considered Roosevelt's appeal.

Nicholas finally bent, but only a little. In a meeting with the American ambassador, he agreed to give up the southern half of Sakhalin Island. An indemnity was still out of the question, but the conversation signaled the Czar's implicit agreement that the talks could continue.

At the same time, Roosevelt tried to pressure the Japanese. Komura stated that Japan would accept no compromise plan that did not include the payment of some sort of indemnity. Roosevelt warned that the world would condemn Japan if it insisted on continuing the war for money alone. He sent a brusque message to the Japanese: "Ethically it seems to me that Japan owes a duty to the world at this crisis. The civilized world looks to her to make peace."

On August 25, the President, keen to test out a new piece of military technology, descended to the floor of Long Island Sound in the Navy's new submarine, the *Plunger*. The diplomats in Portsmouth might have hoped the vessel never made it back to the surface. The President's "interference" had irritated both Witte and Rosen, and the Japanese were "not particularly pleased" with Roosevelt's rather blunt advice. Roosevelt was annoyed too; he wrote his son Kermit that the diplomats were turning his hair gray.

The world, now dreading the worst, watched as the conference verged on collapse over the indemnity issue. At one point Komura and Witte simply stared at each other in silence for eight minutes across the conference table, smoking cigarettes all the while. Witte spent a night in his hotel room, in his own words, "sobbing and praying." The Russians finally received a message from the Czar to "end discussion tomorrow in any case. I prefer to continue the war than to await gracious concessions on the part of Japan." The

Japanese, firm in their conviction that Russia must pay something, still awaited final instructions from Tokyo. The Russians paid their hotel bills. Roosevelt prepared to admit defeat.

But at the last moment the Japanese government gave in. At what would have been the final meeting, Komura asked to meet privately with Witte. He said that Japan was dropping the indemnity demand; it would settle for the southern half of Sakhalin Island. Witte emerged from the meeting and announced, "Well, friends, peace. They agreed to everything."

The world breathed a sigh of relief. Stability had been restored, even if only for a brief time. The U.S. ambassador to Russia thought the conference saved the lives of a quarter of a million men. The press and public praised the President effusively. A French newspaper called him a "grand victor in this battle of giants."

Roosevelt knew these accolades came only because the conference, due to circumstances mostly out of his control, had been successful. He did admit, though, that the peace was a good thing for Russia, a very good thing for Japan, and a "mighty good thing for *me*, too!" In 1906, the President received the Nobel Peace Prize for his efforts.

True to his word, the President sent the Japanese Emperor the skin of the largest bear he had shot on a trip to Colorado earlier in the year. "His Majesty was greatly pleased with the skin, because of the emblematic nature of the gift." And the Russians eventually grew to appreciate Roosevelt as well. Years later, Baron Rosen, who had been so irritated by his summons to Oyster Bay, read an edition of Roosevelt's letters to his children. His conclusion: "It is impossible not to love the man."

President Theodore Roosevelt
Letter to Alice Lee Roosevelt
September 2, 1905

TO ALICE LEE ROOSEVELT

Roosevelt Mss.

Oyster Bay, September 2, 1905

Dear Alice: I hope you will enjoy your Chinese trip. I am curious to hear your Philippine experiences.

Well, I had had pretty vigorous summer myself and by no means a restful one, but I do not care in the least, for it seems now that we have actually been able to get peace between Japan and Russia. I have had all kinds of experiences with the envoys and with their Governments, and to the two latter I finally had to write time after time as a very polite but also very insistent Dutch Uncle. I am amused to see the way in which the Japanese kept silent. Whenever I wrote a letter to the Czar the Russians were sure to divulge it, almost always in twisted form, but the outside world never had so much as a hint of any letter I sent to the Japanese. The Russians became very angry with me during the course of the proceeding because they thought I was only writing to them. But they made the amends in good shape when it was over, and the Czar sent me the following cable of congratulation, which I thought rather nice of him:

Accept my congratulations and warmest thanks for having brought the peace negotiations to a successful conclusion, owing to your personal energetic efforts. My country will gratefully recognize the great part you have played in the Portsmouth peace conference.

It has been a wearing summer, because I have had no Secretary of State and have had to do all the foreign business myself, and as Taft has been absent I have also had to handle everything connected with Panama myself. For the last three months the chief business I have had has been in connection with the peace business, Panama, Venezuela, and Santo Domingo, and about all of these matters I have had to proceed without any advice or help.

It is enough to give anyone a sense of sardonic amusement to see the way in which the people generally, not only in my own country but elsewhere, gauge the work purely by the fact that it succeeded. If I had no brought about peace I should have been laughed at and condemned. Now I am overpraised. I am credited with being extremely longheaded, etc. As a matter of fact I took the position I finally did not of my volition but because events so shaped themselves that I would have felt as if I was flinching from a plain duty if I had acted otherwise. I advised the Russians informally to make peace on several occasions last winter. And to this they paid no heed. I had also consulted with the Japanese, telling them what I had told the Russians. It was undoubtedly due to the Japanese belief that I would act squarely that they themselves came forward after their great naval victory and asked me to bring about the conference, but not to let it be known that they had made the suggestion—so of course this is not to be spoke about. Accordingly I undertook the work and of course got assent of both Governments before I took any public action. Then neither Government would consent to meet where the other wished and the Japanese would not consent to meet at The Hague, which was the place I desired. The result was that they had to meet in this country, and this necessarily threw me into a position of prominence which I had not sought, and indeed which I had sought to avoid—though I feel now that unless they had met here they would never have made peace. Then they met, and after a while came to a deadlock, and I had to intervene again by getting into direct touch with the Governments themselves. It was touch and go, but things have apparently come out right. I say "apparently," because I shall not feel entirely easy until the terms of peace are actually signed. The Japanese people have been much less wise than the Japanese Government, for I am convinced that the best thing for Japan was to give up trying to get any indemnity. The Russians would not have given it: and if the war had gone on the Japanese would simply have spent—that is waste and worse than waste—hundreds of millions of dollars additional without getting back what they had already paid out.

At present we are having a house party for Ted and Ethel. Ted and Ethel count themselves as the two first guests, and then, by the way of a total change, Steve and Cornelia Landon, and finally Jack Thayer and Martha Bacon. Today is rainy and I look forward with gloomy foreboding to a play in the barn with the smallest folks this afternoon. Mother and I have had lovely rides and rows together. I chop a good deal and sometimes play tennis. I am still rather better than James Roosevelt and Jack.

Give my regards to all who are with you and thank the Griscoms especially for their hospitality. *Your loving father*

WOODROW WILSON

CHAPTER 9

MISSION FROM GOD

Woodrow Wilson and the League of Nations

Edith carefully placed a blanket over her husband's paralyzed left arm and dimmed the lights so the bedridden man could barely be seen. The doctor rehearsed a few very simple jokes with him. Then Edith set up two chairs on her husband's "good side" and waited for the guests to arrive. It had been six weeks since anyone but his wife and doctor had seen President Woodrow Wilson.

Edith Wilson ushered the visitors, one Republican Senator and one Democrat, into their carefully placed seats. Wilson recited his rehearsed lines.

"We're praying for you, Mr. Wilson," Republican Albert Fall said.

"Which way, Senator?" asked Wilson. "Which way?"

The Senators had a good laugh before the doctor quickly ushered them out.

Improbably, the ruse succeeded. *The New York Times* reported that the meeting "silenced for good the many wild and often unfriendly rumors of Presidential disability." If only they knew the truth. The master statesman and negotiator had been reduced to a mere shell of himself. But it had to be done. At stake was Wilson's vision—his mission from God, he firmly believed—of a world without war. Wilson's World War I peace treaty, negotiated in Paris with the most powerful leaders of Europe, twisted in the crosswinds of the U.S. Senate. To save the treaty's centerpiece,

Wilson's League of Nations, the President would do anything. He would fight to the death.

Wilson's peace treaty, as all do, started with war. In this case, World War I, the "war to end all wars." From 1914 to 1918, the war engulfed Europe in battle after battle. By the time it ended, an utterly unprecedented 8.5 million people were dead. Wilson had tried to keep America out of the war for as long as possible. He won reelection to the White House in 1916 on a platform of neutrality. But soon after the election, concern grew that Germany might bring the war across the ocean and try to take America by force.

In January 1917, Germany made its first move against the United States. It declared all-out submarine warfare in the Atlantic, deploying U-boats to sneak up on American ships at night and torpedo them.

Then, British intelligence intercepted a telegram from the German government to Mexico and delivered it to President Wilson. The telegram encouraged Mexico to attack the United States. Germany promised its full support, and as a reward, the Germans would deliver to Mexico the states of Texas, Arizona, and New Mexico as the spoils of victory. It was thought to be a forgery until the Foreign Secretary of the German empire surprisingly confirmed the telegram's intent. Wilson released a copy to the press. Anti-German fervor made it impossible for the United States to remain neutral.

Wilson decided that if he had to go to war, victory was not enough. He would fight for a larger principle. Wilson had made a name for himself as a young academic writing books about the role of government, political theory, and progressive ideals. He had spent years thinking about America's place in the world and had long considered the concept of a worldwide organization devoted to peace that would bring nations together to hold one another in check. "I have been thinking a great deal about a remark of Napoleon Bonaparte's," he once told his brother-in-law, "that 'nothing was ever finally settled by force.'" Wilson would go to war, but he would do so only to bring peace to the world . . . for all time. Here was a remarkable, audacious, and supremely naive premise, and an unprecedented approach to foreign relations. But it was the only way Wilson could justify America becoming involved in Europe's conflict.

On April 2, 1917, Wilson made his case for war to the American people with a speech on Capitol Hill. "The world," President Wilson announced, "must be made safe for democracy." This was "a war against all nations," and the United States' motive would "not be revenge . . . but only the vindication of right, of human right, of which we are only a single champion." *The New York Times* wrote that the audience cheered Wilson "as he ha[d] never been cheered in the Capitol in his life."

Edward Douglass White, Chief Justice of the Supreme Court, sat in the most prominent seat in the audience. According to the *Times*, he led the cheers. "[H]e compressed his lips close together as if he were trying to keep tears back . . . and brought his mighty palms together as if he were trying to split them." Wilson's speech touched an emotional chord with the people in the audience and with the people around the country who read about it the next day.

One contemporary scholar called it "the most momentous speech of Wilson's career," and another called it the greatest presidential speech since Lincoln's second inaugural address.

Americans united around the cause. The morning after the speech, George M. Cohan, best known for writing the American classics "Yankee Doodle Dandy" and "Give My Regards to Broadway," wrote a new song called "Over There," which became the unofficial rallying cry of the war.

But to Wilson, the moment was bittersweet. The cheers were tempered by his foreknowledge that a great number of American lives would be lost, and that those losses would fall on his shoulders. He told his secretary, "Think what it was they were applauding. My message today was a message of death for our young men. How strange it seems to applaud that."

This would be the first time America stepped out onto the global stage. And Wilson was determined not to waste the chance to determine the outcome of the war and to shape the postwar world. Three million Americans were drafted, and almost immediately Wilson looked ahead to peace. He put together a committee of the country's leading political scientists and historians and directed them to study the situation in Europe and put together a peace proposal. By the new year, Wilson had used the committee's findings to develop a 14-point peace plan. The plan covered freedom of the seas, the removal of trade barriers, weapons reduction, and a League of Nations to guarantee "political independence and territorial integrity to great and small states alike."

Within days, Wilson proudly unveiled his Fourteen Points to the nation and to the world. "In a very deep sense Mr. Wilson now pledges his country to fight for the liberation of the Belgian and the Pole, the Serb and the Rumanian," wrote the *New York Tribune*. "For [many] the words of the President of the United

States are a promise of freedom after a slavery worse a thousand times than that of the negro."

Reaction at home was extraordinary but reaction abroad was mixed. Europeans perceived Wilson's plan as callow and unrealistic. The European nations had been in almost constant conflict since the Middle Ages. Barely 50 years after its own civil war, how could America show Europe the road to peace? The *Times* of London wrote, "Our chief criticism of the President's speech is that in its lofty flight of an ideal it seems not to take into account certain hard realities of the situation."

Wilson disregarded the criticism and took his message directly to the people. He embarked on an unprecedented propaganda campaign, hoping to get the Fourteen Points into the hands of the Germans and their allies, knowing it might turn the tide. Airplanes dropped leaflets over German territory; soldiers lobbed empty artillery shells stuffed with copies of the speech over enemy lines; the Fourteen Points were translated into a dozen languages, with copies dispersed throughout the world.

The campaign worked. For the first time, the American flag itself became a symbol of hope and recovery, hanging in windows across Europe. The people of the world wanted peace, on Wilson's terms. And they shared his vision for a League of Nations.

It is not exaggeration to say that Wilson's Fourteen Points brought the war to an end. On May 28, 1918, as Americans continued their fight against German soldiers, the new German chancellor wrote to Wilson and said that he would stop the fighting if a peace agreement would be based on the Fourteen Points.

But now, with victory tantalizingly close, Britain and France wanted more; they demanded to reap the spoils of an unconditional surrender, and they sought the total destruction of Germany. Wilson resisted. He knew that a grossly unfair peace plan would only create resentment in Germany and provoke more problems in the future. The principle behind the Fourteen Points was balance and equilibrium. Britain and France held their ground, but Wilson had a trump card to play. The United States' entry into the war had dealt the death knell to Germany; without U.S. support, there was no guarantee Britain and France could finish the job themselves. America's superior strength could not be ignored. Wilson threatened to negotiate his own peace with the Germans and leave the British and French to continue fighting on their own.

As the negotiations proceeded, Wilson turned to the American people and asked them to send the world a message in the 1918 midterm congressional elections. In an open letter to voters in newspapers throughout the country, he wrote: "If you have approved of my leadership . . . I earnestly beg that you will express yourself unmistakably to that effect by returning a Democratic majority to both the Senate and the House." Knowing that a peace conference lay ahead, and hoping to pave the way for easy approval of the resulting treaty in the Senate once it had been negotiated overseas, the President wanted the Congress to know how much Americans supported his plan. But the partisan appeal backfired. The country that had united behind Wilson in going to war now resented his attempt to divide them in brokering the peace. Republicans won a majority in both houses of Congress. The new Senate would have the power to defeat any peace plan.

Despite the election's result, the European powers eventually realized that the risk of Wilson pulling out the American forces was just too great. After months of negotiation, Britain and

France relented, and on November 11, 1918, the Allies and the Germans signed an armistice. "At exactly one minute of eleven," *The New York Times* wrote, "like a final thunder crash at the clearing of a storm, the guns on both sides abruptly ceased . . . the rolling plain was alive with cheering, shouting men, friend and enemy alike . . . . Germans and Americans were coming along the narrow stretch of ground so fiercely fought over, some shyly and awkwardly, like schoolboys."

When America learned of the end of the war, celebration erupted at the Capitol. Forty-eight bonfires were lit, and the crowd sang patriotic songs, tooted horns, and rang bells. Wilson joined in the festivities, his secretary later recalling "how happy he looked . . . [with] a glow of satisfaction of one who realizes he has fought for a principle and won." Wilson felt this had been his destiny, ever since childhood.

Woodrow Wilson recalled that as a young boy he "lived in a dream life . . . when all the world seemed to me a place of heroic adventure." His father, a Presbyterian minister, instilled in Wilson, as a small boy, a belief that he had a mission in life to make the world a better place. Wilson envisioned that one day he would hold political office.

Instead, he became an academic. By his mid-30s, he had been appointed a professor at Princeton University in history and political science (he is still the only American President to hold a doctorate). He wrote articles for major magazines, accepted speaking engagements, and soon became the most famous professor at Princeton. Eventually, the university appointed him president.

But at age 39, Wilson suffered a minor stroke. It weakened

his right arm and left him unable to write. Typical of sufferers of minor strokes, he recovered within a year. The problem returned nine years later, but then subsided. And then in 1906, at age 50, Wilson woke up one morning and to his horror found himself blind in his left eye. Doctors told him the blood vessels behind his eye had hemorrhaged from a severe case of high blood pressure. The only treatment was rest. Wilson took a trip to the rural countryside of Britain to improve his health. Alone in his own wilderness, his sight returned and he had an epiphany. He became convinced that God had a plan for him.

Wilson set his mind to transforming Princeton from a playground for the rich to a serious academic institution that trained the future leaders of the world. Rich alumni fought his efforts to abolish Princeton's elitist "eating clubs," but Wilson, now seeing himself on a mission from a force greater than himself, refused to compromise. For the next four years, he fought the alumni at every turn, knowing his ideas could radically improve higher education; but the board of trustees resisted his efforts, blocking his plans repeatedly. By 1910, he needed to move on.

As fate would have it, Wilson's attempts at reform had earned the attention of local progressive political leaders. They approached him to run for governor of New Jersey. To them, Wilson seemed an ideal candidate: educated, articulate, and possessing a track record of fighting for reform and justice. He swept to victory.

Once Wilson took office, however, he had trouble convincing the state legislature to pass his progressive agenda—including election reform, new corporate anti-corruption regulations, and a proposal to institute a workman's compensation program. At first he appealed to their "better, unselfish natures," but it was not enough to get action. Undeterred, Wilson went directly to the people and asked for their support. He gave a series of speeches around the state to rally the public around his policies so that they would pressure their representatives to enact his agenda. His populism proved successful—and Wilson discovered the political tactic he would use later in the war. If the career politicians refused to bend to his will (which he saw as the will of the people), he would take his case on the road.

Just two years later, his success in New Jersey catapulted Wilson to the Democratic Party's presidential nomination. Promising a better life for the average American, he won that election too. But he saw the victory as part of a larger plan. When the chairman of the Democratic Party approached Wilson seeking a job in the administration, in return for helping him win the election, Wilson responded that it was God, not the Democratic Party, who had placed him in the White House. Wilson had sought and reached his higher calling.

Riding the wave of support that brought him into office, Wilson immediately convinced Congress to pass reform bills creating an income tax, banning child labor, and making loans easier to get for average Americans. Wilson's domestic agenda began to fall into place.

But the new President had never before dealt with international matters. Just a month into Wilson's term, the Mexican president was murdered. As the Mexican people erupted into violence and riots, the idealistic Wilson decided to send troops across the border to help restore order. The effort proved disastrous—a battle between the American soldiers and Mexican rioters left over a hundred dead. Mexican rebels, insulted by the presence of American troops in a purely internal conflict, began to attack American border towns. Wilson continued to send in troops and insert America where few felt it belonged. Although his intentions were noble, the situation proved a failure. In the aftermath, Theodore Roosevelt called Wilson "a ridiculous creature in international matters . . . the very worst man we have ever had in his position." But it illustrated Wilson's deeper sympathies—he wanted to save the world, regardless of national borders. And now, he was finally in a position to do just that.

Wilson and his counterparts in Europe agreed to a peace conference in Paris. Wilson longed to attend the conference himself. It would be the first time a sitting President would visit Europe—and Wilson would have to do more than just visit. Attending the conference would remove the President from the day-to-day affairs of his presidential administration for six months, something unprecedented before or since.

Advisers pleaded with Wilson to stay home. By going to Paris, they argued, he would be just another negotiator at the table. Remaining at home, they felt, would give Wilson more power to influence the conference's direction and the chance to veto the end result if it didn't meet with his approval.

Frank Cobb, who resigned as editor of the *New York World* to advise the President, strongly opposed Wilson making the trip: "In Washington he is a dispassionate judge whose mind is unclouded by all these petty personal circumstances of a conference . . . but if the President were to participate personally in the proceedings, it would be a broken stick . . . he must fight on his own ground and his own ground is Washington. Diplomatic Europe is all enemy soil for him." Going to Paris in order to bicker over a peace treaty was unbecoming for an American President.

Nevertheless, Wilson decided he could not risk being a bystander as his League of Nations was bargained away or weakened to the point of ineffectiveness. He went to Paris himself, and after six months of difficult negotiations, Wilson emerged from the conference with a peace plan that in many respects looked very different from his Fourteen Points, but in one respect looked much the same. His League of Nations survived, intact.

But the Paris trip had weakened Wilson's support at home. Republicans seethed that Wilson had not included any influential leaders from across the political aisle in his delegation. Wilson declined to ask any to join him out of a concern they would impede his progress—he knew he would need to focus on negotiating with foreign leaders; he did not want to have to worry about the Republicans too.

The stress of the conference also took its toll on Wilson's health. He caught the influenza that had been sweeping Europe, suffering from high fever and vomiting. Sick in bed, he continued to work long hours each day. Future President Herbert Hoover, who spent time with Wilson in Paris, noticed changes in Wilson's behavior and mental processes—whereas before he had been willing to listen to advice and was quick to grasp new ideas and make decisions, the illness had slowed him, and he had trouble remembering and digesting new facts and situations. In retrospect, he had likely been suffering a series of small strokes.

Despite the hardships, the peace plan draft that emerged from the Paris conference received nothing but the highest praise.

The League of Nations would bring the countries of the world together to settle disputes, reduce weapons, and avoid another catastrophic world war—relying on economic sanctions rather than violence to keep its member countries at peace. According to the *London Times*: "Those who thought that the League of Nations was only a project of international amiability will change their minds when they read the Covenant published today. . . . Peace and its preservation have been brought down from the clouds." The *Giornale d'Italia* called it "a sublime act of human solidarity." On Valentine's Day, February 14, 1919, Wilson set sail back to America, enthusiastic to tell the nation what he had accomplished. But the Republican Congress would not be giving him a warm welcome.

Leading the opposition to the peace treaty was Senator Henry Cabot Lodge, the powerful chairman of the Senate Foreign Relations Committee. Lodge hated Wilson—so much so that he once told a friend he never expected to hate anyone as much. In part, the dislike stemmed from a petty matter. Before Wilson entered politics, Lodge had been known as "the scholar," but Wilson, with his Ph.D. and university presidency, quickly stole away the title. Lodge also disliked Wilson because he saw the President as a coward who had waited too long to enter the war. After the Germans sank the British passenger ship *Lusitania*, almost four years earlier on May 7, 1915, killing 128 Americans, Lodge had insisted "Wilson is afraid" for not declaring war immediately.

Finally, Lodge hated Wilson because it was rumored (although never proven) that Wilson had cheated on his wife, and Lodge had a singular loathing of adulterers. Lodge had been the cuckolded husband when his wife had an affair with former Secretary of State John Hay. The prickly and puritanical Lodge also resented that just seven months after Wilson's first wife died, he had married another woman. To the Senator this was unconscionable.

Lodge could do nothing to annul Wilson's marriage, but, as chairman of the Senate Foreign Relations Committee, he could sabotage the peace treaty. He and other Republicans opposed the plan, believing the proposed League of Nations would commit U.S. troops to resolve conflicts across the globe. "Would the citizens of the United States volunteer to enter the army for the purpose of settling difficulties in the Balkans?" one Senator asked.

Wilson tried to explain that a single dissent from a country on the Executive Council—of which the United States would be one of five permanent members—could block any military action taken by the League. The United States, and every other member, had veto power.

Nevertheless, the language bothered Lodge and many other Republicans. Binding nations "to respect and preserve against external aggression the territorial integrity and existing political independence of all members of the League" sounded to some like a loss of American sovereignty. This provision might conflict with Congress's constitutional authority to declare war, they argued.

To placate the opposition, Wilson agreed to meet with a group of influential Senators. But it did not help. One Senator complained the meeting was like "wandering with Alice in Wonderland [and having] tea with the Mad Hatter." After spending months in Europe successfully bargaining with his fellow world leaders, it seemed ironic that Wilson was negotiating unsuccessfully at home. Wilson went to Paris personally because he thought his biggest hurdles would be across the ocean; he never imagined his largest obstacle would be Henry Cabot Lodge and the Republican Congress.

Wielding his prodigious Senate power, Lodge began to scheme. Even though he knew a majority of Senators supported the League in its broad sense, he would introduce amendments and make changes that Wilson would find unpalatable. Lodge would try to split the treaty supporters into two camps, neither one large enough to get to the two-thirds support needed for ratification.

But Lodge needed time to build support. So he packed his committee with the Republicans most hostile toward the League—they would help keep the treaty tied up for months. The committee members stalled for two weeks by having the treaty read aloud, line by line. They stalled for six more weeks by allowing citizens from across the country to complain about the treaty in hearings.

To combat Lodge and the risk of defeat on the Senate floor, Wilson embarked on a nationwide speaking tour. As he had proven to himself in New Jersey, and in Germany, armed with the right information, the people would not let him down. "The stage is set," he said, "the destiny disclosed . . . . We cannot turn back. We can only go forward." This would become Wilson's final crusade. And on this issue, compromise was not possible. His mission from God, his destiny, his ultimate legacy would be the League of Nations. Without the League, Wilson said, "I can predict with absolute certainty that within another generation there will be another world war. What the Germans used were toys compared with what they would use [next]."

The President planned to cover 26 cities in 27 days across the continent, giving up to 10 speeches a day from the rear platform of his seven-car train. Though it started out triumphantly, the two dozen reporters aboard the train quickly noticed all was not well. Wilson would smile and wave in front of the crowds but lose his color as soon as he was out of sight. The First Lady had begged her husband to include some time for rest—a week at the Grand Canyon, she suggested—but Wilson refused. "This is a business trip, pure and simple."

Back in Washington, Senator Lodge, hell-bent on destroying the League, dispatched a number of fellow Senators to speak out against it. They followed Wilson wherever he appeared, trying to discredit him with their own speeches. With adversaries now at every stop, Wilson's train rolled on.

Then in Seattle, a camera's flash startled the President and caused him to fall down in his seat. When he spoke, according to a Navy admiral in the crowd, "something seemed to be wrong with President Wilson. He appeared to have lost his customary force and enthusiasm." Wilson later met an Army veteran who recalled, "he looked old—just old."

But most people saw what they wanted to see: a triumphant leader taking America by storm. The newspapers announced his arrival in each city with unabashed glee: "Los Angeles shrieks approval of the President," one paper wrote. A newspaper reported that at another stop, "the spirit of the crowd seemed akin to fanaticism. The throng joined in a continuous and riotous uproar."

In Salt Lake City, Wilson spoke in the Mormon Tabernacle to a crowd of 15,000. The unventilated building trapped the heat, and the sickly President could not keep from perspiring. All through the evening's festivities he changed his clothes repeatedly, soaking them through with sweat each time.

Three days later, Wilson left Pueblo, Colorado (population 65,000—no town was too small for the President), for Wichita, Kansas. At 11:30 that night, Edith Wilson heard a knock on her door. "Can you come to me, Edith? I'm terribly sick," said the President. The headaches were finally too great to bear.

Edith propped her husband up with pillows, and after five hours of twisting and turning to find a position to ease his pain, he finally fell asleep. She kept watch, breathing quietly for fear she would wake him. He awoke at dawn and insisted on shaving and preparing for the first speech of the day. Edith went to find the doctor.

She returned, doctor in tow, to find Wilson fully dressed. Except that as he spoke, saliva dripped from the left side of his mouth. "I must go on," he said. The doctor insisted he couldn't. "[But] if we cancel this trip, Senator Lodge and his friends will say that I am a quitter, that the trip was a failure. And the treaty would be lost." The President tried to walk toward the doctor, but his left side had gone numb. He could not move his left arm or leg. Edith insisted the public not see him this way. One side of his face had fallen, and his words were barely coherent. "It is your life we must consider," the doctor told Wilson.

"Returning to Washington. Nothing to be alarmed about," the doctor wired the White House. He told reporters that the rest of the President's tour had to be canceled due to illness, and the train sped back to the capital.

The next day, newspapers reported that Wilson had suffered a "nervous breakdown." As Wilson lay in bed weak and in pain, the White House issued reports that he needed rest. The *Times* reported three days later that the President was feeling "slightly better" and updated its diagnosis to say Wilson suffered "simply from nervous exhaustion complicated by nervous indigestion." Only a handful of close confidantes knew it was much more.

Doctors hoped a few days of rest would help improve the President's health. Instead, a week after returning home, Wilson collapsed in the White House bathroom. He suffered a massive stroke that completely paralyzed the left side of his body.

For six weeks Wilson was unable to speak. He could see out of just one-half of one eye. And his mental faculties were devastated—he could not read more than a few lines at a time, became paranoid, lost his temper easily, and suffered from a diminished ability to reason through problems. As Wilson lay in bed, gravely ill, his League of Nations was also paralyzed in the Senate, its creator unable to fight and incapable of brokering a compromise.

But no one could know. His wife and doctors decided to keep Wilson's condition a secret for fear of the consequences—he could be relieved of his presidency. Wilson himself seemed unaware of his true condition. He refused to acknowledge anything was wrong.

Lodge brought the peace plan to a vote on the Senate floor but included changes that altered some of Wilson's language. Despite these changes, the heart of the treaty was not affected. Had Wilson been healthy, this would have been an easy victory. He would have told his supporters to vote for the treaty, and it would have passed. But, when Democratic Party leaders came to Wilson and asked him what to do, he instructed them to accept no changes. Following the advice of their leader, Wilson's supporters voted against the League of Nations and it went down in defeat.

Lodge had not prepared for the public outcry that followed. Demand for compromise rang out, and, under political pressure, the treaty was returned for consideration. But once again, Wilson insisted there could be no changes; and once again, unaware of their President's limitations, many of his supporters obeyed. The treaty fell short of the two-thirds majority necessary—this time by just seven votes. Lodge celebrated his defeat of Wilson; what he didn't know was that he had beaten a man who could barely move and hardly reason.

By this time, the 1920 presidential campaign had gotten underway. Wilson, blind to his condition, sought to run for an unprecedented third term. Unaware of their President's condition, the American people likely would have voted him back to the White House in a landslide. But his wife and advisers worked to make sure he did not receive the nomination. Republicans nominated Warren Harding, a genial but unextraordinary man who had no interest in Wilson's League of Nations. Despite repeated calls from the people for the League to be reconsidered, Harding won the election by 7 million votes, and the peace plan never came to another vote.

The consequences of not passing the peace plan were just as Wilson had predicted: 25 million lives were lost just a generation later in World War II, a war that a healthy Woodrow Wilson might have prevented.

Wilson died on February 3, 1924, believing until the end that his principles would eventually prevail and that there would one day be a League of Nations. Prior to his funeral, Wilson's wife noticed that Henry Cabot Lodge's name had found its way onto the list of people attending. She wrote to him, "Your presence would be embarrassing to you and unwelcome to me." He stayed home.

Wilson won the Nobel Peace Prize for brokering a peace plan that was doomed and for conceiving an organization that would never fulfill its mission. But Wilson's dream finally became a reality 20 years after his death. Given a second chance at the end of World War II, the United States not only championed the United Nations but invited it to establish its headquarters in New York.

President Woodrow Wilson
Address to the Joint Session of Congress
on the Fourteen Points
January 8, 1918

Gentlemen of the Congress:

Once more, as repeatedly before, the spokesmen of the Central Empires have indicated their desire to discuss the objects of the war and the possible basis of a general peace. Parleys have been in progress at Brest-Litovsk between Russian representatives and representatives of the Central Powers to which the attention of all the belligerents have been invited for the purpose of ascertaining whether it may be possible to extend these parleys into a general conference with regard to terms of peace and settlement.

The Russian representatives presented not only a perfectly definite statement of the principles upon which they would be willing to conclude peace but also an equally definite program of the concrete application of those principles. The representatives of the Central Powers, on their part, presented an outline of settlement which, if much less definite, seemed susceptible of liberal interpretation until their specific program of practical terms was added. That program proposed no concessions at all either to the sovereignty of Russia or to the preferences of the populations with whose fortunes it dealt, but meant, in a word, that the Central Empires were to keep every foot of territory their armed forces had occupied—every province, every city, every point of vantage —as a permanent addition to their territories and their power.

It is a reasonable conjecture that the general principles of settlement which they at first suggested originated with the more liberal statesmen of Germany and Austria, the men who have begun to feel the force of their own people's thought and purpose, while the concrete terms of actual settlement came from the military leaders who have no thought but to keep what they have got. The negotiations have been broken off. The Russian representatives were sincere and in earnest. They cannot entertain such proposals of conquest and domination.

The whole incident is full of significances. It is also full of perplexity. With whom are the Russian representatives dealing? For whom are the representatives of the Central Empires speaking? Are they speaking for the majorities of their respective parliaments or for the minority parties, that military and imperialistic minority which has so far dominated their whole policy and controlled the affairs of Turkey and of the Balkan states which have felt obliged to become their associates in this war?

The Russian representatives have insisted, very justly, very wisely, and in the true spirit of modern democracy, that the conferences they have been holding with the Teutonic and Turkish statesmen should be held within open not closed, doors, and all the world has been audience, as was desired. To whom have we been listening, then? To those who speak the spirit and intention of the resolutions of the German Reichstag of the 9th of July last, the spirit and intention of the Liberal leaders and parties of Germany, or to those who resist and defy that spirit and intention and insist upon conquest and subjugation? Or are we listening, in fact, to both, unreconciled and in open and hopeless contradiction? These are very serious and pregnant questions. Upon the answer to them depends the peace of the world.

But, whatever the results of the parleys at Brest-Litovsk, whatever the confusions of counsel and of purpose in the utterances of the spokesmen of the Central Empires, they have again attempted to acquaint the world with their objects in the war and have again challenged their adversaries to say what their objects are and what sort of settlement they would deem just and satisfactory. There is no good reason why that challenge should not be responded to, and responded to with the utmost candor. We did not wait for it. Not once, but again and again, we have laid our whole thought and purpose before the world, not in general terms only, but each time with sufficient definition to make it clear what sort of definite terms of settlement must necessarily spring out of them. Within the last week Mr. Lloyd George has spoken with admirable candor and in admirable spirit for the people and Government of Great Britain.

There is no confusion of counsel among the adversaries of the Central Powers, no uncertainty of principle, no vagueness of detail. The only secrecy of counsel, the only lack of fearless frankness, the only failure to make definite statement of the objects of the war, lies with Germany and her allies. The issues of life and death hang upon these definitions. No statesman who has the least conception of his responsibility ought for a moment to permit himself to continue this tragical and appalling outpouring of blood and treasure unless he is sure beyond a peradventure that

the objects of the vital sacrifice are part and parcel of the very life
of Society and that the people for whom he speaks think them
right and imperative as he does.

There is, moreover, a voice calling for these definitions of
principle and of purpose which is, it seems to me, more thrilling and
more compelling than any of the many moving voices with which
the troubled air of the world is filled. It is the voice of the Russian
people. They are prostrate and all but hopeless, it would seem,
before the grim power of Germany, which has hitherto known no
relenting and no pity. Their power, apparently, is shattered. And yet
their soul is not subservient. They will not yield either in principle
or in action. Their conception of what is right, of what is humane
and honorable for them to accept, has been stated with a frankness,
a largeness of view, a generosity of spirit, and a universal human
sympathy which must challenge the admiration of every friend of
mankind; and they have refused to compound their ideals or desert
others that they themselves may be safe.

They call to us to say what it is that we desire, in what, if in
anything, our purpose and our spirit differ from theirs; and I believe
that the people of the United States would wish me to respond,
with utter simplicity and frankness. Whether their present leaders
believe it or not, it is our heartfelt desire and hope that some way
may be opened whereby we may be privileged to assist the people
of Russia to attain their utmost hope of liberty and ordered peace.

It will be our wish and purpose that the processes of peace,
when they are begun, shall be absolutely open and that they shall

involve and permit henceforth no secret understandings of any kind. The day of conquest and aggrandizement is gone by; so is also the day of secret covenants entered into in the interest of particular governments and likely at some unlooked-for moment to upset the peace of the world. It is this happy fact, now clear to the view of every public man whose thoughts do not still linger in an age that is dead and gone, which makes it possible for every nation whose purposes are consistent with justice and the peace of the world to avow nor or at any other time the objects it has in view.

We entered this war because violations of right had occurred which touched us to the quick and made the life of our own people impossible unless they were corrected and the world secure once for all against their recurrence. What we demand in this war, therefore, is nothing peculiar to ourselves. It is that the world be made fit and safe to live in; and particularly that it be made safe for every peace-loving nation which, like our own, wishes to live its own life, determine its own institutions, be assured of justice and fair dealing by the other peoples of the world as against force and selfish aggression. All the peoples of the world are in effect partners in this interest, and for our own part we see very clearly that unless justice be done to others it will not be done to us. The program of the world's peace, therefore, is our program; and that program, the only possible program, as we see it, is this:

I. Open covenants of peace, openly arrived at, after which there shall be no private international understandings of any kind but diplomacy shall proceed always frankly and in the public view.

II. Absolute freedom of navigation upon the seas, outside territorial waters, alike in peace and in war, except as the seas may be closed in whole or in part by international action for the enforcement of international covenants.

III. The removal, so far as possible, of all economic barriers and the establishment of an equality of trade conditions among all the nations consenting to the peace and associating themselves for its maintenance.

IV. Adequate guarantees given and taken that national armaments will be reduced to the lowest point consistent with domestic safety.

V. A free, open-minded, and absolutely impartial adjustment of all colonial claims, based upon a strict observance of the principle that in determining all such questions of sovereignty the interests of the populations concerned must have equal weight with the equitable claims of the government whose title is to be determined.

VI. The evacuation of all Russian territory and such a settlement of all questions affecting Russia as will secure the best and freest cooperation of the other nations of the world in obtaining for her an unhampered and unembarrassed opportunity for the independent determination of her own political development and national policy and assure her of a sincere welcome into the society of free nations under institutions of her own choosing; and, more than a welcome, assistance also of every kind that she may need and may herself desire. The treatment accorded Russia by her sister nations in the months to come will be the acid test of their good will, of their comprehension of her needs as distinguished from their own interests, and of their intelligent and unselfish sympathy.

VII. Belgium, the whole world will agree, must be evacuated and restored, without any attempt to limit the sovereignty which she enjoys in common with all other free nations. No other single act will serve as this will serve to restore confidence among the nations in the laws which they have themselves set and determined for the government of their relations with one another. Without this healing act the whole structure and validity of international law is forever impaired.

VIII. All French territory should be freed and the invaded portions restored, and the wrong done to France by Prussia in 1871 in the matter of Alsace-Lorraine, which has unsettled the peace of the world for nearly fifty years, should be righted, in order that peace may once more be made secure in the interest of all.

IX. A readjustment of the frontiers of Italy should be effected along clearly recognizable lines of nationality.

X. The peoples of Austria-Hungary, whose place among the nations we wish to see safeguarded and assured, should be accorded the freest opportunity to autonomous development.

XI. Rumania, Serbia, and Montenegro should be evacuated; occupied territories restored; Serbia accorded free and secure access to the sea; and the relations of the several Balkan states to one another determined by friendly counsel along historically established lines of allegiance and nationality; and international guarantees of the political and economic independence and territorial integrity of the several Balkan states should be entered into.

XII. The Turkish portion of the present Ottoman Empire should be assured a secure sovereignty, but the other nationalities which are now under Turkish rule should be assured an undoubted security of life and an absolutely unmolested opportunity of autonomous development, and the Dardanelles should be permanently opened as a free passage to the ships and commerce of all nations under international guarantees.

XIII. An independent Polish state should be erected which should include the territories inhabited by indisputably Polish populations, which should be assured a free and secure access to the sea, and whose political and economic independence and territorial integrity should be guaranteed by international covenant.

XIV. A general association of nations must be formed under specific covenants for the purpose of affording mutual guarantees of political independence and territorial integrity to great and small states alike.

In regard to these essential rectifications of wrong and assertions of right we feel ourselves to be intimate partners of all the governments and peoples associated together against the

Imperialists. We cannot be separated in interest or divided in purpose. We stand together until the end. For such arrangements and covenants we are willing to fight and to continue to fight until they are achieved; but only because we wish the right to prevail and desire a just and stable peace such as can be secured only by removing the chief provocations to war, which this program does remove. We have no jealousy of German greatness, and there is nothing in this program that impairs it. We grudge her no achievement or distinction of learning or of pacific enterprise such as have made her record very bright and very enviable. We do not wish to injure her or to block in any way her legitimate influence or power. We do not wish to fight her either with arms or with hostile arrangements of trade if she is willing to associate herself with us and the other peace-loving nations of the world in covenants of justice and law and fair dealing. We wish her only to accept a place of equality among the peoples of the world,—the new world in which we now live,—instead of a place of mastery.

Neither do we presume to suggest to her any alteration or modification of her institutions. But it is necessary, we must frankly say, and necessary as a preliminary to any intelligent dealings with her on our part, that we should know whom her spokesmen speak for when they speak to us, whether for the Reichstag majority or for the military party and the men whose creed is imperial domination.

We have spoken now, surely, in terms too concrete to admit of any further doubt or question. An evident principle runs through the whole program I have outlined. It is the principle of justice to all peoples and nationalities, and their right to live on equal terms of liberty and safety with one another, whether they be strong or weak.

Unless this principle be made its foundation no part of the structure of international justice can stand. The people of the United States could act upon no other principle; and to the vindication of this principle they are ready to devote their lives, their honor, and everything they possess. The moral climax of this culminating and final war for human liberty has come, and they are ready to put their own strength, their own highest purpose, their own integrity and devotion to the test.

RICHARD NIXON WORKING IN THE LINCOLN SITTING ROOM, 1971.

National Archives & Records Administration

CHAPTER 10

THE CHINA CARD

———————◆———————

Nixon and the People's Republic of China

C ruising at a classified altitude, Air Force One chased the
sunset west over the Pacific all through the night of February
20, 1972. Anticipating bed rest at an imminent layover in Guam,
Richard M. Nixon sat awake and alone in his preferred window
seat. Shortly after entering office in 1968, Nixon had ordered the
sleek Boeing 707's interior refurbished. Gone was the open cabin
LBJ had shared with guests, staff, and reporters. Centered around
a cloistered three-room suite, Air Force One became a partitioned
flying sanctum. It was a practical arrangement for a man who'd
earned a reputation as a globe-trotter when Vice President to
Eisenhower by visiting 56 countries over two terms. It was also
the perfect setup for a profoundly secretive man only comfortable
at the center of his own constantly shifting web of intrigue.

As he divided his gaze between the moonlit ocean and his
own reflection that night, Nixon felt that he was "embarking on
a voyage of philosophical discovery as uncertain, and in some
respects as perilous, as the voyages of geographical discovery of
a much earlier time." This voyage was the final hand in a secret
multinational card game.

Nixon was an ace poker player. During his first two months in
the Navy, Lieutenant Nixon won $6,000 through the game (and
later used these winnings to fund his first major political gamble—a
successful run for the U.S. House of Representatives). But now the

stakes were nothing less than the balance of global power—and the "kitty" included Nixon's prospects for reelection later that year.

After Guam, Air Force One would touch down briefly in Shanghai to receive a Red Chinese navigator. From Shanghai, the President, his family, and a small coterie of advisers would be shepherded to the military airfield at Beijing. Nixon, the man who had escalated the war against Communist North Vietnam abroad and had built his reputation as a fierce anti-Communist at home, would become the first American President ever to visit the People's Republic of China.

No American head of state had dared lift the veil of the Kingdom of Heaven since China's bloody fall to Communism after World War II. In the minds of Republican hard-liners, the "Silent Majority" of Americans who had elected the President, and even Nixon's two Democrat predecessors, China was a gigantic nuke-wielding rogue state prepared to overrun the free world at any moment. Johnson had seriously considered bombing China's nuclear installations. Kennedy had declared the People's Republic's atomic saber rattling "a more dangerous situation than any we have faced since the end of the Second World War" (and he had *already* faced the Cuban Missile Crisis).

As Chairman Mao's bloodthirsty "reforms" grew increasingly ruthless and profligate in the late 50s, even his former sponsors in the USSR had been forced to cut ties with China. Thousands of nervous Soviet troops were now deployed along their vast shared border. Nixon was the first U.S. President even to publicly acknowledge the People's Republic of China's chosen name, and that was less than a year prior to this as-yet-unplanned trip. In fact, as recently as 1964, Nixon had publicly maintained his

party's vehemently anti-China stance while stumping for Barry
Goldwater. But "unpredictability is the greatest asset or weapon a
leader can have," Nixon once said. And as his troubled first term
as President wound down, Nixon needed a big win.

Though he had successfully campaigned in 1968 to bring U.S.
troops home from Vietnam, by February 1972, President Nixon had
spread the war into two surrounding countries. The Soviets, meanwhile, under the formidable Leonid Brezhnev, had walked away
from arms limitations talks Nixon initiated with barely a glance
over their shoulder. At home, the President's first two Supreme
Court appointments had been voted down on Capitol Hill, while
his tax reform, no-fault insurance, and school busing bills were at a
stalemate in Congress. In hopes he would kick-start a realignment
of global power in America's favor (and pay priceless domestic dividends for his imminent reelection bid), Nixon had been scrupulously and secretly grooming the China venture for years.

How to best explain Richard Nixon's cagey presidency has
kept historians and journalists busy for decades. He was born
in then-rural Orange County, California, to a father of meager
means and a mother who upheld 200 years of her family's strict
Quaker worship. A pair of near fatal childhood medical episodes
of his own couldn't prepare young Nixon for the devastating loss
of two brothers to tuberculosis.

Working as a carnival barker while vainly awaiting his
brothers' recovery at a sanatorium in Arizona, then later in school
debates and theater and law practice, young Nixon filled a deep
personal void with a relentless pursuit of public approval. As early
as high school, Nixon demonstrated an "ability to kind of slide
round an argument instead of meeting it head on," recalled his

debate instructor. A few years later, he would even mastermind a break-in to confirm his and some fellow students' college grades. No tactic would be off-limits, and no risk would be too great for one who had already lost so much.

Looking back on his career once it lay in post-Watergate ashes, Nixon offered, "I played by the rules of politics as I found them." He began his political life in a postwar world where the stakes had risen sharply as wartime allies became peacetime rivals. Rising anxiety over nuclear "containment," brinksmanship, and domestic Communist conspiracies helped Nixon succeed.

As a member of Joseph McCarthy's House Un-American Activities Committee, the freshman congressman from California cannily tapped into Cold War concerns. The future world leader's dogged pursuit of State Department employee (and Communist spy) Alger Hiss earned Nixon headline name recognition and a second term in Congress. His subsequent bid for a U.S. Senate seat from California offered voters, in his words, "simply the choice between freedom and state socialism." Nixon won by nearly 700,000 votes.

For conservatives like Nixon, the largest and most ominous blot on the new world map was mainland China. After expelling the invading Japanese, Communist strongman Mao Tse-tung had, with the support of the Soviets, forced Nationalist General Chiang Kai-shek to flee to Taiwan. On the island, the general established a government in exile. When Truman sent U.S. troops to intervene in Communist North Korea's invasion of South Korea, Mao made good on his threats to retaliate on North Korea's behalf.

The Korean War over, Eisenhower's Secretary of State, John Foster Dulles, made a point of ignoring the offered handshake of

Chou En-lai, premier and chief foreign minister of China, at the Sino-American peace talks held in Geneva. It was an insult Chou would never forget. It would also be the last time the U.S. and Communist Chinese governments would meet officially for more than a decade. As far as Republicans were concerned, Truman had given China away to the Communists. There would never be enough arms, aid, and rhetoric with which to shower beleaguered Taiwan and the betrayed General Chiang.

Though difficult to pinpoint precisely, hints of Nixon's strategic shift on China appeared early in his '68 presidential campaign. A policy paper Nixon's campaign drafted soon after his nomination stated in part, "we simply cannot afford to leave China forever outside of the family of nations." And after assuming the Oval Office, Nixon promised, during his inaugural address, to usher in a "new era of negotiation."

After a March 1969 Chinese ambush of Soviet border guards patrolling the contested Sino-Soviet border, Nixon knew the time was at hand. While the Western world watched the Chinese and Soviets sporadically clash along their vast frontier, Nixon quietly sent out feelers through backdoor political channels to open a secret dialogue with China.

Mindful of the "hot button" issue Taiwan remained for both the People's Republic and American Republicans, the secretive President cannily employed a clever procedural back door he had built into his own administration. In appointing William Rogers as his Secretary of State, Nixon had rewarded a longtime friend and legal adviser with a position outside his real area of expertise. Rogers could be relied upon to tow the Republican Party line in foreign policy, while Nixon addressed his own agenda through his own means. A scrupulously honest man, a loyal defender of Taiwan's interests, and a personal friend of James Shen (the Taiwanese ambassador to the United States), Rogers could never be trusted with Nixon's China overture. Instead, the President would rely on his National Security Adviser, a German-born Harvard Ph.D., Henry Kissinger.

Throughout his career as an academic and a foreign policy consultant, Kissinger had criticized partisan U.S. politicians like Nixon for conducting international relations on outdated moral grounds. During Nixon's unsuccessful 1960 presidential campaign, Kissinger even declared his future boss "the most dangerous, of all the men running, to have as president." Jewish, foreign-born, pragmatic, and intellectual, Kissinger seemed to be everything Nixon wasn't. But Nixon proved himself, in Kissinger's eyes, to be surprisingly clever and open-minded where world issues were concerned. And in Dr. Kissinger, Nixon had a strategist and diplomat who could operate under the radar.

As much to occupy Secretary of State Rogers as to initiate conventional diplomatic first contact, Nixon ordered the U.S. ambassador to Poland to approach the Chinese. Formal channels between the United States and the People's Republic were so eroded that members of the State Department weren't even sure who their Chinese counterparts were. A small American embassy contingent gamely approached a group of Asians at a Warsaw fashion show and was relieved to discover the stunned diplomats were indeed from the People's Republic. While the dubious Chinese representatives hesitantly agreed to formal meetings with the United States, Kissinger began a parallel series of top secret indirect communications with the Beijing government via go-between Pakistan.

But Nixon's invasion of Cambodia in May 1970 stopped all avenues of diplomacy, driving the Chinese from the bargaining table in Warsaw and closing the secret channel through Pakistan. Undaunted, Nixon went on the public relations offensive, telling *Time* magazine, "If there's anything I want to do before I die, it is to go to China." Privately, he had to believe the Chinese feared the 1.2 million Russian soldiers poised on their shared frontier more than they would admit. The President was also betting that China's unremitting commitment to North Vietnam was in reality as disposable as America's unlimited support to Taiwan would become.

Via Kissinger, Nixon made a direct appeal to Pakistan's President Yahya Khan, urging him to press Chou En-lai about secret high-level U.S.-Chinese talks. Over dinner with the Pakistani leader, Chou agreed, but only if the talks were confined to the subject of Taiwan. Though willing to concede much in return for the invitation for a state visit, Nixon responded that the discussions needed to cover a broader range of issues. Then, once again the secret communications were torpedoed, this time by the U.S.-backed invasion of Laos in early 1971.

Beijing remained discouragingly silent until Chou En-lai made a spectacular play to the media. The premier invited the U.S. table tennis team, then competing in a Japanese tournament, to visit China. The team, their spouses, and the five American journalists permitted to accompany them became the first Americans to visit the People's Republic since Truman's delegation was shown the door in 1949. Chou En-lai had "upped the ante" on Nixon.

Chou told the American athletes they had "opened a new chapter in the relations of the American and Chinese people," and indeed they had. The trip was followed by another series of covert communications with the United States via Pakistan. This time Chou endorsed the U.S. request for a broader base of topics in potential high-level talks. He went even further and invited a U.S. envoy "of ministerial rank" to come to China and hash out the details in person.

Kissinger and Nixon were ecstatic. In the hushed stillness of the White House after hours, they opened a bottle of brandy and toasted Chou's overture. It was, in Kissinger's words, "the most important communication that has come to an American president since the end of World War II." Eyes as ever on the political prize, Nixon's sole stipulation in his enthusiastically affirmative response was that the Chinese receive no other American politicians, especially Democrats.

As Nixon's secret emissary, Kissinger had long since learned to disguise his activities to journalists and political opponents. The National Security Adviser enjoyed Cabinet-level prestige, and his clandestine Air Force One journeys were routinely identified as "training missions conducted to test navigational gear." Often Kissinger would bookend his secret international rendezvous with conspicuous appearances at prominent Washington social events. A popular bachelor on the D.C. party scene, Kissinger would show himself at a soiree on Friday and a dinner on Monday to create the illusion he'd spent the weekend in the nation's capital. In reality, he had slipped away to Andrews Air Force Base to serve his President at some top-secret, high-level meetings, halfway around the world.

For his reconnaissance mission to China, Kissinger's staff informed the press he was embarking on a fact-finding mission throughout Asia. But during a dinner with President Yahya Khan in Pakistan, Kissinger suffered a sudden, carefully rehearsed case of "Delhi Belly" and was taken away by his hosts to recuperate. In a boldly orchestrated operation (code-named "Polo"), the National Security Adviser was actually whisked off to a waiting Pakistani jet. Inside, Kissinger and his aides found themselves face to face with four uneasy representatives of the People's Republic. It wasn't until he was in Beijing, seated at the bargaining table opposite Chou En-lai, that Kissinger was sure he had not been kidnapped.

Chou drove a hard bargain. He required nothing less than binding assurances that the United States was willing to completely reassess its Taiwan policy. Kissinger nimbly played on Chou's anxiety over the threat of a Russian invasion. Chou prodded Kissinger about Nixon's escalation of Vietnam. But both men knew Kissinger wanted only what he had been sent for: an invitation for his President. After 48 hours of nonstop negotiating, the two sides finally hammered out wording that was mutually satisfactory. Kissinger wired Washington the prearranged code word: "Eureka."

Within days of Kissinger's return to the United States, Nixon went on national television, read the full Chinese overture, and shocked the country by saying he had "accepted the invitation with pleasure."

Reaction in the United States was swift and extreme. Labor leader George Meany proposed that Nixon visit Castro in Cuba. "If he's going to visit all the louses of the world," suggested Meany, "why doesn't he visit them all?" Even Republicans accused the President of casually selling out America's most cherished Cold War foundling, Taiwan. John Wayne—whose movie *True Grit* was a Nixon favorite—wrote his fan that the decision to go to China was "a real shocker." Wayne also sent an anti-Communist pamphlet in case the President needed to be reminded that America was still fighting the Cold War.

Secretary of State Rogers was livid. Briefed at the last possible moment, Rogers was given the thankless task of informing his friend, the Taiwanese ambassador, of Nixon's intentions. Ambassador Shen's vitriolic protests about the China trip were ignored. The outraged U.S. Senate crushed Nixon's foreign aid bill with a vote of 41–27 in revenge for being kept in the dark. Senator Ted Kennedy said the President's move in China was a play on "the worst instincts of his party and the nation."

Now, Nixon worked overtime to soothe the bruised egos and outraged interests that he'd willfully circumvented. Cashing in on his efforts on Barry Goldwater's behalf, Nixon successfully persuaded the conservative to come out in support of the China trip. Two future chief executives were given eye-opening lessons in presidential damage control in Nixon's service. Though privately dismissing the Chinese as "a bunch of murdering bums," California Governor Ronald Reagan was recruited by the President to calm Shen's boss, Chiang Kai-shek, in Taiwan.

Hands tied by his President's change in policy, U.S. ambassador to the UN George Bush looked on helplessly as what had only recently been unthinkable had been not only thought, but acted on. In what Bush described as a "moment of infamy," the Warsaw Pact UN delegates closed on Taiwan like wolves. Though the United States voted against an Albanian resolution to admit the Beijing government and expel Taiwan, Nixon's nods toward China had effectively split up the anti-China camp in the UN. The final vote was 76 countries in favor, 35 opposed. Wild applause broke out in the General Assembly at the resolution's passage. The Taiwanese delegation somberly made its final exit from the hall.

But Nixon was already focused on something else—the reaction to his Chinese gambit in Moscow. Within days of Nixon's announcement, the USSR invited the President to resume the stalled SALT negotiations. The Soviet reaction had been perfect—a shift in the balance of world power in America's favor had begun right on cue. With nearly half of his mission already accomplished, Nixon now just had to hang on until the actual trip took place. But the Chinese had a few cards left to play themselves.

Key to Nixon's reelection agenda was the need for complete television coverage of his historic trip. The American public had to see its President functioning as an architect of the Nixon Doctrine's new world order. A closed society for decades, China was reticent to allow the Western press the kind of access that Nixon took for granted. Though Beijing accepted a communications satellite receiver to provide a color television broadcast of the President's arrival, they sharply pared down the list of American journalists they were willing to host.

Even more anxiety resulted from the rumors and intelligence leaking out of China. The Chinese Communist Party teemed with rabid "anti-imperialists" who believed that Mao and Chou had gone too far. Welcoming Nixon, a hated "butcher" and a leader of a nation that had been vilified by every Chinese citizen for more than a generation, was more than many high-ranking Chinese hard-liners could accept. Most vocal in his opposition was Red Army strongman Lin Pao, long considered by Western analysts to be Mao's hand-picked successor. When Lin Pao fell victim to a mysterious plane crash en route to a secret meeting with the Soviets, it sent shock waves through both the Kremlin and the White House.

Leery of Mao's housecleaning and eager to test the limits of China's media reluctance, Nixon sent Kissinger's second in command, General Alexander Haig, on a preliminary tour of the People's Republic a month prior to the President's scheduled arrival. With his GI Joe buzz cut and athletic build, Haig seemed the personification of the American militarism that Chinese hard-liners despised. From the moment Haig arrived at a landing field (decorated with banners denouncing "Capitalist Pigs"), Haig's anti-American Shanghai hosts badgered him about the war in Vietnam and American designs on Asia. The same thing happened when the American delegation was received in Hangzhou. Fortunately, Mao loyalists alerted the Chairman to the political powder keg Haig's visit had become. Beijing quickly saw to it that Haig's provincial hosts were put back in their places, and the American's trip concluded more hospitably than it began. Mission barely accomplished, Haig returned to Washington and told the President he'd intended to cut his trip short, had Mao not intervened. Haig thought Nixon's state visit was at best a gamble and at worst political suicide.

Perhaps all this passed through Nixon's mind as Air Force One, flying low per the Chinese navigator's request, completed the last leg of the journey to Beijing on February 21, 1972. Nixon would recall in his memoirs only that from his window seat, "the small towns and villages" they flew over "looked like pictures I had seen of towns in the middle ages." Touching down in Beijing, the official presidential party of 15 was greeted by three modest formations representing each of China's military services. The morning was cold, and the winter shadows stretched out across the tarmac as Nixon emerged from Air Force One and returned

Chou En-lai's traditional clapped greeting. Mindful of Dulles' snub in Geneva 18 years before, the President stepped forward and took Chou's hand firmly. "When our hands met," Nixon would later say, "one era ended and another began."

That moment, broadcast live around the world, was the showstopper Nixon dreamed it would be. The simple military airfield decorated with billboards bearing revolutionary slogans, Pat Nixon's scarlet coat, the Chinese military band bursting into "The Star-Spangled Banner" were the stuff that would one day inspire an opera. For American viewers and voters back home, all three American television networks broke into their scheduled programming, as they did for Apollo moon landings.

Despite a microscopically detailed itinerary, the Chinese surprised their guests. Before even getting unpacked, Nixon and Kissinger were whisked away to an unscheduled audience with the ailing Chairman Mao. Inside Mao's book-lined study, the California grocer's son and his Harvard academic found themselves face to face with the ferociously intelligent peasant dictator, as much an emperor as the Manchus he'd succeeded and as bloodthirsty a warlord as the brigands he'd exterminated. Together, Mao, Nixon, Kissinger, and Chou En-lai chatted casually for an hour, while a small cadre of Mao's female assistants looked on. Their diplomatic maneuvering nearly at an end, Mao confirmed to his American rival that "Taiwan was a small problem and Russia was a big problem." The Chairman even complimented Nixon on his book, *The Six Crises*.

That night, the two cultures embraced awkwardly, but endearingly, as a Chinese band played "Home on the Range" at a banquet held in the Great Hall of the People. The surreal scene was broadcast around the world. The President told his hosts there was "no reason for us to be enemies" and indirectly chided the Soviets by reminding the Chinese that "neither of us seeks to stretch out our hands and rule the world."

Thanks to Nixon's magnificent orchestration of the two planeloads of press accompanying the presidential party, the rest of the weeklong trip appeared in the media to be made up entirely of sightseeing and banquets. But Nixon and Kissinger worked with the Chinese to draft a communiqué that would justify Nixon's trip for both sides. The most prominent obstacle was still Secretary of State Rogers, who remained appalled at how easily his President had reversed nearly 25 years of U.S. policy. It took an impromptu personal visit to the Secretary's quarters from Chou En-lai himself to persuade Rogers to stand down.

The resulting 1,800-word joint communiqué was issued from Shanghai on February 27. Its five sections detailed the events of the President's visit, made pledges of mutual cooperation between the two nations, and stated newly negotiated rules and common issues. The fourth section was devoted solely to Taiwan and stated in part that "all Chinese on either side of the Taiwan Strait maintain that there is but one China and that Taiwan is a part of China. The U.S. government does not challenge that position." In the interest of *realpolitik*, Nixon had thrown away his Taiwan hand for a new draw of better cards from the mainland.

The seismic diplomatic, and political, tour de force by his President didn't stop Kissinger from worrying as Nixon knocked back many thimble-sized shots of Mai Tai during a final banquet in Shanghai. Having noted that "two glasses of wine were quite enough to make him boisterous, just one more to grow bellicose or sentimental with slurred speech," Kissinger prepared for the worst. But Nixon was as much intoxicated by victory as alcohol, and when the President somewhat unsteadily gushed to those assembled that it had been "the week that changed the world," no one could really find fault with his reasoning.

The next day, Chou bid the President, Mrs. Nixon, and their party good-bye. On board Air Force One, Nixon was already planning his next state visit. This time it would be Russia. (And when his wheels left the runway in Moscow a few months later, he would have a signed U.S.-Soviet SALT agreement. For Nixon, it had been a well-played hand all around.)

Nixon's China venture had been an unqualified success. China was now approachable, and in the process, the Russians had been maneuvered into conciliation. That November, Nixon won by a landslide.

Perhaps not surprisingly, it would be the same Byzantine mastery of secrecy and deception that gave Nixon success in China that ultimately destroyed him. Within two years, a covert scheme taken to ensure the President's reelection would ruin Nixon's career and forever tarnish his reputation. He is a President most remembered for the disgrace of Watergate, yet 30 years on, Nixon's China "card" ensures his legacy of artful statecraft in a game he played so well.

President Richard M. Nixon
Toast to Premier Chou En-lai of the People's Republic of China
Great Hall of the People, Peking
February 21, 1972

Mr. Prime Minister and all of your distinguished guests this evening:

On behalf of all of your American guests, I wish to thank you for the incomparable hospitality for which the Chinese people are justly famous throughout the world. I particularly want to pay tribute, not only to those who prepared the magnificent dinner, but also to those who have provided the splendid music. Never have I heard American music played better in a foreign land.

Mr. Prime Minister, I wish to thank you for your very gracious and eloquent remarks. At this very moment, through the wonder of telecommunications, more people are seeing and hearing what we say than on any other such occasion in the whole history of the world. Yet, what we say here will not be long remembered. What we do here can change the world.

As you said in your toast, the Chinese people are a great people, the American people are a great people. If our two peoples are enemies the future of this world we share together is dark indeed. But if we can find common ground to work together, the chance for world peace is immeasurably increased.

In the spirit of frankness which I hope will characterize our talks this week, let us recognize at the outset these points: We have at times in the past been enemies. We have great differences today. What brings us together is that we have common interests which transcend those differences. As we discuss our differences, neither of us will compromise our principles. But while we cannot close the gulf between us, we can try to bridge it so that we may be able to talk across it.

So, let us, in these next 5 days, start a long march together, not in lockstep, but on different roads leading to the same goal, the goal of building a world structure of peace and justice in which all may stand together with equal dignity and in which each nation, large or small, has a right to determine its own form of government, free of outside interference or domination. The world watches. The world listens. The world waits to see what we will do. What is the world? In a personal sense, I think of my eldest daughter whose birthday is today. As I think of her, I think of all the children in the world, in Asia, in Africa, in Europe, in the Americas, most of whom were born since the date of the foundation of the People's Republic of China.

What legacy shall we leave our children? Are they destined to die for the hatreds which have plagued the old world, or are they destined to live because we had the vision to build a new world?

There is no reason for us to be enemies. Neither of us seeks the territory of the other; neither of us seeks domination over the other; neither of us seeks to stretch out our hands and rule the world.

Chairman Mao has written, "So many deeds cry out to be done, and always urgently. The world rolls on. Time passes. Ten thousand years are too long. Seize the day, seize the hour."

This is the hour, this is the day for our two peoples to rise to the heights of greatness which can build a new and a better world.

In that spirit, I ask all of you present to join me in raising your glasses to Chairman Mao, to Prime Minister Chou, and to the friendship of the Chinese and American people which can lead to friendship and peace for all people in the world.

**PRESIDENT RONALD REAGAN MOTIONS TO A REPORTER
DURING A WHITE HOUSE PRESS CONFERENCE IN THE EAST ROOM, 1981.**

Ronald Reagan Presidential Library

CHAPTER 11

THE ZERO OPTION

◆

Ronald Reagan and the Soviet Union

I n the fall of 1983, while monitoring satellite activity inside a top-secret surveillance bunker just 55 miles from Moscow, Stanislav Petrov, a lieutenant colonel in the Soviet army, heard an alarm sound. He put down his cup of tea and looked up at his computer screen. It appeared that the United States had just launched a nuclear missile. Petrov sat stunned, his hands trembling. It made no sense.

Or perhaps it did. Only months earlier, President Ronald Reagan had begun ratcheting up his rhetoric about the arms race. He had outraged Russian leaders by calling the Soviet Union "the evil empire." Reagan had cut America's domestic programs but poured money into the military. Under his proposed budget, by 1985 the Pentagon would be spending more than $30 million every single hour on defense. More recently, the United States had begun moving a set of medium-range nuclear weapons into Europe. Soviet leaders worried this was just a cover for an invasion—Russia's own contingency plans for nuclear war involved just this kind of deployment.

Further straining tensions, just three weeks before the Soviet military had shot down a Korean airliner, killing all 269 passengers on board, including 61 Americans.

Petrov had to act. He knew Soviet policy required an immediate counter-launch of its own nuclear arsenal should the

United States attack, but that action would surely trigger massive retaliation by the United States. Within minutes, millions of people on both sides of the planet would be dead.

Petrov checked ground radar for corroboration, but it showed no signs of approaching missiles. The older ground system would be minutes behind anyway, and it could hardly be trusted over the year-old, cutting-edge satellite system that Petrov's computer monitored.

Three minutes passed. It must have been a false alarm. After all, Petrov thought, they wouldn't start an attack with just one missile. The alarm sounded again. Lights flashed. Indications of a second missile ran across the screen—and then a third, a fourth, and finally a fifth. At this point, Petrov feared the worst, but he knew that any action on his part would trigger an irreversible chain of events. His standing orders were to send important information up the chain of command, where it would immediately be transmitted to the General Secretary of the Soviet Communist Party, Yuri Andropov. Andropov would no doubt unleash return fire immediately. Instead, Petrov held tight.

All the systems appeared to be working properly, but in his gut, Petrov sensed something might be wrong. Disobeying procedure, he called his superior and reported a false alarm. If he was mistaken, within a quarter of an hour mushroom clouds would envelop city after Russian city with utter devastation, and he would be responsible for having failed to alert the Kremlin leadership. Petrov sweated out the ticking clock.

Four hours later, with no sign of incoming warheads, an investigation team arrived from Moscow. For three days, they held and interrogated Petrov and his colleagues. Ultimately, the

investigators discovered that the alarms had been triggered by no
more than sunlight reflecting off clouds at an unforeseen angle—
a statistical anomaly made it appear that America had let loose
the opening salvo of a nuclear war. In an era of Cold War and
fragile peace, this minor equipment failure had nearly provoked
Armageddon.

Three years later, U.S. President Ronald Reagan arrived
at Hofdi House, a small government guesthouse in Reykjavik,
Iceland. He was seven minutes early for a meeting with the current
Soviet leader, Mikhail Gorbachev.

Reagan's fur-collared overcoat was buttoned all the way up as
he entered the house. Observers noted the sleeves were too long—
an old coat from the depths of his closet, they imagined. A year
ago at the summit in Geneva, Reagan had greeted Gorbachev on a
bitterly cold November morning wearing just his suit jacket. This
was a bit of stagecraft. The 74-year-old Reagan wanted to show
he could stand up to the Russian leader two decades his junior.
As Gorbachev fumbled with his scarf and overcoat, a beaming,
confident Reagan towered over him. Cameras flashed—and the
Russians knew they had lost the first skirmish in the war of images.
This time, perhaps as a polite gesture, Reagan wore a coat.

Gorbachev arrived one minute early, in an overcoat, plaid
scarf, and his trademark fedora. His entrance caught Reagan by
surprise. The President stepped out of the house to greet him.
Reagan made a reference to the time. Gorbachev looked at his
watch and shrugged.

Low expectations had been set for the Reykjavik summit. It
was to be an informal meeting between the two men—a "private

meeting," Reagan had said. But the people of Reykjavik were prepared for history. The streets were lined with merchants selling wool sweaters with pictures of the two leaders, scarves knitted with the stars and stripes on one end and the hammer and sickle on the other, and even gold commemorative ashtrays. A high school gymnasium was transformed into a press room for the 2,000 journalists, complete with local delicacies including herring, smoked lamb, and honey-flavored yogurt. For Reykjavik, this was an event that happened only once in a lifetime. The leaders of the world's competing superpowers were meeting on neutral ground to negotiate for the future of the planet.

There had not been true peace between the two nations since just after World War II. The postwar alliance forged by Josef Stalin and Franklin Roosevelt had fallen apart, and the U.S. and the USSR had since vied for influence worldwide. Starting in Berlin in 1948, the contest between democracy and Communism spread over the years to Hungary, Italy, China, Greece, Vietnam, Cuba, Angola, Grenada, and Afghanistan. With massive outlays of both capital and troops, the nations battled for ideological and strategic supremacy.

The presence of nuclear weapons heightened the stakes as the postwar world took shape. With worries of first-strike and counter-strike capabilities, national defense plans contemplated casualty figures in the hundreds of millions. A nuclear war, both sides knew, would be a war no one could win.

But still, the weapons arsenals continued to grow and the bad feelings continued to rise. In the early 1970s, Richard Nixon and Leonid Brezhnev negotiated a period of détente—the relaxation of tensions—designed to create more cooperation between the two nations. They hoped to increase trade, sign arms control agreements, and lower the overall acrimony on both sides. Despite incremental gains, the "big breakthrough" hadn't happened—the underlying tensions between the two competing systems seemed immutable.

By the time Ronald Reagan won the presidency in 1980, little progress had been made. There had been no significant reductions in arms, and the Soviets were actively expanding their power in Afghanistan, Africa, and Central America. The trade agreements produced by détente (American advisers called one "The Great Grain Robbery" because of its generous terms in favor of the Soviets) were helping support a faltering Soviet economy. Trade deals brokered between the United States and the Soviet Union were allowing the Russians to continue to invest large sums of money in nuclear weapons programs.

Reagan came into office with a new attitude. Unlike his predecessors, he was not willing to prolong the Soviet empire. In his opinion, the United States instead should have been doing everything it could to bring it down. "Nothing proves the failure of Marxism more than the Soviet Union's inability to produce weapons for its military ambitions and at the same time provide for their people's everyday needs," Reagan said. "Stop doing business with them. Let their system collapse."

It was powerful rhetoric and went against established U.S. policy. Past Presidents had looked for temporary peace through stalemate. But Reagan sought to lift the Iron Curtain for good. He wanted to end the Cold War and bring about not a temporary peace but a permanent one, on his terms. It shouldn't have been surprising—although people derided him for being "just an actor," by the time Ronald Reagan won the White House in a landslide election, he had been fighting Communism for almost 40 years. Some have said there was no man better qualified to bring down the Soviet empire, or more committed to the cause. And it all started on a movie set.

On September 27, 1946, Ronald Reagan, then a handsome 35-year-old B-movie actor, reported to the Warner Brothers lot for production on a new film, *Night Unto Night*. On the way to the set, he encountered thousands of picketers outside the studio gates. A strike had been called by Herb Sorrell, head of the Conference of Studio Unions and a member of more than 20 Communist organizations. The Soviet Union's patriarch Vladimir Lenin had once said, "of all the arts, the cinema is the most important," and Sorrell thought his strike could deliver Hollywood to the Communist Party.

The head of Warner Brothers security told the actors and crew to surreptitiously slip past the picket line via the storm drain, but Ronald Reagan refused to be intimidated. So instead the studio sent a bus to transport the actors through the mob of strikers, advising them to lie flat on the floor to avoid getting hit by rocks or soda bottles. Day after day, the bus passed through the picket line in the morning and again at night. While stars and extras alike lay on the floor, one actor sat upright, his head and shoulders visible through the windows. Ronald Reagan had nothing to hide.

As the strike continued, Communist Party members began to threaten Reagan. On the *Night Unto Night* movie set, he received a phone call saying that if he continued to oppose the strike, his face would be disfigured with acid. Reagan had never before thought much about politics—he had grown up in a liberal Democrat family and had voted for Franklin Roosevelt—but the Communist tactics lit a fire inside him. Reagan became a fierce anti-Communist, and he began to speak out in Hollywood about the dangers of Communism. In 1947, his fellow actors elected him president of the Screen Actors Guild, and in that role he served as an informant for the FBI regarding Communist activity in Hollywood.

Fifteen years later, in 1962, Reagan was finishing a decade-long stint as the host of General Electric's weekly drama television series. Part of his job was serving as GE's "ambassador" and traveling the country speaking to workers. His speeches were becoming more and more political, and he had crafted an anti-Communist message that he hoped would strike a chord with audiences.

The 1964 Republican presidential candidate Barry Goldwater had heard one of Reagan's speeches, and he was impressed. He asked Reagan to tape a speech for nationwide television in support of Goldwater's presidential campaign. Reagan crafted his most powerful anti-Communist message yet. "You and I have a rendezvous with destiny," he told the American people. "We will preserve for our children this, the last best hope of man on earth, or we will sentence them to take the last step into a thousand years of darkness."

Reagan's words electrified America. Over $8 million poured in to the Goldwater campaign. *Time* called Reagan's speech "the one bright spot in a dismal campaign," and the *Washington Post* wrote that it was "the most successful national political debut since William Jennings Bryan electrified the 1896 Democratic Convention with his 'Cross of Gold' speech." Reagan was no longer just an actor.

Republican leaders in California convinced Reagan to run for state office, and he won the 1966 gubernatorial election by a million votes. After a second term, he announced his intention to seek the Republican presidential nomination in 1976, as he saw America losing ground to the Russians. Reagan told his son Michael that the biggest reason he wanted to be President was to negotiate with the Soviets. "It's been a long time since they've heard 'nyet' from an American president," he said.

Reagan lost the nomination to incumbent President Gerald Ford, but after four years of President Carter's conciliatory policies toward the Russians, Reagan knew he had to try again. He won the 1980 nomination easily and defeated Carter, under whose watch interest rates and inflation had skyrocketed, America had hostages being held in Iran, and taxes went through the roof. But high on Reagan's list was ending the Soviet threat. The lifelong anti-Communist had made it to the White House, and now things could finally change.

Reagan entered office with a plan—"Peace through Strength." Economic forecasts told him the Soviet empire was on the brink of collapse and that the Russians could not continue to funnel money into an arms race and at the same time keep their people fed. Reagan would exploit Russia's economic weakness by pushing the arms race to its limit until the Soviets had no choice but to give up. "The great dynamic success of capitalism had given us a powerful weapon in our battle against Communism—money," Reagan said.

"The Russians could never win the arms race; we could outspend them forever."

Reagan executed the largest peacetime military buildup in America's history, hoping to force the Russians to make an unpleasant choice—keep up and starve their people, or finally admit defeat. It was a bold strategy, and critics attacked it immediately. Senator Edward Kennedy said, "I reject the absurd theory that we can have fewer nuclear bombs tomorrow only if we build more nuclear bombs today." Even Reagan's advisers urged him it would never work. But President Reagan believed.

From 1980 to 1985, the Pentagon budget would grow by 51 percent—a $330 billion increase in inflation-adjusted dollars. This was a change from past administrations, which had stood idly by as the Russians increased their nuclear arsenal without protest from America. Reagan later enjoyed sharing with audiences a cartoon that illustrated this strategic change. The cartoon showed one Russian general saying to another, "I liked the arms race better when we were the only ones in it."

Coupled with the military buildup, Reagan began a campaign to spread the gospel of freedom throughout the world, hoping to increase resistance against the Soviets within their empire in Eastern Europe and to prevent new countries from falling prey to Communism. The United States funded underground resistance movements in Poland, throughout the Eastern bloc, and in Central America. As part of the plan, Reagan, a former sportscaster, turned to radio. He spread the "Voice of America" and "Radio Liberty" all over Europe, transmitting messages of democracy and freedom and exposing the shortcomings of life under Communism—shortages in consumer products, higher illegitimacy rates, and a lower average lifespan.

The radio campaign was a staggering success. By the end of Reagan's first term, American radio was heard by almost one-fifth of the Soviet adult population at least once a week, and the numbers were even higher elsewhere: 68 percent of Poles, 64 percent of Romanians, and 58 percent of Hungarians all tuned in. A May 1983 survey of 600 Poles found that Ronald Reagan ranked third, behind only the Pope and the Virgin Mary, and ahead of even Solidarity leader Lech Walesa, as the "last hope for Poland."

Reagan took a controversial next step. In 1983, the United States moved immediate-range nuclear missiles into Western Europe, where they would be capable of reaching deep into the Soviet Union. The move was intended to demonstrate to Russia that the United States threat was serious, but it polarized America's allies in NATO, and demonstrators throughout Europe took to the streets. In a way, it worked too well. Reagan became increasingly viewed as a warmonger. His own daughter Patti publicly spoke out against the missile deployment and joined the anti-nuclear movement. And the Russian leaders became nervous.

Reagan had also begun ratcheting up the language in his speeches, calling the Soviet Union "the focus of evil in the modern world" and saying Communism belonged on the "ash heap of history." He refused to negotiate at all with the Russians, hoping they would make the first move toward admitting defeat—but the increasing lack of communication began to have very real consequences. The 269 deaths in the downing of the Korean airliner may have caused serious alarm, but Petrov's brush with potential disaster in the fall of 1983 had brought the countries to the brink of war. The situation degraded further on September 28,

1983, when Soviet leader Andropov said that Russia would make no more efforts at diplomacy until Reagan left the White House.

The President was torn. On the one hand, his strategy seemed to be working. A fall 1983 CIA memo reported that the Soviet Union was headed toward its "terminal phase"; the economic reforms necessary to fix it would need to be so democratic as to kill Communism. But Reagan and his advisers worried that the Korean airliner incident served as merely a preview of things to come; if the Soviet Union went down, it would not go down quietly. Reagan feared the fight to stay alive could end with an unprovoked act of desperation—a deadly nuclear strike.

Ironically, the Soviets felt the same about America. Reagan's increasingly harsh rhetoric led to worries that he was in fact planning an unprovoked first strike of his own. If the price for the end of Communism was the end of the world, it would not be worth it. Looking back at that fall, Reagan would later write, "I began to realize that many Soviet officials feared us not only as adversaries, but as potential aggressors who might hurl nuclear weapons at them in a first strike." Reagan couldn't believe the Soviets would think that about America, but by refusing to meet with their leaders, he had given them little choice.

Faced with these concerns, along with election-year polling showing that many Americans perceived him as ready to risk war (and disapproved of his foreign policy by 49 percent to 38 percent), Reagan decided his campaign to build up America's strength had worked perhaps too effectively, and now was the right time to move toward peace. He dramatically toned down his language and began to open the door for negotiations. "A nuclear war can never be won and must never be fought," he said. "Our dream is to see the day when nuclear weapons will be banished from the face of the earth." This was a far cry from the "evil empire" language of just months prior.

Nancy Reagan played no small part in the effort to dial down her husband's language and move the plan forward. In early 1984, Reagan finally met with Soviet Foreign Minister Andrei Gromyko. According to Mrs. Reagan, "Gromyko came up to me and said 'Does your husband believe in peace?' And I said, 'Well of course.' And he said, 'Well then, will you whisper that in his ear every night?' And I said, 'Yes I will, and I'll whisper it in your ear, too.'"

But Reagan had one more weapon in his arsenal. The Strategic Defense Initiative (SDI) was Reagan's vision of a missile shield that would protect the United States from an incoming nuclear strike. Reagan had been considering the concept since a visit to the Pentagon's North American Aerospace Defense Command in 1979, where he realized the impossibility of the nuclear situation. Once missiles were fired, there were only two options: do nothing and absorb staggering losses, or strike back and exact an almost suicidal vengeance. "Both choices are bad choices," he said. "There has to be another way." SDI would provide that third way—a system of space-based lasers that could pinpoint and destroy ascending ballistic missiles. It would provide a shield, prevention from a nuclear exchange. Advisers saw this as merely a bargaining chip to induce the Russians to agree to a weapons-reduction deal, but Reagan was a true believer.

Reagan desperately wanted to eliminate nuclear missiles entirely, but SDI, to him, would be the safety net. If the United States ever did find itself threatened by nuclear war, a missile-

defense system would be the only way to truly protect the nation.
And Reagan wanted to share the technology and thus protect
the world, if only the Soviets would believe his intentions. In a
televised speech to the nation, Reagan proposed SDI to America,
and Russia, offering to share the technology so that both sides could
find peace. "The idea of mutual assured destruction," Reagan said,
"didn't seem to me to be something that would send you to bed
feeling safe." SDI, he told the world, could "give us the means of
rendering these nuclear weapons impotent and obsolete."

Russian leaders reacted to Reagan's SDI proposal with horror.
They did not trust Reagan's intentions and saw SDI as a threat—a
way that the United States could safely execute a first strike attack
on the Soviets—and live to tell about it. "Let us not mince words,
even if they are harsh ones," insisted Gromyko. "The system
would be used to blackmail the USSR." The Russians feared that
SDI would set off a brand new arms race based around the latest
technology that, given their failing economy, they simply could
not afford. And Reagan's simplistic offer to share the technology
only increased the Russians' distrust. Soviet leader Andropov had
harsh words for SDI: "Engaging in this is not just irresponsible, it
is insane . . . . Washington's actions are putting the entire world in
jeopardy." The stalemate continued, but now with more rancor.

By March 1985, Andropov had died, and his replacement,
Andrei Chernenko, was frail and close to death as well. "How
am I supposed to get anyplace with the Russians," Reagan asked,
"if they keep dying on me?" But Chernenko's successor, Mikhail
Gorbachev, seemed like a new kind of Russian leader. He was a
generation younger than his recent predecessors, and, for the first
time, there was a Soviet leader willing to admit that his country

needed reform. Gorbachev would introduce *glasnost* (openness and freedom) and *perestroika* (economic restructuring) to Russia under his tenure, ultimately freeing thousands of political prisoners and dissidents and trying to address the shortages in food and goods that had become the hallmarks of the failing Soviet economy.

Gorbachev's predecessors had come from military backgrounds and were awed by the power of nuclear weapons. Gorbachev, on the other hand, like Reagan, feared what these weapons could do. Stalin, Khrushchev, and Brezhnev had learned all they could about the nuts and bolts of the Soviet nuclear arsenal, but Gorbachev chose to keep the technology at arm's length. He refused to even pretend to give the command to launch nuclear missiles during military training exercises. Gorbachev saw what past Soviet leaders did not: his economy couldn't support an arms buildup without turning its back on the Russian people. So, like Reagan, he set his mind on eliminating the arms race. "Peace is the value above anything," Gorbachev said. "In the nuclear-cum-space era, a world war is the absolute evil."

Reagan wasted no time and made an important decision. He sent Vice President George Bush to Chernenko's funeral with a summit invitation for Gorbachev. "You can be assured of my personal commitment to working with you and the rest of the Soviet leadership in serious negotiations," Reagan wrote. Reagan, the fervent anti-Communist, offered an olive branch to the new leader of the Soviet state. He wanted to talk.

The two men agreed to meet in Geneva in November 1985. British Prime Minister Margaret Thatcher, Reagan's strongest ally in Europe, called Gorbachev "a man we can do business with," building up hopes for progress at the summit.

Gorbachev arrived, desperate for peace. "[We] will be pulled into an arms race that is beyond our capabilities," he said, "and we will lose it, because we are at the limit of our capabilities." Reagan's "Peace through Strength" doctrine had effectively pushed the Soviet Union to its breaking point. Now in a position of strength, Reagan was ready to deal for peace.

Improbably, when they met, Reagan and Gorbachev bonded almost immediately. "As we shook hands for the first time," Reagan wrote in his autobiography, "I had to admit—as Margaret Thatcher and Prime Minister Brian Mulroney of Canada predicted I would—that there was something likable about Gorbachev. There was warmth in his face and his style, not the coldness bordering on hatred I'd seen in most senior Soviet officials I'd met until then."

The two men went for a walk along the shore of Lake Leman, chatted about Reagan's film career, and tried to find common ground. They agreed to hold two more summits. On television, the world saw the two men, seated and talking by a crackling fire. If nothing else, the image made peace seem possible for the first time in decades. For that, Reagan came home to a cheering public. "I haven't gotten such a reception since I was shot," he said.

The second summit, a year later in Reykjavik, has been called one of the most extraordinary encounters in the annals of diplomacy.

Inside Hofdi House, the summit began with the two leaders alone—no ministers or advisers. Gorbachev offered everything Reagan could have possibly imagined, making more concessions than the Soviet Union had offered in 25 years. Reagan, without consulting his Secretary of State, military leaders in the Pentagon, or U.S. allies, responded by proposing the complete elimination of nuclear weapons by 1996. The men met face to face for almost 10 hours.

When the advisers joined the talks, Secretary of State George Shultz was shocked to discover that Gorbachev had laid "gifts at our feet." Gorbachev had even volunteered drastic reductions in Russia's conventional forces. "This was something that we'd always considered a prerequisite to a nuclear arms reduction agreement," Reagan wrote, "but never expected to get in Iceland. George and I couldn't believe what was happening. We were getting amazing agreements."

Never before had such reductions in arms been discussed. The threat of nuclear war could come to an end with one shake of the hand. Finally, Gorbachev announced that everything he had proposed hinged on one condition. The United States would have to scrap SDI.

Before the summit, former President Nixon had called SDI America's ultimate bargaining chip and advised the President to use it to get the best deal possible. But Reagan knew that SDI was what had brought Gorbachev to the table. It represented the world's best hope for guaranteed peace.

"There is no way we are going to give up research to find a defense weapon against nuclear missiles," Reagan said. He stood up and put on his coat.

"The meeting is over. George [Shultz], we're leaving."

Gorbachev tried to persuade Reagan to stay.

"I don't think you want a deal," Reagan said.

"I don't know what more I could have done," answered Gorbachev.

The press criticized President Reagan for walking away. But even though the meeting broke down, Reagan knew the pieces were in place. Both sides, at least in principle, had agreed to a nuclear-free world. In Reagan's words, "we [were] closer than ever before to agreements that could lead to a safer world without nuclear weapons." Nobody had ever imagined an end to the Cold War. Previous Presidents had worked from the premise that it could only be contained. Even Gorbachev admitted it. "Reykjavik was a breakthrough," he said. "Reykjavik will eventually produce results."

Margaret Thatcher would later pinpoint the Reykjavik summit as the point when the Cold War really came to an end. A year later, Reagan and Gorbachev met at the White House and signed an agreement of historic proportions. Gorbachev accepted Reagan's "zero option," eliminating both sides' intermediate-range nuclear missiles from Europe, this time without insisting on the termination of SDI. He had no choice. He needed the agreement, and Reagan had proven he would not relent. The threat was gone. The Cold War was over.

In May 1988, Gorbachev invited Reagan to Moscow. Reagan spoke in front of a crowd of students, with a bust of Lenin as a backdrop, and told them that democracy was on its way: "Your generation is living in one of the most exciting, hopeful times in Soviet history. It is a time when the first breath of freedom stirs the air and the heart beats to the accelerated rhythm of hope, when the accumulated spiritual energies of a long silence yearn to break free. We do not know what the conclusion will be of this journey.

But we're hopeful that the promise of reform will be fulfilled."

A reporter later asked Reagan, as he was touring Red Square, "You still think you are in an evil empire, Mr. President?"

"No," Reagan said. "I was talking about another time. Another era."

Reagan's overture to Gorbachev would have a profound impact on the world. In 1989, the Berlin Wall came down after 40 years. Communist nations became democracies overnight. Finally, in 1992, after a coup tried to oust Gorbachev, the USSR faltered and became a free, democratic nation.

Today, in a bleak town 30 miles from Moscow, in a second-floor apartment, Stanislav Petrov lives alone. The weapons he once protected no longer exist, having been melted down for the raw uranium. Out of embarrassment, Soviet leaders never publicly recognized his prescient service. A year after the incident, he retired from a 27-year military career. His only reward was a telephone he received without having to wait the usual years for installation, only today, he is so poor the phone service has been cut off.

The world owes Petrov a deep debt of gratitude for his sound judgment. And it also owes Ronald Reagan for changing his direction, and thereby changing the world.

My fellow Americans, thank you for sharing your time with me tonight.

The subject I want to discuss with you, peace and national security, is both timely and important. Timely, because I've reached a decision which offers a new hope for our children in the 21st century, a decision I'll tell you about in a few minutes. And important because there's a very big decision that you must make for yourselves. This subject involves the most basic duty that any President and any people share, the duty to protect and strengthen the peace.

At the beginning of this year, I submitted to the Congress a defense budget which reflects my best judgment of the best understanding of the experts and specialists who advise me about what we and our allies must do to protect our people in the years ahead. That budget is much more than a long list of numbers, for behind all the numbers lies America's ability to prevent the greatest of human tragedies and preserve our free way of life in a sometimes dangerous world. It is part of a careful, long-term plan to make America strong again after too many years of neglect and mistakes.

Our efforts to rebuild America's defenses and strengthen the peace began 2 years ago when we requested a major increase in the defense program. Since then, the amount of those increases we first proposed has been reduced by half, through improvements in management and procurement and other savings.

The budget request that is now before the Congress has been trimmed to the limits of safety. Further deep cuts cannot be made without seriously endangering the security of the Nation. The choice is up to the men and women you've elected to the Congress, and that means the choice is up to you.

Tonight, I want to explain to you what this defense debate is all about and why I'm convinced that the budget now before the Congress is necessary, responsible, and deserving of your support. And I want to offer hope for the future . . .

The defense policy of the United States is based on a simple premise: the United States does not start fights. We will never be an aggressor. We maintain our strength in order to deter and defend against aggression—to preserve freedom and peace.

Since the dawn of the atomic age, we've sought to reduce the risk of war by maintaining a strong deterrent and by seeking genuine arms control. "Deterrence" means simply this: making sure any adversary who thinks about attacking the United States, or our allies, or our vital interests, concludes that the risks to him outweigh any potential gains. Once he understands that, he won't attack. We maintain the peace through our strength; weakness only invites aggression.

This strategy of deterrence has not changed. It still works. But what it takes to maintain deterrence has changed. It took one kind of military force to deter an attack when we had far more nuclear weapons than any other power; it takes another kind now that the Soviets, for example, have enough accurate and powerful nuclear weapons to destroy virtually all of our missiles on the ground. Now, this is not to say that the Soviet Union is planning to make war on us. Nor do I believe a war is inevitable—quite the contrary. But what must be recognized is that our security is based on being prepared to meet all threats.

There was a time when we depended on coastal forts and artillery batteries, because, with the weaponry of that day, any attack would have had to come by sea. Well, this is a different world, and our defenses must be based on recognition and awareness of the weaponry possessed by other nations in the nuclear age.

We can't afford to believe that we will never be threatened. There have been two world wars in my lifetime. We didn't start them and, indeed, did everything we could to avoid being drawn into them. But we were ill-prepared for both. Had we been better prepared, peace might have been preserved.

For 20 years the Soviet Union has been accumulating enormous military might. They didn't stop when their forces exceeded all requirements of a legitimate defensive capability. And they haven't stopped now. During the past decade and a half, the Soviets have built up a massive arsenal of new strategic nuclear weapons—weapons that can strike directly at the United States . . .

Some people may still ask: Would the Soviets ever use their formidable military power? Well, again, can we afford to believe they won't? There is Afghanistan. And in Poland, the Soviets denied the will of the people and in so doing demonstrated to the world how their military power could also be used to intimidate.

The final fact is that the Soviet Union is acquiring what can only be considered an offensive military force. They have continued to build far more intercontinental ballistic missiles than they could possibly need simply to deter an attack. Their conventional forces are trained and equipped not so much to defend against an attack as they are to permit sudden, surprise offensives of their own.

Our NATO allies have assumed a great defense burden, including the military draft in most countries. We're working with them and our other friends around the world to do more. Our defensive strategy means we need military forces that can move very quickly, forces that are trained and ready to respond to any emergency.

Every item in our defense program—our ships, our tanks, our planes, our funds for training and spare parts—is intended for one all-important purpose: to keep the peace. Unfortunately, a decade of neglecting our military forces had called into question our ability to do that.

When I took office in January 1981, I was appalled by what I found: American planes that couldn't fly and American ships that couldn't sail for lack of spare parts and trained personnel and insufficient fuel and ammunition for essential training. The inevitable result of all this was poor morale in our Armed Forces, difficulty in recruiting the brightest young Americans to wear the uniform, and difficulty in convincing our most experienced military personnel to stay on.

There was a real question then about how well we could meet a crisis. And it was obvious that we had to begin a major modernization program to ensure we could deter aggression and preserve the peace in the years ahead.

We had to move immediately to improve the basic readiness and staying power of our conventional forces, so they could meet—and therefore help deter—a crisis. We had to make up for lost years of investment by moving forward with a long-term plan to prepare our forces to counter the military capabilities our adversaries were developing for the future.

I know that all of you want peace, and so do I. I know too that many of you seriously believe that a nuclear freeze would further the cause of peace. But a freeze now would make us less, not more, secure and would raise, not reduce, the risks of war. It would be largely unverifiable and would seriously undercut our negotiations on arms reduction. It would reward the Soviets for their massive military buildup while preventing us from modernizing our aging and increasingly vulnerable forces. With their present margin of superiority, why should they agree to arms reductions knowing that we were prohibited from catching up?

Believe me, it wasn't pleasant for someone who had come to Washington determined to reduce government spending, but we had to move forward with the task of repairing our defenses or we would lose our ability to deter conflict now and in the future. We had to demonstrate to any adversary that aggression could not succeed, and that the only real solution was substantial, equitable, and effectively verifiable arms reduction—the kind we're working for right now in Geneva.

Thanks to your strong support, and bipartisan support from the Congress, we began to turn things around. Already, we're seeing some very encouraging results. Quality recruitment and retention are up dramatically—more high school graduates are choosing military careers, and more experienced career personnel are choosing to stay. Our men and women in uniform at last are getting the tools and training they need to do their jobs.

Ask around today, especially among our young people, and I think you will find a whole new attitude toward serving their country. This reflects more than just better pay, equipment, and leadership. You the American people have sent a signal to these young people that it is once again an honor to wear the uniform. That's not something you measure in a budget, but it's a very real part of our nation's strength.

It'll take us longer to build the kind of equipment we need to keep peace in the future, but we've made a good start.

We haven't built a new long-range bomber for 21 years. Now

we're building the B-1. We hadn't launched one new strategic submarine for 17 years. Now we're building one Trident submarine a year. Our land-based missiles are increasingly threatened by the many huge, new Soviet ICBMs. We're determining how to solve that problem. At the same time, we're working in the START and INF negotiations with the goal of achieving deep reductions in the strategic and intermediate nuclear arsenals of both sides.

We have also begun the long-needed modernization of our conventional forces. The Army is getting its first new tank in 20 years. The Air Force is modernizing. We're rebuilding our Navy, which shrank from about a thousand ships in the late 1960s to 453 during the 1970s. Our nation needs a superior navy to support our military forces and vital interests overseas. We're now on the road to achieving a 600-ship navy and increasing the amphibious capabilities of our marines, who are now serving the cause of peace in Lebanon. And we're building a real capability to assist our friends in the vitally important Indian Ocean and Persian Gulf region.

This adds up to a major effort, and it isn't cheap. It comes at a time when there are many other pressures on our budget and when the American people have already had to make major sacrifices during the recession. But we must not be misled by those who would make defense once again the scapegoat of the Federal budget.

The fact is that in the past few decades we have seen a dramatic shift in how we spend the taxpayer's dollar. Back in 1955, payments to individuals took up only about 20 percent of the Federal budget. For nearly three decades, these payments steadily increased and, this year, will account for 49 percent of the budget. By contrast, in 1955 defense took up more than half of the Federal budget. By 1980 this spending had fallen to a low of 23 percent. Even with the increase that I am requesting this year, defense will still amount to only 28 percent of the budget.

The calls for cutting back the defense budget come in nice, simple arithmetic. They're the same kind of talk that led the democracies to neglect their defenses in the 1930s and invited the tragedy of World War II. We must not let that grim chapter of history repeat itself through apathy or neglect.

This is why I'm speaking to you tonight—to urge you to tell your Senators and Congressmen that you know we must continue to restore our military strength. If we stop in midstream, we will send a signal of decline, of lessened will, to friends and adversaries alike. Free people must voluntarily, through open debate and democratic means, meet the challenge that totalitarians pose by compulsion. It's up to us, in our time, to choose and choose wisely between the hard but necessary task of preserving peace and freedom and the temptation to ignore our duty and blindly hope for the best while the enemies of freedom grow stronger day by day.

The solution is well within our grasp. But to reach it, there is simply no alternative but to continue this year, in this budget, to provide the resources we need to preserve the peace and guarantee our freedom.

Now, thus far tonight I've shared with you my thoughts on the problems of national security we must face together. My predecessors in the Oval Office have appeared before you on other occasions to describe the threat posed by Soviet power and have proposed steps to address that threat. But since the advent of nuclear weapons, those steps have been increasingly directed toward deterrence of aggression through the promise of retaliation.

This approach to stability through offensive threat has worked. We and our allies have succeeded in preventing nuclear war for more than three decades. In recent months, however, my advisers, including in particular the Joint Chiefs of Staff, have underscored the necessity to break out of a future that relies solely on offensive retaliation for our security.

Over the course of these discussions, I've become more and more deeply convinced that the human spirit must be capable of rising above dealing with other nations and human beings by threatening their existence. Feeling this way, I believe we must thoroughly examine every opportunity for reducing tensions and for introducing greater stability into the strategic calculus on both sides.

One of the most important contributions we can make is, of course, to lower the level of all arms, and particularly nuclear arms. We're engaged right now in several negotiations with the Soviet Union to bring about a mutual reduction of weapons. I will report to you a week from tomorrow my thoughts on that score. But let me just say, I'm totally committed to this course.

If the Soviet Union will join with us in our effort to achieve major arms reduction, we will have succeeded in stabilizing the nuclear balance. Nevertheless, it will still be necessary to rely on the specter of retaliation, on mutual threat. And that's a sad commentary on the human condition. Wouldn't it be better to save lives than to avenge them? Are we not capable of demonstrating our peaceful intentions by applying all our abilities and our ingenuity to achieving a truly lasting stability? I think we are. Indeed, we must.

After careful consultation with my advisers, including the Joint Chiefs of Staff, I believe there is a way. Let me share with you a vision of the future which offers hope. It is that we embark on a program to counter the awesome Soviet missile threat with measures that are defensive. Let us turn to the very strengths in technology that spawned our great industrial base and that have given us the quality of life we enjoy today.

What if free people could live secure in the knowledge that their security did not rest upon the threat of instant U.S. retaliation to deter a Soviet attack, that we could intercept and destroy strategic ballistic missiles before they reached our own soil or that of our allies?

I know this is a formidable, technical task, one that may not be accomplished before the end of this century. Yet, current technology has attained a level of sophistication where it's reasonable for us to begin this effort. It will take years, probably decades of effort on many fronts. There will be failures and

setbacks, just as there will be successes and breakthroughs. And
as we proceed, we must remain constant in preserving the nuclear
deterrent and maintaining a solid capability for flexible response.
But isn't it worth every investment necessary to free the world
from the threat of nuclear war? We know it is.

In the meantime, we will continue to pursue real reductions
in nuclear arms, negotiating from a position of strength that can
be ensured only by modernizing our strategic forces. At the same
time, we must take steps to reduce the risk of a conventional
military conflict escalating to nuclear war by improving our
nonnuclear capabilities.

America does possess—now—the technologies to attain
very significant improvements in the effectiveness of our
conventional, nonnuclear forces. Proceeding boldly with these
new technologies, we can significantly reduce any incentive that
the Soviet Union may have to threaten attack against the United
States or its allies.

As we pursue our goal of defensive technologies, we
recognize that our allies rely upon our strategic offensive power
to deter attacks against them. Their vital interests and ours are
inextricably linked. Their safety and ours are one. And no change
in technology can or will alter that reality. We must and shall
continue to honor our commitments.

I clearly recognize that defensive systems have limitations and
raise certain problems and ambiguities. If paired with offensive

systems, they can be viewed as fostering an aggressive policy, and no one wants that. But with these considerations firmly in mind, I call upon the scientific community in our country, those who gave us nuclear weapons, to turn their great talents now to the cause of mankind and world peace, to give us the means of rendering these nuclear weapons impotent and obsolete.

Tonight, consistent with our obligations of the ABM treaty and recognizing the need for closer consultation with our allies, I'm taking an important first step. I am directing a comprehensive and intensive effort to define a long-term research and development program to begin to achieve our ultimate goal of eliminating the threat posed by strategic nuclear missiles. This could pave the way for arms control measures to eliminate the weapons themselves. We seek neither military superiority nor political advantage. Our only purpose—one all people share—is to search for ways to reduce the danger of nuclear war.

My fellow Americans, tonight we're launching an effort which holds the promise of changing the course of human history. There will be risks, and results take time. But I believe we can do it. As we cross this threshold, I ask for your prayers and your support.

Thank you, good night, and God bless you.

AGAINST
THE ENEMY

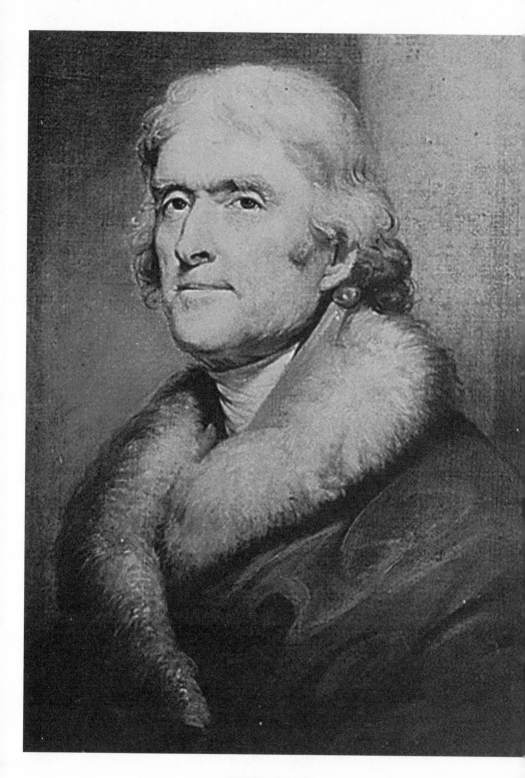

THOMAS JEFFERSON

Copy of a painting by Rembrandt Peale, ca. 1805. National Archives & Records Administration.

CHAPTER 12

LIFE, LIBERTY, AND THE PURSUIT OF SMUGGLERS

Thomas Jefferson and the Embargo Acts

It was 3:30 in the afternoon on June 22, 1807, about 10 miles off the coast of Virginia. The *USS Chesapeake* had just set sail for the Mediterranean under the command of Commodore James Barron. The crew, spread out over the deck, taking advantage of the sunny weather, noticed a ship following close behind. Just a few lengths from the *Chesapeake* lurked the British frigate *HMS Leopard*. The *Leopard* signaled it had an important message to deliver.

Reluctantly, Commodore Barron granted permission for the *Leopard* to send over a messenger. A young lieutenant rowed over to the *Chesapeake* and presented Barron a note. It demanded that Barron allow the crew of the *Leopard* to search the *Chesapeake* for British deserters. Barron replied that he knew of no deserters and that under instructions from the U.S. government, he could not under any circumstances let the crew of another ship board. "It is my disposition to preserve harmony," Barron wrote back, "and I hope this answer to your dispatch will prove satisfactory."

This was not the first time a British ship had approached an American vessel at sea. The British had been doing this regularly for the past few years. And often they *did* find deserters on board. Given the Napoleonic Wars, British sailors were often at risk of capture by the French; they would desert and defect when they reached American ports. America had remained neutral in the war, so to be an American sailor was safer. The British seamen would switch allegiances and sail back to Europe on American ships that carried exports abroad. And the British ships in America would have to sail back home with skeleton crews.

What made Britain especially angry was how the American government granted British sailors citizenship papers quickly and easily. So, the British stopped recognizing these defections and instituted a policy designed to repatriate their sailors. They would intercept American ships, search for deserters, and "impress" any British seamen they found on board. As the war continued, and the British became more desperate to retain their sailors, the practice became more intrusive. British captains often made "mistakes" and seized American sailors who had never been British citizens. To make life even more inconvenient for American seafarers, the British government began to station frigates permanently off the U.S. coast for the sole purpose of searching all incoming and outgoing ships, regardless of any prior suspicion of deserters.

The *Leopard* was one of these searcher ships and had been watching from Lynnhaven Bay on the Virginia coastline as the *Chesapeake* set sail.

Just minutes after the British lieutenant returned to the *Leopard*, his request denied, the *Leopard* pulled closer to the *Chesapeake* and its captain again shouted his demand to search the ship.

Commodore Barron stood on the deck of his ship, unsure what to do. These were neutral waters—he surely had no obligation to let the British board. To buy time, he shouted back that he did not hear what the British captain had said. Then, in case of violence, he ordered his men to prepare for action. But the *Chesapeake* crew barely had a chance to move from the deck when the *Leopard* fired a cannon shot that smashed through the *Chesapeake*'s bow. The ship was under attack.

The *Leopard* kept firing, three broadsides in 15 minutes, damaging the masts, the sails, and the rigging. The assault killed 3 sailors and wounded 18 more. As Barron lowered his flag in surrender, a member of his crew finally fired the *Chesapeake*'s first and only shot, at this point simply for honor's sake. The *Chesapeake* all but sunk, two British lieutenants boarded the ship and searched for deserters. They found four men who belonged to Britain—including one hiding in the *Chesapeake*'s coal storage hole. One of the four would be hanged for his offenses while serving in the King's fleet.

The *Chesapeake*, riddled with holes, dead and dying men strewn across its deck, crawled back to its Virginia port. News quickly spread of the attack. Despite the presence of deserters on board, the British actions outraged Americans. Ironically, these were the very same waters where a quarter-century earlier, the British navy had been defeated in the Battle of Yorktown, ensuring American independence. Now, this independence was very much in doubt—Americans no longer felt safe in their own harbors.

On June 28, 1807, 4,000 people turned out for the funeral of one of the *Chesapeake* sailors who had died of his wounds. Men wore black fabric bands on their arms to mourn him and his fellow slain comrades. The city of Norfolk, Virginia, passed a resolution refusing to repair or resupply any British ships in port. "This country," President Thomas Jefferson wrote, "has never been in such a state of excitement since the battle of Lexington." All signs pointed to war.

In fact, all signs had been pointing to war for years. For the past four years, France and Britain had been fighting for supremacy over Europe in battles that would ultimately last another decade and kill between 500,000 and 700,000 people. At various times, Austria, Prussia, Russia, Sweden, and Germany all found themselves part of the bloody battles, as France fought to wrest control of the high seas from Great Britain, and the British fought to stop France from conquering the entire European continent. A new country, celebrating its freedom across the Atlantic Ocean, wanted no part of this Old World conflict. But the offenses had been piling up, and with its freedom and safety threatened, it seemed doubtful that America would find a way to avoid joining the fray. The *Chesapeake* incident was only the most recent in a line of growing assaults against America by the European powers.

America's Minister to Great Britain, James Monroe, estimated that prior to 1807, the British had seized 528 American merchant ships—nearly $30 million worth of vessels and cargo (approximately $460 million today)—and imprisoned thousands of American sailors without cause. The British, with their world-class navy, indisputably controlled the seas. In the months preceding the *Chesapeake* incident, they had all but cut off American trade with France, a crucial partner and essential ally. More recently, the British had prohibited U.S. ships from trading anywhere along the entire European coast unless they stopped first at a British port—and paid a tax. The Revolutionary War, just 30 years earlier, remained on the minds of many Americans. That war had been fought in part to escape unfair taxation, which made Britain's new policies even more of an affront. Effectively, the British now threatened to return America to colonial status.

The French, unfortunately, were no more charitable toward America than were the British. Napoleon's Berlin Decree claimed the right to confiscate any vessels and goods arriving in France by way of Britain, no matter who owned them—and usually it was Americans who owned them. With America's freedom of the seas under challenge—by both countries—the United States had clear justification to declare war against Britain, France, or both.

American citizens clamored for a response. After all, animosity was high between America and Britain even in peaceful times—in times like these, the ill feelings only escalated. President Jefferson needed to act. Most Americans assumed that with Jefferson in the White House, war was a certainty. After all, the 64-year-old President was a man of bold action. He had overcome concerns about the constitutionality of acquiring new land when he purchased the Louisiana Territory from Napoleon four years earlier; he conceived and underwrote the historic and unprecedented Lewis and Clark expedition into the West; and he turned societal mores on their head by maintaining an affair with a pretty slave girl three decades his junior.

More to the point, he had already proven his willingness to wage war. When American shipping fell prey to Barbary Coast pirates, Jefferson dispatched a naval squadron and fought for four years to protect American commerce and freedom on the seas. The pirates had been exacting bribes from the United States since the country's inception—as ambassador to France in 1785, Jefferson had warned that paying for safe transit would only lead to more attacks, but he was ignored. By 1800, payments in ransom and tribute had risen to 20 percent of America's annual government revenues.

When Jefferson took office, he vowed to stop the payments—and when the pirates (and the North African leaders supporting them) demanded $225,000 on Jefferson's inauguration day, he refused and sent warships to the Mediterranean. After American forces staged a daring hostage rescue and then a land attack on the city of Derna (commemorated in a popular Marine battle anthem—"to the shores of Tripoli"), the pirates surrendered. The U.S. military had proven itself capable of handling an overseas conflict.

Jefferson's willingness to make bold moves and not shy away from conflict only added to his legend. There seemed to be nothing he could not do. In a time when the rigors of daily life were enough to keep most men occupied, Jefferson became a master inventor, scientist, violinist, agriculturalist, religious scholar, and architect. (He even introduced ice cream to the United States.) And the assumption he would lead the United States to war was only strengthened by the knowledge that Jefferson's animus toward the British ran deep. After all, he had written the Declaration of Independence, and if the British had been successful in quelling America's revolution, he would likely have been one of the first to be hanged.

Throughout his administration, Jefferson tried not to let England forget that America was a different place, on a different continent, with a different kind of people. He made a point of insulting British notions of formality and their antiquated norms and customs.

Characteristic of this attitude, in Jefferson's first term as President, he invited Anthony Merry, the First British Minister to the United States, to a state dinner in Merry's honor at the White House. Merry arrived, accompanied by his wife, with Secretary

of State James Madison. Merry stood tall in his velvet and gold
trimmed coat and, as tradition held, wore his sword on his belt. President Jefferson was nowhere to be found.

While Madison frantically searched the grounds, Jefferson appeared from his study to greet his guests—dressed in his morning attire, complete with slippers and a robe. Merry was aghast, and it only got worse. Jefferson had invited the French Charge d'Affaires, Louis Andre Pichon, to join them at dinner despite the ongoing wars between England and France and the personal antagonism between the two men.

The dinner bell rang, and instead of escorting Mrs. Merry to the table, as proper custom held, Jefferson took Dolly Madison's hand as the rest of the guests were left to scramble for seats. In place of a traditional rectangular table that would have allowed for Merry to sit as the guest of honor, Jefferson used a round table. Throughout dinner, Jefferson tossed one of his slippers in the air with his foot and then would catch it with his big toe. Insulted by these perceived slights, Merry insisted on leaving just as dinner ended.

Jefferson enjoyed the evening immensely. He obviously knew the "right" way to behave—he had lived under British rule and spent a great deal of time in Europe—but he simply had no interest in following tradition. Going to dinner with the British minister in his bathrobe was just another reason why Jefferson had fought for independence. Though a full-fledged aristocrat, Jefferson rejected the idea of aristocracy and embraced the small farmer and common man. (To that end, he opened his residence to the public each Fourth of July so that any American could commemorate the creation of the country with one of its founders, the President.) If anyone was inclined to go to war against England, it was Jefferson.

As much as Jefferson despised the British, reveled in bold action, and knew of the popular outcry for war, he also knew America could not win a war against England, and he certainly did not want to get embroiled in the ongoing Napoleonic conflicts. The United States in 1807 did not have a standing army, and barely had a navy. Jefferson, in fact, had turned over protection of the coastline largely to the individual state militias, reducing the navy to a supporting player. Jefferson knew America, and its handful of naval ships, could certainly not compete with the British Royal Navy, which was over 500 ships strong and a force that controlled the oceans worldwide.

As it was, the United States tried to resist British attacks on its ships and sailors, but it couldn't. The Monroe-Pinckney Treaty, negotiated between the United States and Britain in early 1807, provided an informal promise by Britain to stop capturing innocent American soldiers, but the promise had no teeth and did nothing to slow the inflammatory incidents at sea. Britain knew the United States had no military might to fight back.

According to Jefferson's Treasury Secretary, Albert Gallatin, a war would increase the nation's debt and taxes, and "progress in every respect would be interrupted." But Jefferson had to do something. He decided to step back and think more strategically. The United States could not win a war, but maybe he could take steps to prevent further violence—and also harm Britain and France in the process.

Jefferson called a Cabinet meeting to discuss the situation. He took Congress's recent defense appropriations and fortified the nation's most exposed ports—New York, New Orleans, and Charleston. He asked the states to ready 100,000 militiamen in case war became necessary. And, finally, he issued a proclamation ordering all armed British ships to leave American waters immediately. The proclamation forbade United States citizens from approaching these ships or providing them with supplies. Only "a vessel forced by distress or charged with public dispatches" would even be allowed within American waters.

Despite Jefferson's good intentions, the proclamation proved weak. American waters extended only three miles out to sea— even the *Chesapeake* incident had taken place farther out than that. Besides, enforcement was impossible. The British belittled the idea of the United States imposing any limitation at all on the world's greatest naval power. British commanders openly ignored the new rules. They continued to chase American ships and demanded they be allowed to search for deserters. In one case, the governor of Virginia ordered militiamen to the scene. But soldiers on shore could do little against a ship at sea, and the inconsequential U.S. Navy and Coast Guard were helpless.

Undeterred, Jefferson now looked to protect his men already at sea. By the government's best estimate, 40,000 American sailors were out somewhere on the ocean. If tensions escalated, these men would be unprotected targets for the British. Jefferson was afraid the British might seize American ships one by one, and there would be nothing the United States could do. So he began by calling back all American ships in the Mediterranean (where the *Chesapeake* had been headed) and simultaneously reached out to allies around the world to garner sympathy and help in the struggle.

Jefferson first turned to the Russians, who had good relations with Britain, hoping he could convince their leaders to talk with the British Prime Minister and help put a stop to the impressments of American ships and sailors. The Russians refused.

Jefferson next turned to the French and tried to win the friendship of French Minister General Turreau in support of their common fight against the British. In perfect unaccented French, Jefferson told Turreau that "if the English do not give us the satisfaction we want, we will take Canada, which wants to enter the union." But then he had to admit the U.S. military actually had "no officers." Turreau reported back to his government that Jefferson "does not want war, and that Mr. Madison dreads it still more. I am convinced that these two personages will do everything that is possible to avoid it . . . the actual Administration has nothing to gain and everything to lose by war." Like the Russians, Turreau realized there was no advantage in helping Jefferson—as an ally, America had nothing to offer in the way of military strength.

In truth, Jefferson hoped he could find a diplomatic way out of the conflict. Despite his passionate hatred of everything British, the prospect of war would not have excited him even if the United States had a chance at victory. At his core, Jefferson was a pacifist. Contrary to contemporaries like Alexander Hamilton and Aaron Burr, Jefferson never fought a duel, never served in the military, and never, as far as historical records can determine, played any part in taking a human life. He wrote a letter that emphasized his hope of preserving peace in this struggle: "[I have] the belief that a just and friendly conduct on our part will procure justice and friendship from others. In the existing contest, each of the combatants will find an interest in our friendship."

It was under these conditions that Jefferson took an extraordinary and unprecedented step. He decided that if America could not harm Britain with its military, he would instead take advantage of Britain's dependence on American imports of raw materials and goods, like cotton and textiles. He had planned for war and had begun to ready for war, but Jefferson then resisted the calls for violence. Instead he proposed an embargo, an end to all trade between America and England.

The embargo Jefferson envisioned would serve two purposes: it would keep American sailors off the seas, and it would inflict enough pain on England's economy to change its naval policies. In Jefferson's mind, this action was flawless—the British would soon realize how much they needed American imports, and they would meekly curtail their oppressive actions. Jefferson wrote: "Our commerce is so valuable to them [the European belligerents] that they will be glad to purchase it when the only price we ask is to do us justice. I believe that we have in our hands the means of peaceable coercion."

The reality was not quite so simple. Though Congress eagerly passed the embargo, almost immediately its wisdom was called into doubt by the very people it aimed to keep safe. As soon as the bill passed, port cities erupted in a fever of activity, scrambling ships out to sea. Anyone who could carry a box found himself recruited to help load vessels. Even empty ships set sail, hoping to find cargo elsewhere, since a ship would be of no use if docked in port. Sailors panicked. The embargo would render them unemployed—to them, worse than the potential danger of capture at sea. Businessmen rushed to get every last commodity aboard a departing ship, hoping for a windfall once the world realized these would be the very last sacks of flour available, thus driving up prices.

The embargo's immediate effects proved disastrous to Americans, not the British. Closing the seaports put 30,000 seamen out of work. New England's economy, almost completely dependent on foreign trade, came to a halt. In New York, busy ports that had recently been filled with bales of cotton, wool, rice, sugar, tea, rum, and wine turned into ghost towns. Not only did the embargo ruin the shipping companies but also the underwriters and insurance brokers who had made a living off the sea trade. Retail outlets located near ports no longer had customers. Daily foot traffic vanished. In major cities, public works projects were started just to give the many idle hands something to do. In Philadelphia, the chamber of commerce put sailors to work making rope.

Even worse, the embargo encouraged rampant scheming about ways to get around it. Enterprising businessmen snuck goods up across the Canadian border at Lake Champlain, forcing Jefferson to send troops to halt the traffic. Others looked south to Florida—and Jefferson had to send reinforcements down there as well. Traders sought every edge they could find to keep their businesses alive, forcing Jefferson to deploy massive amounts of resources simply to enforce the new laws.

As Americans looked for ways around the embargo, Jefferson was forced to extend the ban to cover more and more loopholes. Initially, ships had been allowed to sail along the coast, delivering needed goods down the eastern seaboard from one state to another. But shippers figured out they could present false itineraries to customs agents, load their ships, and then leave for points unknown. To combat this, Jefferson banned all coastal trade—but this measure then led to food shortages throughout the country.

People were unable to get the flour and sugar they desperately needed, while piles of fresh produce and baked goods rotted on wharves and docks. Americans were starving in a country that had an abundance of food, but the food was marooned onshore, unable to get where it was needed.

Jefferson relented, if only a little. He authorized governors to grant "special permits" for domestic transport only to those shippers in whom they had the utmost confidence. But governors quickly succumbed to pressure from influential merchants and began granting false permits and turning a blind eye to the resulting commerce. Major ports developed an underground trade in these permits. Jefferson tried to crack down—soon enough, he himself was examining applications case by case, considering the merits of every bale of cotton and barrel of rum for interstate transport. The system became unmanageable.

One man, a middle-aged fur trader who had come to America from Germany with the singular goal of becoming rich in the New World, forged a letter to Jefferson from an imaginary Chinese nobleman, seeking permission to charter a ship and pass through the blockade to return to his family. Jefferson, who sought to improve relations with China, approved the request. The ship sailed with box after box of "baggage," which was unloaded in China, and then sailed back full of Chinese manufactured goods. With prices for these goods skyrocketing due to the embargo, the man—John Jacob Astor—found himself transformed from a mere fur trader to a financial baron whose family would retain wealth and prominence for generations.

As enterprising merchants found even more loopholes, Jefferson cast his net wider and wider. He extended the embargo to cover the movement of goods even by "carts, wagons, and sleds"—anything that might carry items across a border and from there to a ship.

The effect of the embargo on the nation's economy was staggering. U.S. exports declined by almost 80 percent in a year (from $103 million to $22 million), and imports declined by almost 60 percent (from $145 million to $58 million). Even the most conservative estimates of smuggling topped $6 million. Revenue from duties on American shipping fell from $16 million per year to a few hundred thousand dollars. Approximately 50,000 sailors and 100,000 men nationwide were out of work. In New York City alone, 1,300 men were thrown into debtors prison, including 1,150 for debts of less than $25. In the South, "stay laws" were passed limiting debt collection because so many plantations went bankrupt.

New England newspapers wrote of the "Dambargo," and as one historian wrote, "if England bled, or France, under the [embargo], the United States bled faster." Instead of bringing England to its knees, the British seemed to be coping perfectly well. Manufacturing towns sprang up in England. And to compensate, British traders opened new markets in Spain to ship their exports.

Jefferson grew frustrated. In his 1808 State of the Union address, he appealed to the people to try their hardest to cooperate with the embargo. He acknowledged that "the suspension of our foreign commerce, produced by the injustice of the belligerent powers and the consequent losses and sacrifices of our citizens are subjects of just concern" but pleaded that Americans give the embargo a chance to work.

As 1808 came to a close, the embargo was almost universally **293** considered a failure. John Armstrong, the U.S. Minister to France, wrote, "Here it is not felt, and in England . . . it is forgotten." A hundred years later, Senator Henry Cabot Lodge claimed that "[n]o civilized nation today would seek the possible injury of its enemies by its own certain impoverishment. . . . The theory of the Embargo was wholly false."

As one of Jefferson's last acts as President, just days before he left the White House, he signed a repeal of the Embargo Act, acknowledging its failure but continuing to believe that if not for the smuggling it would have worked. He later insisted that "a continuance . . . for two months longer would have prevented our eventual war [the War of 1812]."

At the time, Jefferson feared that his embargo had been a disaster, and as he returned to his hilltop estate of Monticello in nearby Virginia, he worried about his historical legacy and reputation. The embargo seemed to have done nothing to change the situation. After it was lifted, the British continued to arrest American ships and impress their sailors. By 1810, perhaps close to 15,000 Americans were serving on British ships against their will. Britain had promised, once the embargo was lifted, to let American ships sail free, but they still did as they pleased with impunity.

Faced with no other options, and a citizenry demanding America demonstrate its mettle, President Madison reluctantly declared war against England in 1812. On a summer day in 1814, President Madison fled for safety as the British set the White House and the Capitol aflame, the rest of Washington saved only by a rainstorm. Jefferson, 71 now, closely followed events from his home. To his relief, the war ended not with British conquest but with a truce. America successfully turned back the threat. Much of the credit belonged to Jefferson's "failed" embargo, which bought the country time to build up its military, at least enough to withstand a British onslaught. Jefferson's courage to stick with his plan, political pressures be damned, may have saved the New World's freedom.

Like Jefferson, Commodore Barron had also refused to yield to pressure. In the aftermath of the *Chesapeake* drama, six officers on the ship brought charges against Barron for neglect in not preparing the ship more quickly to fight. He fought the charges. After a trial, the Navy suspended Barron for five years without pay. In 1820, a fellow commodore accused Barron of surrendering meekly to the British. After a long argument, Barron killed him in a duel.

Jefferson lived another decade after the end of the War, planning the University of Virginia from the ground up, which he would see as his ultimate legacy. He composed his own epitaph— "Here was buried Thomas Jefferson, Author of the Declaration of Independence, of the Statute of Virginia for religious freedom, and the Father of the University of Virginia"—leaving out a number of his accomplishments, not least of which being his time as President. The embargo, by this time, had been forgotten and forgiven.

Just after midnight on July 4, 1826, a dying Jefferson asked his doctor, "This is the fourth?" The doctor answered that it was. Jefferson murmured, "Ah." Jefferson summoned his servants, said good-bye, and took his final breath.

TO THE SENATE AND HOUSE OF REPRESENTATIVES OF THE UNITED STATES:

It would have been a source, fellow citizens, of much gratification, if our last communications from Europe had enabled me to inform you that the belligerent nations, whose disregard of neutral rights has been so destructive to our commerce, had become awakened to the duty and true policy of revoking their unrighteous edicts. That no means might be omitted to produce this salutary effect, I lost no time in availing myself of the act authorizing a suspension, in whole or in part, of the several embargo laws. Our ministers at London and Paris were instructed to explain to the respective governments there, our disposition to exercise the authority in such manner as would withdraw the pretext on which the aggressions were originally founded, and open a way for a renewal of that commercial intercourse which it was alleged on all sides had been reluctantly obstructed. As each of those governments had pledged its readiness to concur in renouncing a measure which reached its adversary through the incontestable rights of neutrals only, and as the measure had been assumed by each as a retaliation for an asserted acquiescence in the aggressions of the other, it was reasonably expected that the occasion would have been seized by both for evincing the sincerity of their profession, and for restoring to the commerce of the United States its legitimate freedom. The instructions to our ministers with respect to the different belligerents were necessarily modified with reference to their different circumstances, and to the condition annexed by law to the executive power of suspension, requiring a degree of security to our commerce which would not result from a repeal of the decrees of France. Instead of a pledge, therefore, of a suspension of the embargo as to her in case of such a repeal, it was presumed that a sufficient inducement might be found in other considerations, and particularly in the change produced by a compliance with our just demands by one belligerent, and a refusal by the other, in the relations between the other and the United States. To Great Britain, whose power on the ocean is so ascendant, it was deemed not inconsistent with that condition to state explicitly, that on her rescinding her orders in relation to the United States their trade would be opened with her, and remain shut to her enemy, in case of his failure to rescind his decrees also. From France no answer has been received, nor any indication that the requisite change in her decrees is contemplated. The favorable reception of the proposition to Great Britain was the less to be doubted, as her orders of council had not only been referred for their vindication to an acquiescence on the part of the United States no longer to be pretended, but as the arrangement proposed, while it resisted the illegal decrees of France, involved, moreover, substantially, the precise advantages professedly aimed at by the British orders. The arrangement has nevertheless been rejected.

This candid and liberal experiment having thus failed, and no other event having occurred on which a suspension of the embargo by the executive was authorized, it necessarily remains in the extent originally given to it. We have the satisfaction, however, to reflect, that in return for the privations by the measure, and which our fellow citizens in general have borne with patriotism, it has had the important effects of saving our mariners and our vast mercantile property, as well as of affording time for prosecuting the defensive and provisional measures called for by the occasion. It has demonstrated to foreign nations the moderation and firmness which govern our councils, and to our citizens the necessity of uniting in support of the laws and the rights of their country, and has thus long frustrated those usurpations and spoliations which, if resisted, involve war; if submitted to, sacrificed a vital principle of our national independence.

Under a continuance of the belligerent measures which, in defiance of laws which consecrate the rights of neutrals, overspread the ocean with danger, it will rest with the wisdom of Congress to decide on the course best adapted to such a state of things; and bringing with them, as they do, from every part of the Union, the sentiments of our constituents, my confidence is strengthened, that in forming this decision they will, with an unerring regard to the essential rights and interests of the nation, weigh and compare the painful alternatives out of which a choice is to be made. Nor should I do justice to the virtues which on other occasions have marked the character of our fellow citizens, if I did not cherish an equal confidence that the alternative chosen, whatever it may be, will be maintained with all the fortitude and patriotism which the crisis ought to inspire.

The documents containing the correspondences on the subject of the foreign edicts against our commerce, with the instructions given to our ministers at London and Paris, are now laid before you.

The communications made to Congress at their last session explained the posture in which the close of the discussion relating to the attack by a British ship of war on the frigate *Chesapeake* left a subject on which the nation had manifested so honorable a sensibility. Every view of what had passed authorized a belief that immediate steps would be taken by the British government for redressing a wrong, which, the more it was investigated, appeared the more clearly to require what had not been provided for in the special mission. It is found that no steps have been taken for the purpose. On the contrary, it will be seen, in the documents laid before you, that the inadmissible preliminary which obstructed the adjustment is still adhered to; and, moreover, that it is now brought into connection with the distinct and irrelative case of the orders in council. The instructions which had been given to our ministers at London with a view to facilitate, if necessary, the reparation claimed by the United States, are included in the documents communicated.

Our relations with the other powers of Europe have undergone no material changes since your last session. The important negotiations with Spain, which had been alternately suspended and resumed, necessarily experience a pause under the extraordinary and interesting crisis which distinguished her internal situation.

With the Barbary powers we continue in harmony, with the exception of an unjustifiable proceeding of the dey of Algiers toward our consul to that regency. Its character and circumstances are now laid before you, and will enable you to decide how far it may, either now or hereafter, call for any measures not within the limits of the executive authority.

With our Indian neighbors the public peace has been steadily maintained. Some instances of individual wrong have, as at other times, taken place, but in nowise implicating the will of the nation. Beyond the Mississippi, the Iowas, the Sacs, and the Alabamas, have delivered up for trial and punishment individuals from among themselves accused of murdering citizens of the United States. On this side of the Mississippi, the Creeks are exerting themselves to arrest offenders of the same kind; and the Choctaws have manifested their readiness and desire for amicable and just arrangements respecting depredations committed by disorderly persons of their tribe. And, generally, from a conviction that we consider them as part of ourselves, and cherish with sincerity their rights and interests, the attachment of the Indian tribes is gaining strength daily—is extending from the nearer to the more remote, and will amply requite us for the justice and friendship practised towards them. Husbandry and household manufacture are advancing among them, more rapidly with the southern than the northern tribes, from circumstances of soil and climate; and one of the two great divisions of the Cherokee nation have now under consideration to solicit the citizenship of the United States, and to be identified with us in laws and government, in such progressive manner as we shall think best.

In consequence of the appropriations of the last session of Congress for the security of our seaport towns and harbors, such works of defence have been erected as seemed to be called for by the situation of the several places, their relative importance, and the scale of expense indicated by the amount of the appropriation. These works will chiefly be finished in the course of the present season, except at New York and New Orleans, where most was to be done; and although a great proportion of the last appropriation has been expended on the former place, yet some further views will be submitted by Congress for rendering its security entirely adequate against naval enterprise. A view of what has been done at the several places, and of what is proposed to be done, shall be communicated as soon as the several reports are received.

Of the gun-boats authorized by the act of December last, it has been thought necessary to build only one hundred and three in the present year. These, with those before possessed, are sufficient for the harbors and waters exposed, and the residue will require little time for their construction when it is deemed necessary.

Under the act of the last session for raising an additional military force, so many officers were immediately appointed as were necessary for carrying on the business of recruiting, and in proportion as it advanced, others have been added. We have reason to believe their success has been satisfactory, although such returns have not yet been received as enable me to present to you a statement of the numbers engaged.

I have not thought it necessary in the course of the last season to call for any general detachments of militia or volunteers under the law passed for that purpose. For the ensuing season, however, they will require to be in readiness should their services be wanted. Some small and special detachments have been necessary to maintain the laws of embargo on that portion of our northern frontier which offered peculiar facilities for evasion, but these were replaced as soon as it could be done by bodies of new recruits. By the aid of these, and of the armed vessels called into actual service in other quarters, the spirit of disobedience and abuse which manifested itself early, and with sensible effect while we were unprepared to meet it, has been considerably repressed.

Considering the extraordinary character of the times in which we live, our attention should unremittingly be fixed on the safety of our country. For a people who are free, and who mean to remain so, a well-organized and armed militia is their best security. It is, therefore, incumbent on us, at every meeting, to revise the condition of the militia, and to ask ourselves if it is prepared to repel a powerful enemy at every point of our territories exposed to invasion. Some of the States have paid a laudable attention to this object; but every degree of neglect is to be found among others. Congress alone have power to produce a uniform state of preparation in this great organ of defence; the interests which they so deeply feel in their own and their country's security will present this as among the most important objects of their deliberation.

Under the acts of March 11th and April 23rd, respecting arms, the difficulty of procuring them from abroad, during the present situation and dispositions of Europe, induced us to direct our whole efforts to the means of internal supply. The public factories have, therefore, been enlarged, additional machineries erected, and in proportion as artificers can be found or formed, their effect, already more than doubled, may be increased so as to keep pace with the yearly increase of the militia. The annual sums appropriated by the latter act, have been directed to the encouragement of private factories of arms, and contracts have been entered into with individual undertakers to nearly the amount of the first year's appropriation.

The suspension of our foreign commerce, produced by the injustice of the belligerent powers, and the consequent losses and sacrifices of our citizens, are subjects of just concern. The situation into which we have thus been forced, has impelled us to apply a portion of our industry and capital to internal manufactures and improvements. The extent of this conversion is daily increasing, and little doubt remains that the establishments formed and forming will—under the auspices of cheaper materials and subsistence, the freedom of labor from taxation with us, and of protecting duties and prohibitions—become permanent. The commerce with the Indians, too, within our own boundaries, is likely to receive abundant aliment from the same internal source, and will secure to them peace and the progress of civilization, undisturbed by practices hostile to both.

The accounts of the receipts and expenditures during the year ending on the 30th day of September last, being not yet made up, a correct statement will hereafter be transmitted from the Treasury. In the meantime, it is ascertained that the receipts have amounted to near eighteen millions of dollars, which, with the eight millions and a half in the treasury at the beginning of the year, have enabled us, after meeting the current demands and interest incurred, to pay two millions three hundred thousand dollars of the principal of our funded debt, and left us in the treasury, on that day, near fourteen millions of dollars. Of these, five millions three hundred and fifty thousand dollars will be necessary to pay what will be due on the first day of January next, which will complete the reimbursement of the eight percent stock. These payments, with those made in the six years and a half preceding, will have extinguished thirty-three millions five hundred and eighty thousand dollars of the principal of the funded debt, being the whole which could be paid or purchased within the limits of the law and our contracts; and the amount of principal thus discharged will have liberated the revenue from about two millions of dollars of interest, and added that sum annually to the disposable surplus. The probable accumulation of the surpluses of revenue beyond what can be applied to the payment of the public debt, whenever the freedom and safety of our commerce shall be restored, merits the consideration of Congress. Shall it lie unproductive in the public vaults? Shall the revenue be reduced? Or shall it rather be appropriated to the improvements of roads, canals, rivers, education, and other great foundations of prosperity and union, under the powers which Congress may already possess, or such amendment of the constitution as may be approved by the States? While uncertain of the course of things, the time may be advantageously employed in obtaining the powers necessary for a system of improvement, should that be thought best.

Availing myself of this the last occasion which will occur of addressing the two houses of the legislature at their meeting,

I cannot omit the expression of my sincere gratitude for the repeated proofs of confidence manifested to me by themselves and their predecessors since my call to the administration, and the many indulgences experienced at their hands. The same grateful acknowledgments are due to my fellow citizens generally, whose support has been my great encouragement under all embarrassments. In the transaction of their business I cannot have escaped error. It is incident to our imperfect nature. But I may say with truth, my errors have been of the understanding, not of intention; and that the advancement of their rights and interests has been the constant motive for every measure. On these considerations I solicit their indulgence. Looking forward with anxiety to their future destinies, I trust that, in their steady character unshaken by difficulties, in their love of liberty, obedience to law, and support of the public authorities, I see a sure guaranty of the permanence of our republic; and retiring from the charge of their affairs, I carry with me the consolation of a firm persuasion that Heaven has in store for our beloved country long ages to come of prosperity and happiness.

FRANKLIN ROOSEVELT ABOARD THE *USS INDIANAPOLIS*, 1936.

Franklin Roosevelt Presidential Library and Museum

CHAPTER 13

THE GARDEN HOSE

Franklin Roosevelt and the Lend-Lease Act

W hen Winston Churchill looked out his window on Sunday morning, September 15, 1940, he saw clear skies overhead. The Prime Minister had hoped for rain, or at least clouds; but the good visibility was perfect—for German bombers. Every day for the last two months, Nazi airplanes, sometimes thousands at a time, had attacked Great Britain. Today would be no exception.

Adolf Hitler, who had defeated France and now dominated continental Europe, had focused his country's military might on bringing Britain to its knees. The German air campaign, Churchill knew, was only a prelude to what Hitler called Operation Sea Lion, an invasion of Britain by the juggernaut German army.

Only 22 miles of water separated the Wehrmacht from the English shore. And, as the American attaché in London said, Britain was "no more fortified or prepared to withstand invasion in force than Long Island." The British army, smaller than the German, had left most of its artillery and tanks behind when the Nazis chased it off the Continent in the summer. Desperate to stave off calamity, the British had experimented with setting the seas on fire. Churchill considered drenching the beaches with mustard gas.

So far, though, heroic efforts by the outnumbered Royal Air Force had disrupted Hitler's plans. On this Sunday morning, the Prime Minister decided to visit the RAF command center outside London and observe the action. When he descended to the operations room, a bomb-proof chamber 50 feet below ground, the commanding officer greeted him saying, "I don't know whether anything will happen today. At present all is quiet." Churchill took a seat in the back of the room.

Within 15 minutes, radar picked up wave after wave of German aircraft ("Forty plus!" "Sixty plus!") heading for the English coast. Twenty people scurried around a large map set on a table, pushing discs around that showed the enemy's position. Soon the map showed over a thousand incoming aircraft. Light bulbs on the wall showed available British squadrons. One by one, as Churchill stared, all the lights went out. Alarmed, he asked the commander, "What other reserves have we?" and received the reply, "There are none." Every British plane available had taken to the air.

When the Germans appeared in the sky over London, RAF fighters were waiting for them. Furious dogfights broke out. Burning planes fell out of the air, sometimes, but not always, followed by parachuting pilots. Sergeant Ray Holmes, piloting an RAF Hurricane, zeroed in on a German bomber and began firing. Holmes expected the plane to try to evade him, but it maintained its course (the crew had already bailed out), and the Hurricane slammed into the bomber's tail. As the German plane spiraled downward its bombs dropped out, two of them landing on Buckingham Palace. Holmes bailed out of his fighter and parachuted onto an apartment house. He kissed two girls in the garden below, went to look at the bomber's wreckage outside Victoria Station, and then headed back to his barracks.

Before the day was over, 55 more Nazi aircraft went down (the British lost twenty-five). Churchill went home and took a nap. Two days later British intelligence learned that Hitler had decided to postpone Operation Sea Lion. Britain held on.

But the danger, as Churchill knew, had hardly ended. The invasion by land had been delayed, not canceled. And even if the Führer never sent his legions across the Channel, he might still force Britain to surrender. Nazi planes and submarines were preying on British shipping. If Germany gained mastery of the seas, then it could gradually starve the British into submission. Hitler might prefer a knockout blow, but he would gladly accept a slow stranglehold.

Churchill's problems did not end there. Surviving a long war would take money, and the British government did not have it. When invasion appeared imminent, the Prime Minister had decided to leave "financial problems on the laps of the Eternal Gods." But now, facing a possibly protracted struggle, Churchill recognized that his country would need a more earthly source.

In the meantime, the bombing of Britain continued. Two nights after his visit to the command center, Churchill met in London with his chiefs of staff. A raid began, and the Prime Minister led his generals outside to observe. Sirens wailed, bombs exploded, and antiaircraft fire filled the sky. On the other side of a park a building burned.

Churchill, an observer remembered, stepped away from a protective concrete wall and with "chin thrust out, the long cigar in his mouth," he growled: "By God we'll get the B's for this." But he knew they couldn't do it alone. As his people braced each sunset for another night of bombing, the Prime Minister's thoughts turned to the west. Only one country—one man—might save Britain.

Franklin Roosevelt understood, even before many in Europe, that Hitler had to be stopped. From the beginning he believed the

German dictator a "wild man" with a "Joan of Arc complex . . . a self-nominated reincarnation of Julius Caesar and Jesus Christ." In 1938, Germany's ambassador in Washington, in a report to Berlin, called the American President "Hitler's most dangerous enemy."

Two years later, Roosevelt watched in alarm as the Germans swept over France and then attacked Britain. Nazi Germany, he believed, did not only threaten democratic rule in Europe, but it also posed a grave threat to the United States. Hitler had aligned his country with Japan, America's antagonist in the Pacific. If Germany defeated Britain, and especially if it captured the British navy, then the Axis powers would control the oceans. If they decided to isolate America from the rest of the world, the vastly inferior American navy would be unable to prevent them.

Worse, the Germans had infiltrated Latin America. Brazil already had a Fascist government filled with Nazi sympathizers, and a German military mission had opened in Argentina. Hitler might not be crazy enough to attack the United States from the south, but he might well seize the Panama Canal. The tiny American army, which in 1940 had fewer troops than Switzerland's, could not hope to stop him.

But even if these dangers had not existed, the President still would have fought to save Britain. In the long term, Roosevelt believed, America could never coexist peacefully with Nazi Germany or Imperial Japan. To him, the thought that the United States could survive as "a lone island in a world dominated by the philosophy of force" was a "delusion."

Unfortunately, most of his fellow Americans seemed to have succumbed to that very idea. In order to defeat tyranny abroad, the President would first have to overcome the isolationists here at home.

In a country to which many had to escape upheaval in their homeland, isolationism had always been a powerful political force. Protected from most of the rest of the world by two oceans, many Americans saw little reason to send their sons abroad to fight wars that, in their minds, did not affect them.

The country's experience in World War I had confirmed this outlook. The United States entered the war buoyed by Woodrow Wilson's idealist rhetoric. But after 50,000 American soldiers lost their lives, the nation watched helplessly as the other Allied powers indulged their cynicism and thirst for revenge at Versailles. The Allies, including Britain, then failed to pay war debts they owed to the United States. When Roosevelt occupied the White House, most Americans believed that America's entry into World War I had been a mistake. In 1935 Ernest Hemingway summed up their feelings: "No European country is our friend nor has been since the last war and no country but one's own is worth fighting for." As the tension in Europe began to increase again, isolationist feeling stiffened.

Roosevelt argued that geography no longer provided an adequate defense (if a hostile power captured Bermuda, he said, "it is a matter of less than three hours for modern bombers to reach our shores"). But as a political force, isolationists were too powerful for the President to ignore, and he often bowed to their wishes. In 1932, during his first run for the White House, he renounced his support for the League of Nations. When Congress passed a Neutrality Act three years later, Roosevelt grudgingly signed it.

His internationalist friends criticized what they viewed as the sacrifice of his principles. His wife, Eleanor, refused to speak to him for days when he renounced the League. Roosevelt believed he had simply done what he had to. "Have you ever stopped to consider," he wrote one friend, "that there is a difference between ideals and the methods of obtaining them?"

And when, hoping to avert another global conflict, he did try to take a more forceful role abroad, isolationists fought him at every step. In 1937 he proposed sanctions against Japan; subsequently, two congressmen said he should be impeached. In early 1939, after Hitler marched into Czechoslovakia, Roosevelt asked Congress to repeal the Neutrality Act. It refused.

Even after Hitler conquered France and turned toward Britain, isolationists opposed giving aid to the democracies. Doing so, they believed, would inevitably bring the United States into the war. Others believed the United States had to act, and in the summer and fall of 1940 the public debate grew rancorous. Discussion of the issue dominated public life. To keep fights from breaking out, a restaurant in New York posted a sign: "Please refrain from discussing the war situation at the bar." The historian Arthur Schlesinger Jr., who lived through Vietnam and other grave national crises, later said that "none so tore apart families and friendships as the great debate of 1940–41."

Almost no one, however, wanted America itself to enter the war. Senator Robert Taft said this would be "even worse than a German victory." A poll showed that less than 6 percent of Americans thought the country should fight. Princeton students formed an organization called "Veterans of Future Wars" and demanded that the government pay them $1,000 bonuses now, before they fought and died. At another school, students demonstrated with banners saying, "Let God Save The King. The Yanks Aren't Coming."

As Americans argued, Britain faced catastrophe. The Germans shifted tactics and began bombing London and other cities primarily after sunset. At the time no good defense existed against nighttime attacks (less than 1 percent of Luftwaffe bombing missions at night resulted in the loss of a plane). On October 15, 1940, alone, German planes dropped almost 400 tons of explosives on London. German submarines continued to torpedo British shipping.

Churchill and Roosevelt had met only once, in London 20 years earlier. Roosevelt had thought Churchill rude ("a stinker ... lording it over all of us"), but in 1939 he began a secret correspondence with the future Prime Minister. The arrangement, which continued throughout the war, was unique; no similar example exists of the leaders of two separate governments communicating privately so often. The President (code-named "Sylvia") risked the ire of the isolationists if this exchange had become public knowledge.

As Britain's prospects darkened, Churchill (code-named "Former Naval Person") used this private channel to plead with Roosevelt for American aid. He briefed the President on both the desperate military situation ("We can't go on like this") and the looming financial emergency ("We shall go on paying dollars as long as we can, but I should like to feel reasonably sure that when we can pay no more, you will give us the stuff all the same").

For Roosevelt, the crisis came at the worst possible time. The year 1940 was an election year, and the isolationist vote would desert him in droves if he took any step that might lead the United States into war. Late in the summer, a poll showed Wendell Willkie, the Republican nominee, beating Roosevelt in the general election. If Willkie won, the British might never get what they needed.

Despite his fear of what might happen in the interval, the President knew that a meaningful aid program, and a showdown with the isolationists in Congress, would have to wait.

Perhaps more than any other American President, Franklin Roosevelt understood the value of patience. In 1920, he seemed to have it all. His son James remembered him as "the handsomest, strongest, most glamorous, vigorous, physical father in the world." Women stopped in the street to watch him walk by. Though Roosevelt was only 38, and Assistant Secretary of the Navy at the time, the Democrats chose him as their vice presidential candidate. At the national convention he made a huge splash when, eager to get to the podium and give a speech, he leaped over several rows of chairs to get there. The Republican, Warren Harding, won the election that year, but a long career on the national stage clearly awaited the attractive young New Yorker.

But one day the next summer, after a swim with his children, he felt strangely tired. The next morning his left leg buckled as he walked to the bathroom, and by the following day he could not stand up. Within two weeks a doctor gave him the devastating news—it was polio.

Having almost achieved his highest ambition, he now had to rebuild his life. Doctors feared the blow would crush him, but he remained, to their surprise, "wonderfully cheerful . . . a remarkable patient." For seven years he devoted himself to regaining the use of his muscles. He learned to walk using crutches and painful, heavy leg braces, but the effort exhausted him. "I must get down the driveway today—all the way down the driveway."

In 1924 he returned to the Democratic National Convention

to make another speech, and he insisted on walking to the podium. A year earlier, when he had tried to return to his job at a bond firm in New York, his crutch had slipped on the floor of the office building's lobby, and he had fallen down in front of a crowd of people, his hat rolling across the ground. The experience did not deter him. His son James escorted him to the dais: "his fingers dug into me like pincers . . . . His face was covered with perspiration." Roosevelt would walk the final 15 feet alone. Slowly, and in full view of 12,000 delegates, he lurched across the stage. An observer said that no one in Madison Square Garden seemed to breathe. When he finally reached the podium, he threw back his head and beamed in triumph. The delegates cheered for three minutes. As they did, the sun broke through clouds above and shone through the Garden's skylight on him.

But the delegates who cheered him also doubted his capacity to hold office ("Were it not for his precarious health . . . "). Roosevelt knew that if he wanted to have a political career, he would have to learn how to make people forget his disease. When he had dinner at the home of friends, the hosts wondered how he would move into the drawing room, as was customary, following the meal. Not wanting to make him uncomfortable, they planned to remain at the table until their visitor left. But Roosevelt got down from his chair, said "See me get into the next room," and crawled, face up and dragging his legs behind him, out the door. Somehow it didn't seem unusual. Eleanor said, "He deliberately did something to distract you, so that you were never conscious of seeing anything but that wonderful head."

By 1928, the charm had cast its spell, and New York elected him governor. More than one person would later marvel at the

President's seeming "serenity" during the many crises of his time in office. Roosevelt would reply, "If you spent two years in bed trying to wiggle your big toe, after that anything else would seem easy!"

The President needed every bit of his composure in the summer of 1940. Facing a strong challenge from Willkie, he knew that isolationists would pounce on any hint that he intended to involve America in the war. But the critical situation in Europe could not be ignored. A desperate Churchill, whose cables to Roosevelt normally took a careful, ingratiating tone, became impatient: "I cannot see why, with the position as it is, you do not send me at least 50 or 60 of your oldest destroyers . . . . Mr. President, with the greatest respect I must tell you that in the long history of the world this is a thing to do *now*."

Roosevelt was forced to agree. He negotiated a deal with the British to exchange the destroyers for naval bases in the Caribbean. Knowing that isolationists in the Senate would reject the agreement, he authorized the transfer under existing legislation. Many questioned the legality of the move, but the President went ahead anyway. "Congress is going to raise hell about this," said Roosevelt, "but even another day's delay may mean the end of civilization."

The deal could have cost him the election. The *St. Louis Post-Dispatch* howled: "Mr. Roosevelt today committed an act of war. He also became America's first dictator." And even though Willkie personally favored aid to Britain, he still tried to use the transfer to capture the isolationist vote. Sending the destroyers to Britain without the approval of Congress was, he said, "the most

arbitrary and dictatorial action ever taken by any President of the
United States."

Trying to reassure the voters, the President said repeatedly that America would not enter the war "except in cases of attack." But the pressure on him increased. Newspapers that had supported him in the past, including *The New York Times*, had come out against a third term. Finally, in a speech just days before the election, Roosevelt told a crowd: "Your boys are not going to be sent into any foreign wars" and left out the qualification.

A speechwriter pointed out the omission, and Roosevelt snapped, "If somebody attacks us, then it isn't a foreign war, is it?" But the change made a difference. Listening to the President's speech on the radio, Willkie cursed: "That hypocritical son of a bitch! This is going to beat me."

He was right. On November 5, Roosevelt won reelection handily.

Across the Atlantic, Churchill awaited the results with "profound anxiety." No one but Roosevelt, he believed, could ensure the passage of an effective aid package. And as the campaign in America drew to a close, Hitler began bombing other British cities in addition to London. A raid on Coventry leveled the city's center and killed 400; a week later three separate raids on Birmingham killed twice as many. At the same time, Britain's coffers were nearly empty. On November 23, the British ambassador stepped off a plane in New York and told reporters, "Well boys, Britain's broke; it's your money we want."

Prior to the election, Roosevelt had been forced to use an inadequate, piecemeal approach to aid the British. But the time for half-measures had passed; the isolationists in Congress must be confronted. As he left for a post-election vacation on board the Navy cruiser USS *Tuscaloosa*, Roosevelt told his Cabinet to "use your imaginations" to come up with a plan.

Over the next week, administration officials met frantically to discuss what the President should propose. Some favored an outright gift to the British, but Congress would almost certainly reject this. Unfortunately, loans would not work either. Americans had not forgotten the unpaid British debts from World War I. With no other ideas, the officials essentially put off the question. In a cable to Roosevelt, they suggested that the United States begin constructing arms factories using both American and the remaining British funds. This would get things started until Congress could take up the aid question when it convened in January.

As the Cabinet met, the *Tuscaloosa* steamed through the Caribbean. Roosevelt whiled away the warm days fishing, watching movies, and playing poker with friends. But on December 9, a seaplane delivered an urgent message from Churchill. In a 10-page letter that the Prime Minister considered "one of the most important" he ever wrote, Churchill outlined the need for immediate aid to his country.

"Unless we can establish our ability to feed this island," said the Prime Minister, "to import the munitions of all kind which we need . . . and do all this with the assurance of being able to carry it on till the spirit of the Continental Dictators is broken, we may fall by the way. . . ." The time drew near when Britain would "no longer be able to pay cash for shipping and other supplies. . . . You may be certain that we shall prove ourselves ready to suffer and sacrifice to the utmost for the Cause. . . . The rest we leave with confidence to you and your people."

For two days the President, interrupting his other activities, brooded over Churchill's letter. On the second day after receiving it, he refused to see anyone. Britain had to be helped—now. When Roosevelt received the Cabinet's stopgap proposal, he didn't like it (with admirable understatement, one official later said the President had been "a tiny bit displeased"). In a return cable he instructed that the issue should rest until he returned to Washington. There—they waited to see what the President would come up with.

On a spring evening 23 years before, a group of eminent Republicans gathered in a private room at the Metropolitan Club in New York for dinner. The gathering included the governor of New Jersey, a former Secretary of State, an ex-Secretary of the Navy, and J. P. Morgan Jr. By far the most notable member of the party, however, was a former President, Theodore Roosevelt. All the men were enemies of the White House's current occupant, Woodrow Wilson.

One month earlier, Kaiser Wilhelm II, desperate to reverse Germany's fortunes in the First World War, had declared unrestricted submarine warfare in the Atlantic. German U-boats were ordered to sink any ship making for an Allied port. The order would doubtless result in the loss of American ships—and lives. But Wilson wished to keep the United Sates out of the war and went to great lengths to do so. He had severed relations with Germany following the Kaiser's order but refused, for six weeks, to do anything further that might provoke the Kaiser. The men gathered at the Metropolitan Club, most of them infuriated by the President's position, discussed the situation.

At some point a tall, athletic-looking man, much younger than the others, came into the room. His presence at the dinner, if it had been known, would have raised eyebrows. He was a Democrat and, as Assistant Secretary of the Navy, a prominent member of Wilson's administration. But, like "Cousin Theodore" and the others, he too favored a declaration of war against Germany.

As the group talked, Franklin Roosevelt may have recounted a suggestion he had made to the President a few weeks earlier. Wilson wanted to arm American merchant ships so that the vessels could defend themselves against forced searches by German submarines. But the President believed he needed the approval of Congress.

Franklin Roosevelt, an attorney, explored the law and found an old statute that, he believed, would allow Wilson to lease guns to ship owners without asking Congress. Despite urging from several Cabinet members, the President refused to exploit the loophole. But when he sent a request to arm the merchant ships to Capitol Hill, antiwar Senators filibustered and killed the measure. After weeks of delay, Wilson finally relented and armed the ships under the authority of the old law.

As President Roosevelt stared out over the Caribbean, Churchill's letter in his lap, he may have remembered the episode. His circumstances differed from Wilson's; he would need Congress's approval to provide significant foreign aid. But instead of just giving the British an outright gift, or proposing a loan program that would be easy for isolationists to attack, why not lease America's allies what they needed?

When the President returned to Washington on December

16, he had formulated his plan of attack. He called a press
conference the next day and explained his concept in brilliantly
homespun terms:

> *Suppose my neighbor's home catches fire . . . if he*
> *can take my garden hose and connect it up with his*
> *hydrant, I may help him to put out his fire. Now,*
> *what do I do? I don't say to him before that operation,*
> *"Neighbor, my garden hose cost me $15; you have*
> *got to pay me $15 for it." . . . I don't want $15—I*
> *want my garden hose back when the fire is over.'*

Two weeks later, in a Fireside Chat, Roosevelt explicitly said
that the United States could not afford to let Britain fall: "We
well know that we cannot escape danger by crawling into bed and
pulling the covers over our heads. . . . We must be the great arsenal
of Democracy." Roosevelt placed no limits on how much the
United States would do. One historian has called the speech the
most extreme commitment ever made by an American President.

Roosevelt challenged the isolationists as directly and as
fearlessly as he could. The bill he sent to the Capitol was no less
bold than his public statements. If passed, it would give him
the power to "lease, lend, or otherwise dispose of" arms to any
nation whose security was "related," in the President's view, to
America's. It included no meaningful provision for repayment.

Isolationists, perhaps realizing their hour had come, responded
to the proposal with venomous outrage. Their assaults centered
on two points. First, as one isolationist wailed, the bill would
"abolish the Congress for all practical purposes." *The Chicago
Tribune* labeled it "the Dictator Bill." Second, the law would

provoke Germany to attack America and thus draw the United States into the war. The president of the University of Chicago said that "the American people are about to commit suicide," and an isolationist Senator said that the law would "plow under every fourth American boy."

Roosevelt called the last statement "the most dastardly, unpatriotic thing . . . that has been said in public life in my generation." But the argument found support. The head of the most prominent organization that had lobbied for aid to the British turned against the President, agreeing that the legislation would lead the United States into the conflict.

For the next two months, the debate raged. Congressional hearings on the bill drew the largest crowds anyone had ever seen. Charles Lindbergh, who believed a German victory in Europe inevitable, testified against the measure. The bill's opponents tried to eviscerate it with a series of amendments.

But the crisis in Europe, together with the President's flash of inspiration and his masterful presentation of the idea to the public, turned the tide. On March 8, 1941, the Lend-Lease Bill passed Congress. An elated Churchill called the law "the most unsordid act in the history of any nation . . . a new Magna Carta." Hitler realized he had a new enemy.

The President, for his part, declared isolationism dead. At the White House Correspondents' dinner the next night, he declared: "This decision is the end of any attempts at appeasement in our land; the end of urging us to get along with the dictators, the end of compromise and the forces of oppression."

The American war machine cranked into gear, ending the Great Depression and preparing industry to respond quickly to the events that lay ahead. Its output was staggering. By the end of the war, America had produced 300,000 airplanes, 107,000 tanks, and 20 million guns for the Allied war effort.

In August 1941, Roosevelt and Churchill met each other for the second time in their lives aboard an American ship off the coast of Newfoundland. After the leaders discussed the war situation, Churchill invited the President to a church service aboard the *HMS Prince of Wales* the following morning. Roosevelt, who wanted to acknowledge the importance of the occasion, was determined to walk onto the British ship under his own power.

When the President's boat pulled up alongside the next morning, Churchill waited on the deck of his ship as Roosevelt made his way across the gangway. The Prime Minister saw that every step was causing the President pain. A witness remembered looking at Roosevelt and seeing a "calm, carved face, the face of a St. George who has trampled the dragon under him."

When Roosevelt reached his chair, he flashed the famous grin. As the two delegations sang "Onward, Christian Soldiers," Churchill believed the voices of the Americans and British "completely intermingled. . . . Every word seemed to stir the heart."

Later, as the President's ship pulled away, an officer thanked the Prime Minister for the conference. "It's an honor for us all," replied Churchill. "You have seen a great man this day."

President Franklin Roosevelt
Radio Address from the White House
December 29, 1940

MY FRIENDS:

This is not a fireside chat on war. It is a talk on national security, because the nub of the whole purpose of your President is to keep you now, and your children later, and your grandchildren much later, out of a last-ditch war for the preservation of American independence and all of the things that American independence means to you and to me and to ours . . .

Never before since Jamestown and Plymouth Rock has our American civilization been in such danger as now.

For, on September 27th, 1940, this year, by an agreement signed in Berlin, three powerful nations, two in Europe and one in Asia, joined themselves together in the threat that if the United States of America interfered with or blocked the expansion program of these three nations—a program aimed at world control—they would unite in ultimate action against the United States.

The Nazi masters of Germany have made it clear that they intend not only to dominate all life and thought in their own country, but also to enslave the whole of Europe, and then to use the resources of Europe to dominate the rest of the world.

It was only three weeks ago their leader stated this: "There are two worlds that stand opposed to each other." And then in defiant reply to his opponents, he said this: "Others are correct when they say: With this world we cannot ever reconcile ourselves . . . . I can beat any other power in the world." So said the leader of the Nazis.

In other words, the Axis not merely admits but the Axis proclaims that there can be no ultimate peace between their philosophy of government and our philosophy of government.

In view of the nature of this undeniable threat, it can be asserted, properly and categorically, that the United States has no right or reason to encourage talk of peace, until the day shall come when there is a clear intention on the part of the aggressor nations to abandon all thought of dominating or conquering the world.

At this moment, the forces of the states that are leagued against all peoples who live in freedom are being held away from our shores. The Germans and the Italians are being blocked on the other side of the Atlantic by the British, and by the Greeks, and by thousands of soldiers and sailors who were able to escape from subjugated countries. In Asia the Japanese are being engaged by the Chinese nation in another great defense.

In the Pacific Ocean is our fleet.

Some of our people like to believe that wars in Europe and in Asia are of no concern to us. But it is a matter of most vital concern to us that European and Asiatic war-makers should not gain control of the oceans which lead to this hemisphere.

One hundred and seventeen years ago the Monroe Doctrine was conceived by our Government as a measure of defense in the face of a threat against this hemisphere by an alliance in Continental Europe. Thereafter, we stood (on) guard in the Atlantic, with the British as neighbors. There was no treaty. There was no "unwritten agreement."

And yet, there was the feeling, proven correct by history, that we as neighbors could settle any disputes in peaceful fashion. And the fact is that during the whole of this time the Western Hemisphere has remained free from aggression from Europe or from Asia.

Does anyone seriously believe that we need to fear attack anywhere in the Americas while a free Britain remains our most powerful naval neighbor in the Atlantic? And does anyone seriously believe, on the other hand, that we could rest easy if the Axis powers were our neighbors there?

If Great Britain goes down, the Axis powers will control the continents of Europe, Asia, Africa, Australia, and the high seas—and they will be in a position to bring enormous military and naval resources against this hemisphere. It is no exaggeration to say that all of us, in all the Americas, would be living at the point of a gun—a gun loaded with explosive bullets, economic as well as military.

We should enter upon a new and terrible era in which the whole world, our hemisphere included, would be run by threats of brute force. And to survive in such a world, we would have to convert ourselves permanently into a militaristic power on the basis of war economy.

Some of us like to believe that even if (Great) Britain falls, we are still safe, because of the broad expanse of the Atlantic and of the Pacific.

But the width of those (these) oceans is not what it was in the days of clipper ships. At one point between Africa and Brazil the distance is less from Washington than it is from Washington to Denver, Colorado—five hours for the latest type of bomber. And at the North end of the Pacific Ocean America and Asia almost touch each other.

Why, even today we have planes that (which) could fly from the British Isles to New England and back again without refueling. And remember that the range of a (the) modern bomber is ever being increased.

During the past week many people in all parts of the nation have told me what they wanted me to say tonight. Almost all of them expressed a courageous desire to hear the plain truth about the gravity of the situation. One telegram, however, expressed the attitude of the small minority who want to see no evil and hear no evil, even though they know in their hearts that evil exists. That telegram begged me not to tell again of the ease with which our American cities could be bombed by any hostile power which had gained bases in this Western Hemisphere. The gist of that telegram was: "Please, Mr. President, don't frighten us by telling us the facts."

Frankly and definitely there is danger ahead—danger against which we must prepare. But we well know that we cannot escape danger (it), or the fear of danger, by crawling into bed and pulling the covers over our heads.

Some nations of Europe were bound by solemn non-intervention pacts with Germany. Other nations were assured by Germany that they need never fear invasion. Non-intervention pact or not, the fact remains that they were attacked, overrun, (and) thrown into (the) modern (form of) slavery at an hour's notice, or even without any notice at all. As an exiled leader of one of these nations said to me the other day, "The notice was a minus quantity. It was given to my Government two hours after German troops had poured into my country in a hundred places."

The fate of these nations tells us what it means to live at the point of a Nazi gun. The Nazis have justified such actions by various pious frauds. One of these frauds is the claim that they are occupying a nation for the purpose of "restoring order." Another is that they are occupying or controlling a nation on the excuse that they are "protecting it" against the aggression of somebody else.

For example, Germany has said that she was occupying Belgium to save the Belgians from the British. Would she then hesitate to say to any South American country, "We are occupying you to protect you from aggression by the United States?"

Belgium today is being used as an invasion base against Britain, now fighting for its life. And any South American country, in Nazi hands, would always constitute a jumping-off place for German attack on any one of the other republics of this hemisphere.

Analyze for yourselves the future of two other places even nearer to Germany if the Nazis won. Could Ireland hold out? Would Irish freedom be permitted as an amazing pet exception in an unfree world? Or the Islands of the Azores which still fly the flag of Portugal after five centuries? You and I think of Hawaii as an outpost of defense in the Pacific. And yet, the Azores are closer to our shores in the Atlantic than Hawaii is on the other side.

There are those who say that the Axis powers would never have any desire to attack the Western Hemisphere. That (this) is the same dangerous form of wishful thinking which has destroyed the powers of resistance of so many conquered peoples. The plain facts are that the Nazis have proclaimed, time and again, that all other races are their inferiors and therefore subject to their orders. And most important of all, the vast resources and wealth of this American Hemisphere constitute the most tempting loot in all of the round world.

Let us no longer blind ourselves to the undeniable fact that the evil forces which have crushed and undermined and corrupted so many others are already within our own gates. Your Government knows much about them and every day is ferreting them out.

Their secret emissaries are active in our own and in neighboring countries. They seek to stir up suspicion and dissension to cause internal strife. They try to turn capital against labor, and vice versa. They try to reawaken long slumbering racist and religious enmities which should have no place in this country. They are active in every group that promotes intolerance. They exploit for their own ends our own natural abhorrence of war. These trouble-breeders have but one purpose. It is to divide our people, to divide them into hostile groups and to destroy our unity and shatter our will to defend ourselves.

There are also American citizens, many of then in high places, who, unwittingly in most cases, are aiding and abetting the work of these agents. I do not charge these American citizens with being foreign agents. But I do charge them with doing exactly the kind of work that the dictators want done in the United States.

These people not only believe that we can save our own skins by shutting our eyes to the fate of other nations. Some of them go much further than that. They say that we can and should become the friends and even the partners of the Axis powers. Some of them even suggest that we should imitate the methods of the dictatorships. But Americans never can and never will do that.

The experience of the past two years has proven beyond doubt that no nation can appease the Nazis. No man can tame a tiger into a kitten by stroking it. There can be no appeasement with ruthlessness. There can be no reasoning with an incendiary bomb. We know now that a nation can have peace with the Nazis only at the price of total surrender.

Even the people of Italy have been forced to become accomplices of the Nazis, but at this moment they do not know how soon they will be embraced to death by their allies.

The American appeasers ignore the warning to be found in the fate of Austria, Czechoslovakia, Poland, Norway, Belgium, the Netherlands, Denmark and France. They tell you that the Axis powers are going to win anyway; that all of this bloodshed in the world could be saved, that the United States might just as well throw its influence into the scale of a dictated peace, and get the best out of it that we can.

They call it a "negotiated peace." Nonsense! Is it a negotiated peace if a gang of outlaws surrounds your community and on threat of extermination makes you pay tribute to save your own skins?

Such a dictated peace would be no peace at all. It would be only another armistice, leading to the most gigantic armament race and the most devastating trade wars in all history. And in these contests the Americas would offer the only real resistance to the Axis powers.

With all their vaunted efficiency, with all their (and) parade of pious purpose in this war, there are still in their background the concentration camp and the servants of God in chains.

The history of recent years proves that the shootings and the chains and the concentration camps are not simply the transient tools but the very altars of modern dictatorships. They may talk of a "new order" in the world, but what they have in mind is only (but) a revival of the oldest and the worst tyranny. In that there is no liberty, no religion, no hope.

The proposed "new order" is the very opposite of a United States of Europe or a United States of Asia. It is not a government based upon the consent of the governed. It is not a union of ordinary, self-respecting men and women to protect themselves and their freedom and their dignity from oppression. It is an unholy alliance of power and pelf to dominate and to enslave the human race.

The British people and their allies today are conducting an active war against this unholy alliance. Our own future security is greatly dependent on the outcome of that fight. Our ability to "keep out of war" is going to be affected by that outcome. Thinking in terms of today and tomorrow, I make the direct statement to the American people that there is far less chance of the United States getting into war if we do all we can now to support the nations defending themselves against attack by the Axis than if we acquiesce in their defeat, submit tamely to an Axis victory, and wait our turn to be the object of attack in another war later on.

If we are to be completely honest with ourselves, we must admit that there is risk in any course we may take. But I deeply believe that the great majority of our people agree that the course

that I advocate involves the least risk now and the greatest hope
for world peace in the future.

The people of Europe who are defending themselves do not ask us to do their fighting. They ask us for the implements of war, the planes, the tanks, the guns, the freighters which will enable them to fight for their liberty and for our security. Emphatically we must get these weapons to them, get them to them in sufficient volume and quickly enough, so that we and our children will be saved the agony and suffering of war which others have had to endure.

Let not the defeatists tell us that it is too late. It will never be earlier. Tomorrow will be later than today . . .

This nation is making a great effort to produce everything that is necessary in this emergency—and with all possible speed. And this great effort requires great sacrifice.

I would ask no one to defend a democracy which in turn would not defend everyone in the nation against want and privation. The strength of this nation shall not be diluted by the failure of the Government to protect the economic well-being of its (all) citizens.

If our capacity to produce is limited by machines, it must ever be remembered that these machines are operated by the skill and the stamina of the workers. As the Government is determined to protect the rights of the workers, so the nation has a right to expect that the men who man the machines will discharge their full responsibilities to the urgent needs of defense.

The worker possesses the same human dignity and is entitled to the same security of position as the engineer or the manager or the owner. For the workers provide the human power that turns out the destroyers, and the (air)planes and the tanks.

The nation expects our defense industries to continue operation without interruption by strikes or lockouts. It expects and insists that management and workers will reconcile their differences by voluntary or legal means, to continue to produce the supplies that are so sorely needed.

And on the economic side of our great defense program, we are, as you know, bending every effort to maintain stability of prices and with that the stability of the cost of living.

Nine days ago I announced the setting up of a more effective organization to direct our gigantic efforts to increase the production of munitions. The appropriation of vast sums of money and a well coordinated executive direction of our defense efforts are not in themselves enough. Guns, planes, (and) ships and many other things have to be built in the factories and the arsenals of America. They have to be produced by workers and managers and engineers with the aid of machines which in turn have to be built by hundreds of thousands of workers throughout the land.

In this great work there has been splendid cooperation between the Government and industry and labor, and I am very thankful.

American industrial genius, unmatched throughout all the world in the solution of production problems, has been called upon to bring its resources and its talents into action. Manufacturers of watches, of farm implements, of linotypes, and cash registers, and automobiles, and sewing machines, and lawn mowers and locomotives are now making fuses, bomb packing crates, telescope mounts, shells, and pistols and tanks.

But all of our present efforts are not enough. We must have more ships, more guns, more planes—more of everything. And this can only be accomplished if we discard the notion of "business as usual." This job cannot be done merely by superimposing on the existing productive facilities the added requirements of the nation for defense.

Our defense efforts must not be blocked by those who fear the future consequences of surplus plant capacity. The possible consequences of failure of our defense efforts now are much more to be feared.

And after the present needs of our defense are past, a proper handling of the country's peacetime needs will require all of the new productive capacity—if not still more.

No pessimistic policy about the future of America shall delay the immediate expansion of those industries essential to defense. We need them.

I want to make it clear that it is the purpose of the nation to build now with all possible speed every machine, every arsenal, every (and) factory that we need to manufacture our defense material. We have the men—the skill—the wealth—and above all, the will.

I am confident that if and when production of consumer or luxury goods in certain industries requires the use of machines and raw materials that are essential for defense purposes, then such production must yield, and will gladly yield, to our primary and compelling purpose.

So I appeal to the owners of plants—to the managers—to the workers—to our own Government employees—to put every ounce of effort into producing these munitions swiftly and without stint. (And) With this appeal I give you the pledge that all of us who are officers of your Government will devote ourselves to the same whole-hearted extent to the great task that (which) lies ahead.

As planes and ships and guns and shells are produced, your Government, with its defense experts, can then determine how best to use them to defend this hemisphere. The decision as to how much shall be sent abroad and how much shall remain at home must be made on the basis of our overall military necessities.

We must be the great arsenal of democracy. For us this is an emergency as serious as war itself. We must apply ourselves to our task with the same resolution, the same sense of urgency, the same spirit of patriotism and sacrifice as we would show were we at war.

We have furnished the British great material support and we will furnish far more in the future.

There will be no "bottlenecks" in our determination to aid
Great Britain. No dictator, no combination of dictators, will
weaken that determination by threats of how they will construe
that determination.

The British have received invaluable military support from
the heroic Greek army and from the forces of all the governments
in exile. Their strength is growing. It is the strength of men and
women who value their freedom more highly than they value
their lives.

I believe that the Axis powers are not going to win this war. I
base that belief on the latest and best of information.

We have no excuse for defeatism. We have every good reason
for hope—hope for peace, yes, and hope for the defense of our civilization and for the building of a better civilization in the future.

I have the profound conviction that the American people
are now determined to put forth a mightier effort than they have
ever yet made to increase our production of all the implements of
defense, to meet the threat to our democratic faith.

As President of the United States I call for that national
effort. I call for it in the name of this nation which we love and
honor and which we are privileged and proud to serve. I call upon
our people with absolute confidence that our common cause will
greatly succeed.

PRESIDENT HARRY TRUMAN SIGHTING A SHOTGUN AT SUN VALLEY, IDAHO, 1948.

Truman Presidential Library

CHAPTER 14

ALWAYS DO RIGHT

———————◆———————

Harry Truman and the Berlin Airlift

On March 5, 1948, General Lucius Clay, American military governor of Germany, sent a top-secret cable from Berlin to Washington reporting "a new tenseness in every Soviet individual with whom we have official relations." War, he reported, might erupt with "dramatic suddenness." Secretary of the Army Kenneth Royall checked to see how long it would take to move atomic bombs closer to Russia.

At the end of World War II, the Americans, British, French, and Russians had carved up Berlin, as they had the German nation, like a giant pie, and each had claimed a slice. However, the former Nazi capital lay deep within the Russian-designated Eastern zone of Germany like an Allied island surrounded by a Soviet sea. The victors had hardly occupied the pummeled ruins of the metropolis when their awkward four-power system began to disintegrate.

On the heels of the Soviet-backed coup in Czechoslovakia in February 1948, the Western Allies publicized their intention to merge their three German zones into an independent nation of West Germany. Immediately, Russian antagonism escalated sharply. Soon after Clay's warning, Soviet governor Marshal Vassily Sokolovsky stomped out of an Allied Control Council meeting and declared the committee void. Then, on March 30, the Soviets pronounced that all military transport on the single rail line from the Western zones of Germany into Berlin would be subject to inspection.

Ruth Andreas-Friedrich—who as a leading member of an underground anti-Nazi movement had survived Hitler, had narrowly escaped rape by her Soviet liberators, and had scavenged through rubble for scraps of food—likened the disputes of her military overlords to "a dance on the edge of a volcano." Ruth worried. "Our vegetables, our fruit, our potatoes—nearly all our food is obtained from the neighboring provinces. In a twinkling the occupying power there could sever our lifeline . . . . If necessary, will the Western Allies supply three million Berliners with potatoes? With fruit, vegetables, coal and electricity?" She was not so sure.

However, General Clay had no intention of cowering to Soviet intimidation. When the Pentagon denied him permission to resist the Soviets by force, he instead sent a group of twin-propeller C-47 cargo planes over the Soviet zones at 5,000 feet, where they would be easy targets for Soviet antiaircraft fire or fighters. "Clay's pigeons," as the daring pilots were called, could not know whether the Soviet fighter planes, which swarmed menacingly through the air corridors, would take them down. Luckily, the American planes landed in Berlin without incident. They then returned to the Rhein-Mein airbase at Frankfurt to be loaded with supplies for the American garrison in Berlin.

A few days later, normal rail service resumed. But the Soviets arbitrarily arrested Allied officers and attempted to blockade Gatow airport in the British zone of Berlin and the central railway administration in the American section until forced out at gunpoint. Worst of all, a Soviet Yak-3 buzzed and then collided with a British

passenger flight, killing both crews and 10 civilians. Simultaneously,
Soviet-backed Communist district leaders told Berliners they must
register to boycott the Western Allies' plans for an independent
West Germany. "Perhaps the time will come," they warned, "when
the card you receive for signing must be shown in order to prove
that you really stand on the side of the people."

Back in the United States, President Harry S Truman delivered
a series of impromptu fundraising speeches for the Democratic
Party from the back of the *Ferdinand Magellan*, his armor-plated
presidential Pullman railroad car. In Eugene, Oregon, Truman
stressed his resolve to stand up to Soviet aggression. He promised
to contain the spread of Communism. As proof of his commitment,
he cited a plan, just approved by Congress, that his Secretary of
State, General George C. Marshall, had engineered to bolster
impoverished European countries by offering massive financial
aid. Then, in an off-the-cuff remark, recalling his meeting with
Soviet dictator Joseph Stalin at Potsdam in July 1945, he told the
crowd, "I like old Joe! He is a decent fellow."

Back on the train, Undersecretary of State Robert Lovett put
through an urgent call to Clark Clifford, Truman's trusted White
House aide, who tactfully advised the President not to repeat the
remark ever again. "Well, I guess I goofed," Truman conceded.

To many, such gaffes, and the homespun modesty with which
the President owned up to them, proved that he was just the "little
man from Missouri," a failed small-town haberdasher turned
farmer turned county judge then sent up to Washington as Senator
by famously corrupt Kansas City political boss Tom Pendergast.
However, by forming a Senate committee to investigate military
contract inefficiencies and frauds, this little man distinguished

himself enough to gain the Democratic nomination as Franklin D. Roosevelt's fourth-term running mate. But when Roosevelt died on April 12, 1945, as General Omar Bradley explained, "Truman did not appear to be at all qualified to fill Roosevelt's large shoes."

President Truman later conceded that he was still "an innocent idealist" when he met the Soviet dictator at Potsdam. He knew that the "little-son-of-a-bitch," as he sometimes referred to Stalin, had sent more people to their deaths than even Hitler. Nevertheless, "old Joe," wearing simple khakis and a single red-ribboned gold star, had charmed him.

Truman admired the fact that Stalin was an attentive listener and direct speaker, qualities that he also excelled at. Moreover, after the President flew in a renowned pianist to play his favorite Chopin waltz and personally turned his sheet music, Stalin had returned the honor by sending for his best Moscow musicians to perform at a banquet, which Truman described as "a wow."

The President's deep personal loyalty had gotten him into trouble before. He had appointed so many hometown buddies to his staff that detractors accused him of making the White House seem like "the lounge of the Lion's Club of Independence, Missouri." Truman's warm impression of Stalin dangerously prevented him from believing just how ruthless the dictator would prove to be.

On June 18, 1948, the United States, Great Britain, and France went forward with plans to introduce the Deutsche mark as the new currency in their Western German zones. Berlin was temporarily exempt, pending agreement from its four-power council.

The Soviets not only withheld their consent, they banned the Western money in Soviet-controlled Eastern Germany and in Berlin and initiated plans to introduce their own new legal tender. The next morning Berliners learned that they had two new currencies—one Western, one Eastern. Irate citizens stormed City Hall. As the crowd burst through the door, many were trampled underfoot. Others were beaten as the demonstration turned violent.

At 11 p.m. on June 23, the Soviet news agency in Germany announced that all traffic into and out of the Soviet zones of Berlin had been halted. Rail lines and waterways were also closed. The notice further decreed that neither coal nor electricity would be supplied to the Western sectors. By morning, shipments of milk and vegetables from the Soviet-controlled provinces were stopped and accounts at the central bank, located in the Eastern sector, were frozen. Like a medieval fortress surrounded, West Berlin was under siege.

The official excuse for these changes was "technical difficulties." However, as Joseph Stalin intended, they were universally interpreted as a threat to starve 2.5 million people unless the Americans, British, and French abandoned plans to create an independent nation of West Germany and to introduce the new Deutsche mark in Berlin. Stalin might even convince his former allies to pull out of Berlin altogether.

American troops were briefed. One company commander grimly informed his men, "Gentlemen, you should know this. If the Russians decide to come in, we all have about two hours to live." The three Western Allies combined had only about 6,500 troops in Berlin, compared with a Soviet total of 18,000, with an additional 300,000 and numerous heavy tanks in the surrounding Eastern German zone.

If President Truman was slow to believe that Stalin would let an entire city go hungry, Colonel Frank Howley, the American commandant in Berlin, had no doubts. At an early meeting of the city's four-power Kommandatura, he had argued that the meager 1,250 calories allotted to the lowest category of ration recipients be increased. "You can't kick a lady when she's down," he told the Soviet deputy.

"Why, my dear Colonel Howley, that is the best time to kick them," came the reply.

"You mean food is political?"

"Of course," said the Soviet, with a condescending smile.

Without consulting General Clay or the State Department, Colonel Howley took to the airwaves and promised that the Americans would not leave. He admitted that there were only enough supplies to last 30 days but emphatically told listeners, "this much I do know. The American people will not stand by and allow the German people to starve." He concluded by giving "the Russians something to chew on besides black bread . . . . [W]e have heard a lot about your military intentions. Well, this is all I have to say on the subject. If you do try to come into our sector you had better be well prepared. We are ready for you."

Power shortages meant that few in the Western sectors could hear Howley's messages, so he sent vans with loudspeakers to broadcast updates through the streets. Neighborhoods were broken into groups, which received electricity for two hours a day on a rotating basis. Ruth Andreas-Friedrich had power from midnight until 2 a.m.

Even before the blockade began, Colonel Howley, with General Clay's support, had coordinated a makeshift airlift of food and coal. As bad as things were, neither believed that the Soviets were ready to shoot down Allied planes. That day, 34

American and British flights landed in Berlin with 80 tons of food
and medical supplies. However, Howley's experts calculated that
the Western sectors required a daily minimum of 4,500 tons of
food, coal, and other supplies. Only once in aviation history—
over the "Hump" of the Himalayas in the China-India-Burma
theater during World War II—had a massive supply mission by
air ever succeeded. Berlin needed almost twice as much tonnage
as that operation had hauled at its peak.

Clay concluded that it would be "absolutely impossible"
to supply the city exclusively by planes. The logistics were too
daunting: air access was restricted to three narrow corridors; the
two airports in the Western sectors, like the rest of the bombed-
out city, were in a calamitous state of disrepair; and the United
States had only about 100 war-weary C-47s stationed in the area.
Great Britain had only six equivalent models.

In spite of these limitations, British Air Commodore Reginald
Waite, the Royal Air Force staff expert on the Control Council,
independently assessed that a massive airlift could work. He
convinced British military governor Sir Brian Robertson, who
wired London for an additional squadron of planes to get it
started. Although dubious, Clay lent his support by requisitioning
as many American planes as he could.

That done, Clay frantically telexed the Pentagon and State
Department to launch his own plan. He had assembled a 6,000-
member armed convoy, complete with armor, artillery, and a
combat engineering battalion, to drive straight through the Soviet
zone to Berlin on the autobahn. All he needed was permission to
give the order.

Horrified, Undersecretary of State Robert Lovett told Clay

that after blowing up a couple of bridges, "the Soviets would just sit up on the hillside and laugh." Secretary of the Army Kenneth Royall warned that Berlin's currency reform was not something to go to war over and urged him to evacuate American dependents from the city.

When news from Berlin reached President Truman, he summoned Secretary of Defense James Forrestal, Undersecretary of State Lovett, and Secretary of the Army Royall to the Oval Office. After updating him, they admitted that they could find no documents legally guaranteeing American use of access routes into Berlin. This came as a bitter disappointment. In spite of the President's repeated emphasis on this point, every time the issue had been raised at the Allied Control Council, the Soviets had vetoed it. Now, it was too late.

Truman asked his advisers to come back with more information. In the meantime, he ordered two squadrons of B-29s, the type of planes that had dropped the atomic bombs on Japan, to Europe. The B-29s heading into Soviet range were not equipped for that purpose, but Stalin could not know that. Truman, a poker fanatic, understood the value of a good bluff.

With the habitual spring in his step and a twinkle behind his thick glasses, Truman gave no outward sign of worry. Nor did he betray any concern that the papers had just reported Thomas E. Dewey's nomination as the Republican candidate for President, as if the self-satisfied governor of New York had already won the election. That evening he dined with the First Lady out on the South Lawn and lingered to take in the view. Jotting down observations ("A mockingbird imitates robins, jays, redbirds, crows, hawks—but has no individual note of its own. A lot of people like that."), he concluded it was "a lovely evening."

The next afternoon at the Pentagon, Army General Omar Bradley, Air Force General Lauris Norstad, and Navy Secretary John Sullivan joined Forrestal, Lovett, and Royall for the first high-level discussion of an appropriate American response. They narrowed their options to three: the United States could withdraw from Berlin (a position most favored), attempt to stay and forge a diplomatic solution, or prepare to wage war with the Soviet Union on a major scale. Clay's proposed convoy, which they dubbed the "shoot our way into Berlin" policy, was quickly dismissed. No one even mentioned the airlift option.

The generals received a shock when they learned, mid-meeting, that the British had announced that they would not pull out of Berlin under any circumstances. Bradley had just dispatched Major General Albert Wedemeyer to London to discuss plans to evacuate the German capital.

They were further dismayed when, as Lovett began to outline the various alternatives to Truman at the White House, the President cut him off with a roar: "There is no discussion on that point. We stay in Berlin—period." He seemed as bull-headed as the Brits. Certainly, he was earning his nickname as "the contrariest mule of Missouri."

As respectfully as he could, Royall asked, "Mr. President, have you thought this through?" and pointed out that such a stance might ignite World War III.

"We will have to deal with the situation as it develops," Truman answered, "but the essential position is that we are in Berlin by terms of an agreement and that the Russians have no right to get us out by either direct or indirect pressure."

The President's advisers knew better than to argue that this was a difficult or unpopular course. In response to such statements, Truman would point to a framed motto of Mark Twain's, written in the author's hand, that he had hung in the Oval Office. "Always do right!" it read. "This will gratify some people and astonish the rest."

With the President remaining firm about staying in Berlin, the discussion quickly turned to how best to hold their position. To everyone's relief, the President rejected Clay's armed convoy. Truman also dismissed a suggestion to retaliate by closing ports and the Panama Canal to Russian ships. Without prompting, the President decided that the airlift was the best idea. He ordered that it be expanded into a full-scale operation until a diplomatic solution could be found. Most of his advisers, like Clay, doubted that an airlift could feed 2.5 million people, but Truman never asked them what they thought, nor did he promise that his plan would work.

From across the continental United States, Alaska, and the Caribbean, American planes, including 39 C-54 Skymasters capable of hauling 10-ton loads, departed for Germany. Anyone and everyone with wings—press officers, operations specialists, even General Curtis LeMay, commander of the U.S. Air Force in Europe—was put on flight duty and took turns flying double shifts for "Operation Vittles." Likewise, pilots from all over the British Commonwealth arrived to muscle "Operation Plane Fare." Berliners referred to both missions as *die Luftbrücke* —"the air bridge." The steady hum of the engines overhead that once meant bombs now promised survival in the form of coal, flour, yeast, Spam, canned fruits, and dehydrated potatoes and vegetables. Within weeks, the makeshift airlift begun by Colonel Howley and the British on June 24 had become a full-fledged mission.

At first, scheduling was haphazard and confused. Air traffic control refused to bend its regulation of 25 minutes between flights until Brigadier General Joseph Smith, director of the American operation, bluntly ordered them to ignore the rulebooks and land a plane in Berlin every five minutes. Heavy rain in early July delayed numerous flights. Shortages of propellers, tires, and engine parts canceled others. On July 8, an American C-47 crashed into a mountain west of Wiesbaden, killing everyone on board, the mission's first casualties. But by mid-July, airlift planes loaded, flew, unloaded, returned, refueled, reloaded, and took off again in a steady beat, one landing every four minutes even as Soviet aircraft teased the corridors. Operation Vittles set a record on the 15th with 1,450 tons delivered in 24 hours.

That same day President Truman also scored a victory. After patiently waiting in the wings throughout the evening of the 14th, at just after midnight he captured the Democratic nomination. At 2 a.m., looking remarkably fresh in his crisp linen suit, he fired up the lackluster convention with what *Life* magazine termed a "Li'l Abner Ozark style speech" in which he dared the Republicans to make good on their "poppycock" campaign promises by calling Congress into a special summer session to begin July 26 (which he informed listeners was "Turnip Day" in Missouri) so that they would have the opportunity to pass laws to halt rising prices and to promote civil rights and education, which they claimed to support. "They can do this job in fifteen days, if they want to," he taunted. "They will still have time to run for office."

Diplomatic efforts to end the blockade made little progress. On July 3, General Clay, with the British and French governors, had called on Marshal Sokolovsky, who insisted that "technical difficulties" would continue until the plan for a separate West German government was abandoned. Official denouncements of the blockade failed to even get a response. All the Soviets had to do, they thought, was wait. As one London newspaper put it, "[E]very expert knows that aircraft, despite their immense psychological effect, cannot be relied upon to provision Berlin in the winter months."

Stalin seriously underestimated just how stubbornly patient the President could be. He should have consulted with First Lady Bess Truman. It had taken nine years from the evening that Truman first showed up with a pie plate at her mother's door, but his dogged perseverance eventually won him the hand of his boyhood Sunday school crush.

The President worried privately that "Russia might deliberately choose to make Berlin the pretext for war." But, he vowed, "We'll stay in Berlin—come what may. . . . I don't pass the buck, nor do I alibi out of any decision I make." In order to stand his ground, he battled his own military advisers almost as much as he did Stalin.

To the President's annoyance, his "muttonhead Secretary [of the] Army" ordered Clay home from Germany to testify before the National Security Council, which, in Truman's opinion, "stirred up a terrific how-dy-do for no good reason."

However, by this time, Operation Vittles' remarkable progress had swayed the general's convictions. Clay argued that he was certain that Berlin could hold firm if the mission received additional planes and resources.

Truman listened carefully and then asked Air Force Chief

of Staff General Hoyt Vandenberg for his opinion. Vandenberg warned that concentrating too many planes in Germany would leave America vulnerable in other parts of the world. He also thought that massing too many aircrafts in Germany would make it easy for the Soviets to destroy the Air Force in one attack.

Truman interrupted sternly to ask if he would prefer them to drive an armed convoy into Berlin. Without waiting for a response, the President stated that, in his view, the airlift posed the fewest problems. He ordered a vast increase in the number of large-capacity C-54s assigned to the mission; then he affirmed that he, the President, was willing to take the risk.

Ever the naysayer, Vandenberg worried that Berlin had insufficient landing facilities. This time, Clay jumped in to say that he'd already picked out a suitable spot for a new airport in the French sector. Truman ordered the general back to Germany to get it built.

Shortly afterward, Major General William Tunner, who had directed the successful "Hump" airlift in the Himalayas, arrived in Berlin to take Operation Vittles to a new level. With a system of runway jeeps staffed by the most attractive girls the German Red Cross could find, pilots received instructions and purchased snacks without ever leaving their planes. Flights landed every three minutes. On August 12, American and British pilots delivered a combined total of 4,742 tons of cargo to Berlin, exceeding the minimum daily requirement for the first time.

First Lieutenant Gail S. Halvorsen and his flight crew began to drop their candy rations to groups of waving children who waited by the airport fence. As he approached, he wiggled his wing flaps while his sergeant shoved out the small packages, each with a handkerchief parachute to break its fall. Some weeks later, after spotting a large stack of letters addressed to "Onkel Wachelflügel" (Uncle Wiggle Wings), the "Schokoladenflieger" (Chocolate Pilot) Halvorsen decided they had better stop—but not until they made one final, double-sized drop. The next day, his superior confronted him with a copy of the *Frankfurter Zeitung* and bellowed, "You almost hit a reporter on the head with a candy bar in Berlin yesterday. He's spread the story all over Europe." From around the world, "Operation Little Vittles" soon received mountains of donated chocolate, candy, and handkerchiefs, which Uncle Wiggle Wings distributed throughout the city, even over the Eastern sector until the Soviets lodged an official complaint.

Diplomatic efforts proceeded less well. For much of the summer, Western ambassadors were told that Stalin's Foreign Minister, Vyacheslav Molotov, was away on vacation. When he returned in late July, his office reported that since nothing had changed the Westerners had no reason to see him. American ambassador General Walter Bedell Smith and his Allied colleagues managed to meet directly with Stalin, who seemed ready to abandon his demand against the formation of West Germany. But when, as instructed, they followed up with Molotov, he denied this. By mid-September, talks broke down completely. And when the Western Allies next tried to contact Stalin, they were told that he was now on vacation.

On the streets of Berlin, Ruth and her compatriots vacillated "between hope and despair. But vacillating gets to be quite strenuous too," she noted, "if one isn't the dog that fights for the bone, but the bone the dogs are fighting for."

Riots, demonstrations, and police attacks ravaged Berlin

with increasing ferocity. The city police force had broken into two separate entities, and the Eastern branch arrested most of its Western counterparts. As Berlin's population turned on itself, City Hall was stormed. When the municipal council withdrew to the American sector, Ruth Andreas-Friedrich mused, "Perhaps by tomorrow we will have two city governments and along the sector boundary a Chinese wall with battlements and watchtowers." Indeed, things were heading that way.

On September 9, 250,000 demonstrators gathered at the Platz der Republik to protest the attacks on City Hall. Attendance exceeded that of the largest Nazi rallies, which had been compulsory. The Eastern police pointed guns at the crowd as several men attempted to tear the Soviet flag down from the Brandenburg Gate. Shots rang out and a 15-year-old boy, shielding a woman from the line of fire, was killed. Twenty-two others were wounded.

Truman confessed to his diary, "I have a terrible feeling . . . that we are very close to war. I hope not." His Cabinet pressed to learn if he was prepared to use the atomic bomb. The President replied that he prayed never to be forced to make such a decision again. However, if events necessitated such a step, the first man in history to authorize such an attack said that he could do so again.

Despite these worries, on September 17 Truman set off in his armor-plated railway car on a vigorous 33-day campaign tour, determined to fight hard against Republican Tom Dewey. He refused to get disheartened, even when all 50 writers polled by *Newsweek* predicted he would lose. "I know every one of these fifty fellows," he remarked. "There isn't one of them has enough sense to pound sand in a rat hole." The unexpectedly large crowds who shouted "Give 'em Hell, Harry" wherever he stopped delighted him. But as he waged his own desperate battle for the presidency, he did not neglect those struggling against the odds to maintain Berlin. General Clay cabled, "We are not quite holding our own." In Dallas, Truman had Ambassador Smith discreetly slipped aboard his railway car.

His most recent meeting with Molotov had yielded nothing, Smith reported. In consultation with Secretary of State Marshall, Truman decided that there was no further point in trying to negotiate. A final, last-ditch effort, made at the behest of the French and British, provoked a sharp denial that a blockade even existed. The matter was referred to the United Nations Security Council. Here, too, it became quickly apparent, when the council's Soviet representative kept repeating *"Blokada nyet"* (There is no blockade), that it was going to be a long, cold winter in Berlin.

Desperate, the President considered sending his buddy, Chief Justice Fred Vinson, to Moscow to negotiate with Stalin, even as his Secretary of State grappled with the Security Council in Paris. Truman knew that the scheme was improbable but was ready to try almost anything. "If only we could get Stalin to unburden himself to someone on our side," the President later recalled. "I thought perhaps we might get somewhere." However, he abandoned the plan, which his speechwriters had cooked up as a publicity stunt, the moment that Marshall objected.

While Truman campaigned in the American West, the Joint Chiefs undertook a full policy reappraisal. In their view, the airlift could not be sustained on an indefinite basis without weakening other national security needs. They pointedly criticized the decision to stay in Berlin in the first place and recommended evacuation as soon as possible. To risk war on behalf of Berlin, they concluded, was "neither militarily prudent nor strategically sound." Lovett thought the Joint Chiefs must have gotten a case of the "jitters."

Furious, Truman scheduled a National Security Council meeting to take place upon his return. This time, the President felt no qualms about summoning Clay to his side from Germany. Before the committee, the general highlighted the airlift's new efficiency, which resulted from the recent merging of the American and British operations into a single, streamlined effort, but stressed that it urgently needed more planes in order to succeed.

The President asked for opinions from everyone present. Not one supported Clay. But when the meeting concluded, Truman asked him back to his office, where he remarked, "I'm afraid you're very unhappy, General. Don't be. You're going to get them." Truman ordered that the planes be sent to Germany immediately.

Against all odds, the underdogs began to triumph. Less than two weeks later, at 4 a.m. on the morning after Election Day, one of Truman's Secret Service men wakened him with the news that he was already leading the race by 2 million votes. Contrary to headlines in the first-edition papers, the President had won the election.

Berlin's fate remained uncertain. In mid-November a thick blanket of fog settled over Germany. The airlift's pace slackened sharply despite heroic efforts to keep the flights going. On the 27th the airlift shut down completely for 15 hours. The Soviet-backed Eastern press played up every delay. So, although supplies were low, to boost morale Clay distributed 50 pounds of coal per family (more for those with children) to celebrate surviving Germany's worst conditions. But the Teutonic weather gods hadn't finished with them yet. On the 30th, only 10 planes managed to land in 24 long hours. As the fog lingered into December, Ruth Andreas-Friedrich wondered, "Is Heaven in league with the Soviets?"

In spite of the weather and bullying threats from the Eastern police, 86.3 percent of eligible voters in West Berlin went to the polls on December 5 to elect their mayor and city council. It was a tremendous showing on behalf of the democratic privileges they were struggling to keep. Berlin continued to stand strong.

The New Year brought 34 airlift casualties, poor weather, and further electricity cuts. Ever so subtly, however, the atmosphere began to shift. The British Parliament voted that Operation Plane Fare should be considered a long-term program. The skies cleared and the airlift regained its momentum. As Howley told reporters: "It must be obvious to even the most dense Communist that their tactics have failed. Neither the blockade at the Elbe nor the ice of winter has stopped the airlift."

On January 20, 1949, President Truman, smiling broadly, delivered his inaugural address, which he composed entirely himself and devoted wholly to promoting peace and democracy throughout the world. The immense throngs responded with sustained applause and cheered as the surviving members of his World War I company escorted his car through the parade. An armada of 700 planes flew overhead.

Not long afterward, Stalin gave a veiled indication that he might be ready to negotiate. In a prepared response to a Western journalist's question about what conditions he required to end the blockade, he neglected to mention the currency issue, which had always been his biggest gripe.

After consulting with Truman, Dean Acheson, who had recently replaced Marshall as Secretary of State, instructed the American ambassador to the United Nations to casually ask his Soviet counterpart whether there was any significance to Stalin's omission. A month passed before the answer came back that yes, the currency question was important, but it could be discussed at a meeting of the foreign ministers. Slowly, and very quietly, Stalin was backing down. Next, the American ambassador asked his Soviet colleague if the blockade would be lifted if such a meeting were scheduled. He'd have to inquire was the response.

Worried that things were going too well and that his pilots would lose their edge, airlift director "Willy the Whip" Tunner gave Berlin an Easter parade of coal-carrying planes that landed at an extraordinary rate of almost one per minute and hauled 12,941 tons of coal into the city in a mere 24 hours. If Stalin still held out hope that his blockade might work, Operation Vittles squashed it.

In May, Stalin capitulated without gaining any of his desired concessions. At one minute after midnight on May 12, the lights went on in the Western sectors, the roadblocks were lifted, and the first trains started down the rail lines as spectators looked on in full evening dress. Harry Truman and Operation Vittles won their battle by dropping chocolates, not bombs, over Berlin.

On January 15, 1953, in his farewell address, President Truman promised the American people that a time would come when the Soviet regime collapsed of its own accord. "Nobody can say for sure when that is going to be, or exactly how it will come about," he conceded, but he had "not a doubt in the world that a change will occur." In the intervening years, the Cold War had blown hot in the battlegrounds of Korea. Then, in 1961 the Soviets erected the fortified wall dividing East from West Berlin that Ruth Andreas-Friedrich had envisioned. But just as Truman predicted, the Soviets and their East German government eventually crumpled, and in 1989 the wall came down. When the American garrison made a last parade through the streets of Berlin on June 18, 1994, an old twin-engine C-47, which had been among the first to supply the city, flew over the crowd in final victory.

President Harry Truman   **359**
Address at Mechanics Hall in Boston
October 27, 1948

Thank you, my good friends and fellow citizens . . . .

Yesterday, the free peoples of the world were threatened by the black menace of fascism. The American people helped to save them. Today, the free peoples of the world are threatened by the red menace of communism.

And again, the American people are helping to save them.

I think that I speak for every loyal American—Democrat and Republican alike—when I say that we detest what Communists stand for, and what they have done to the free peoples under their control.

If the people of some other country freely choose a Communist form of government, that is their own business. But we don't want any Communist government in the United States of America.

And if the people of other countries don't want communism, we don't want to see it imposed upon them against their will.

We have been taking positive and successful action, everywhere in the world, to halt the threat of communism . . . .

I want you to get this straight now.

I hate communism. I deplore what it does to the dignity and freedom of the individual. I detest the godless creed it teaches.

I have fought it at home. I have fought it abroad, and I shall continue to fight it with all my strength.

This is one issue on which I shall never surrender . . .

The Communists don't want me to be President, because this country, under a Democratic administration, has rallied the forces of all the democracies of the world to safeguard freedom and to save free people everywhere from Communist slavery.

Our goal is peace—a lasting peace in the world.

It is our conviction that peace in this atomic age is an absolute necessity. But only a peace that is based on human rights and freedom will be a lasting peace.

I propose to keep on doing my level best to win a lasting peace.

That must be done, not only for the people of the United States, but for people everywhere in the world.

In March of last year I announced a fundamental decision of your Government, designed to preserve the freedom of the world. In stating that doctrine, I said: "It must be the policy of the United States to support free peoples who are resisting attempted subjugation by armed minorities or by outside pressures."

Our first step under that doctrine was to give economic and military aid to Greece and Turkey, two countries right under the shadow of Communist domination.

The whole world knows of the success of this policy. Now, the Communists will never forgive me for that . . .

In Germany, we have taken the frank and firm position that communism must not spread its tentacles into the Western Zone.

We shall not retreat from that position.

We shall feed the people of Berlin, and the people of Germany will be given their chance to work out a decent life under a democratic government.

Now, the Communists hate me for that, too . . .

Communism thrives on misery. Human suffering nourishes the Communist menace. That menace withers away where there is prosperity, justice, and tolerance.

The real threat of communism in this country lies in the danger of another major depression. The real threat of communism lies in widespread unemployment and arrogant injustice, such as we had in 1932.

The real threat of communism in this country grows out of

the Republican policies of the 80th Congress—policies which threaten to put an end to American prosperity.

The real threat of communism in this country grows out of the submission of the Republican Party to the dictates of big business, and its determination to destroy the hard-won rights of American labor.

You can fight communism on November 2nd with a Democratic vote . . .

All I can say is that I'm proud to be a Democrat. We are engaged in a great crusade—a crusade for freedom, for tolerance, for the rights and welfare of all the people . . .

This fight is Roosevelt's fight.

And now it is my fight.

More than that, it is your fight.

And I'm proud to be making this fight with you for the things in which we believe.

With your help, and your courage, and your enthusiasm, we are going to win this fight on November the 2nd.

PRESIDENTIAL CANDIDATE JOHN KENNEDY, 1960.

CHAPTER 15

DEFEAT IS AN ORPHAN

———————•———————

John Kennedy and the Bay of Pigs

At 4:32 p.m. on the afternoon of April 17, 1961, "Pepe" San Román crouched down on a Cuban beach, surrounded by smoke, cracks of gunfire, and the roar of fighter planes. Despite the commotion, he tried his best to concentrate on dots and dashes as he tapped out a message in Morse code: "AM DESTROYING ALL MY EQUIPMENT AND COMMUNICATIONS. TANKS ARE IN SIGHT. I HAVE NOTHING TO FIGHT WITH. AM TAKING TO THE WOODS. I CANNOT WAIT FOR YOU." The 28-year-old commander of Brigade 2506 was outnumbered and trapped on a strip of sand between the sea and miles of dense swampland. Everywhere he looked, his soldiers were being killed.

In a last effort, Pepe grabbed his radio handset and somehow got through: "You can hear the guns!" he shouted. "I am ordering the retreat!"

"Hold on!" a voice on the radio begged Pepe. "We're coming. We're coming with everything!"

"How long?" asked Pepe. He was desperate. Over the last 12 hours he'd been promised reinforcements repeatedly, each promise sounding emptier than the last.

"Three to four hours," the voice stammered through the radio.

That was too long to wait. The Central Intelligence Agency had promised to be "above, below, and alongside" Pepe and his brigade of Cuban exiles, but it was obvious that help would not be arriving in time. Without saying another word, Pepe signaled his men to destroy their communications equipment. They smashed it with the butts of their rifles and then fired at it with their submachine guns until there was nothing left but twisted bits of metal and wire. Brigade 2506 was in this alone now.

Pepe needed to find his men cover. All he could see around him were razed beach cottages and leveled palm trees. It looked as if a hurricane had blown through and beaten the landscape flat. The brigade would be easy to spot from Castro's planes.

Pepe instructed his unit to escape into the swamps, and they broke formation and ran. Days passed while the group of soldiers wandered aimlessly in the marshes. After pressing through the sweltering wilderness for nearly a week, Pepe's men exhausted their provisions and, finally forced into the open, were caught. "Shoot us!" one soldier yelled as he was taken prisoner. "But in the name of humanity, give us water first!"

Castro's soldiers packed the captured fighters into trucks. They stuffed one transport so tightly that the men within tore off their clothing, screaming and banging on the walls to be let out of the suffocating heat. When the convoy arrived at Havana a few hours later, nine of the men had died from asphyxiation. And their ordeal was just beginning. For the next 20 days the men were tortured and interrogated, often by Castro himself. They were kept in an overcrowded prison where every 100 men shared a small hole in the ground as a toilet. One month, then three months, then Christmas passed, but no one came to their rescue. The Cuban exiles sat in the fetid darkness, with nothing to do but wait.

Three months earlier, in January 1961, John F. Kennedy rode toward his presidential inauguration. Inside the limousine

sat Dwight D. Eisenhower, his aging and legendary predecessor.
As their motorcade advanced along the snow-lined Pennsylvania
Avenue, Kennedy tried to break the silence with small talk.

Kennedy asked whether President Eisenhower had read
The Longest Day, a recently published history of the Normandy
landings in 1944. No, Eisenhower answered, he had not. And why
would he? As Supreme Commander of the Allied Expeditionary
Forces, Eisenhower had conceived, supervised, and executed
every aspect of the most important invasion in history. There was
no need for him to read about it.

Eisenhower thought that the President-elect, his junior
by over 25 years, was merely a "young whippersnapper." Even
Kennedy's closest associates felt he was not ready to take on
America's highest office. "You have plenty of time," an old friend
told him before the presidential race. "Why not wait?"

But Kennedy knew that time was not on his side. Stricken by
Addison's disease, an often terminal gland failure, Kennedy had
already been given the Catholic death rites four times. Surviving
brushes with death left in Kennedy the need to take action when
opportunity arose. He did not know how long he had left to live,
and waiting around while time passed was not an option.

"I look at the others in the race," Kennedy said as he launched
into his campaign, "and I say to myself, well, if they think they
can do it why not me?" The election was close, but Kennedy
came out on top, defeating veteran politician Richard Nixon by a
margin of just over 100,000 votes.

During his inaugural address, Kennedy told a hopeful crowd
that the torch had been passed to a new generation of Americans.
The 43-year-old President backed his words by bringing young

advisers to his administration. None of Kennedy's recruits had held public office before he called them to Washington from around the country. "We'll learn together," he told Robert McNamara, his newly appointed Secretary of Defense.

Though Kennedy barely knew any of these men, he had confidence in their intellect. "You can't beat brains," said Kennedy. Vice President Lyndon Johnson was in awe of the advisers who would come to be called "the best and the brightest." But after telling Sam Rayburn how smart Kennedy's idea men were, the salty Speaker of the House remained unimpressed. He told Johnson he wished just one of them had run for county sheriff.

Even Kennedy was not fully confident that the country could be run by new blood alone. Half of the appointees to his administration, mostly intelligence and military advisers, were Eisenhower men. Most of Eisenhower's staff had been in Washington for over a decade, making legendary reputations for themselves during World War II and its Cold War aftermath.

Yet these men were from an elder generation and were not exactly charmed by Kennedy's youth. Long-time CIA Director Allen Dulles, almost 25 years older than Kennedy, was accustomed to taking orders from a man like Eisenhower—a Republican and a retired five-star general. Dulles had little interest in sharing his expertise with the neophyte President.

But there was one thing Dulles was eager to share with Kennedy. Immediately after Kennedy took office, Dulles and CIA Deputy Director Richard Bissell briefed him on a "situation" that had developed around Fidel Castro. In 1959 Castro had rallied popular support in Cuba and forced the existing Batista regime out of government. Like the revolutions in Russia 30 years before, the upheaval in Cuba swiftly turned into a Communist takeover.

Dulles and Bissell, both stern men in their mid-60s, explained earnestly to Kennedy that the fiery Cuban dictator could turn into another Stalin. They advised the President that he could not allow a Communist dictatorship to exist a mere 90 miles from U.S. shores. In fact, the two men added, they already had a plan to stop it.

As soon as Castro rose to power, Eisenhower had directed Dulles and Bissell to develop a plan of invasion. He gave only one stipulation: "Our hand should not show in anything." Covert action was quick, quiet, and efficient, and it allowed Eisenhower to avoid the political entanglements of declaring war.

It turned out that Eisenhower could use all the political help he could get. Near the end of his term and just weeks before a U.N. summit on nuclear disarmament was to be held in Paris, the USSR shot down a U-2 spy plane over Soviet airspace. The summit meetings were a complete fiasco. Soviet Premier Nikita Khrushchev demanded that Eisenhower apologize for the reconnaissance mission, angrily storming out of the first day of meetings and condemning the "underhanded tactics of the west." Understandably, Eisenhower paid less and less attention to the CIA's plan to invade Cuba.

Dulles and Bissell, however, continued to develop the operation without Eisenhower. By the time Kennedy won office, he had inherited not only the tensions between the United States and the USSR but the well-polished plan to depose Castro as well. Throughout the first week of his presidency, Dulles and Bissell continued to brief Kennedy on their strategy for Cuba, but the men were vague and their meetings offered little in the way of hard facts.

One member of the Joint Chiefs under Kennedy would later say that CIA briefings on Cuba were "very peculiar" and seemed to address "specific items out of context." For instance, neither Dulles nor Bissell would agree to walk the President through the plan of invasion step by step. When he requested that they do just that, the intelligence chiefs would find a way to lose the President in the details. It seemed that the older men thought they would be better off running the show as they had under Eisenhower— without the President's consent.

Kennedy didn't see it their way and called meeting after meeting to discuss the top secret invasion. After several weeks, the President was finally able to gather an outline for himself. Under Eisenhower, the CIA had been training a force of exiled, anti-Castro Cubans, or brigadistas, at a secret Guatemalan base. The CIA's plan was to land these brigadistas on the southern coast of the island. The force would then create a tiny base on the shore that would grow larger as they scouted the area. A few days later, officers preselected to run a provisional government would land in the secured zone and declare it an independent country. The new nation would request U.S. military protection, while the exile fighters canvassed the countryside, recruiting villagers to take up arms and attack Castro's armies. Fighting alongside the U.S. military, the exile force and their recruits would wrest control of the country away from Castro.

Kennedy agreed with the CIA's basic idea but thought their plan required too much visible U.S. involvement. "Perhaps the assault could be supported by American planes, ships, and supplies?" Kennedy asked the Joint Chiefs of Staff. "Could not such a force be landed gradually and quietly... taking shape as a Cuban force within Cuba, not an invasion force sent by Yankees?"

The CIA presented a new plan to Kennedy, and he rejected it again for the same reasons. "Too spectacular," Kennedy said this time. "It sounds like D-Day. You have to reduce the noise level of this thing." Kennedy explained that he wanted no political risk, even if it meant greater military risk. He refused to have a war on his hands. "The minute I land one U.S. marine, we're in this up to our necks," the President told Dulles and Bissell. "The best possible plan," he concluded, "has not yet been presented." Though the first plan had taken over a year to create, Kennedy gave Bissell four days to finalize another version.

Kennedy had good reason to urge the CIA to rush its plan along. The invasion was becoming, as an aide said, "as top secret as Christmas." The previous October, Cuba's Foreign Minister had loudly and publicly accused the United States of training exiles in Guatemala to attack Castro. *The Nation* magazine printed an editorial entitled "Are We Training Cuban Guerillas?" in November. The following January, *The New York Times* ran a front-page description of the Guatemala camp, "U.S. Helps Train an Anti-Castro Force at Secret Guatemalan Air-Ground Base," and that month *Time* also published a frighteningly accurate description of the operations. President Kennedy was dismayed by the media leaks. "I can't believe what I'm reading . . . . Castro doesn't need agents over here. All he has to do is read our papers. It's all laid out for him."

Bissell presented President Kennedy a third plan on March 15, as requested. This version of the operation, code-named Operation Zapata, met all the President's requirements for secrecy. The brigadistas would invade at an isolated beach called Bahia de

Cochinos, or Bay of Pigs, on the southwest part of the island. The bay was in a quiet, relatively unpopulated area that would make for a smooth beach landing during the night. The United States would provide the Cuban exiles with old Navy boats for transportation from Guatemala and munitions to storm the beach. Castro had a small air force, so Bissell planned to provide air support a few days before the soldiers were to approach the island. In order to further disguise U.S. involvement, Bissell suggested they use vintage World War II B-26 bombers the Cuban exiles could have bought on the open market.

When Bissell explained Operation Zapata to Kennedy, it seemed as if the CIA had thought of everything. The President approved the plan and scheduled the preliminary air strikes to begin in four weeks, though he reserved the right to call off the actual invasion up to 24 hours beforehand.

With a final schedule in place, the Cuban exile force stepped up its training program in Guatemala. The core group of Brigade 2506, like their commander Pepe San Román, had worked under Batista and fought alongside the Cuban President in his struggle against Castro. Some, however, were newcomers—civilians recruited secretly by the CIA to bolster the number of troops. Many were Cuban, but a few were disillusioned, college-aged Americans looking for adventure and a quick dollar. Believing a CIA report that claimed that the people in a popular uprising against Castro would do most of the fighting and that Castro's army "is without experience in coordinated offensive action," the American recruits boarded in fancy hotels and generally enjoyed the luxury of their situation. One wrote in a letter that he was spending most of his time at the pool, drinking, ironically enough, Cuba Libres.

Back in Washington, with only two weeks to go before Operation Zapata went into action, Kennedy received a 4,000-word memo from William Fulbright that made him second-guess his approval of the operation. Fulbright was the Chairman of the Senate Foreign Relations Committee, and his memo argued strongly against military action in Cuba for political reasons. It would be impossible to disguise U.S. involvement, Fulbright argued, and if the invasion met with resistance or failed to incite an uprising in its support, the United States would be forced to use overt military force to support it. "If we came to that," Fulbright's memo stated, "even under the paper cover of legitimacy, we would have undone the work of thirty years [in trying to stabilize Latin America]." Fulbright recommended that it was a far better idea for the President to seek a diplomatic solution.

Unable to decide between the hawkish CIA plan and a more diplomatic solution, President Kennedy invited Fulbright to the White House to present his case against the CIA's plan. Ten days before the air strikes were scheduled to begin, Fulbright delivered an eloquent and impassioned speech that outlined his case against military action in Cuba. When he sat down at the end of his talk, not one of Kennedy's advisers reacted. "What do you think," the President asked his men, "yes or no?" No one answered. The room was quiet except for the sound of Kennedy's fingers drumming repeatedly on the table. Finally, a foreign policy staffer who'd been in the White House since the Roosevelt era broke the silence. "There has to be a confrontation with Castro sooner or later," he said, "so . . . I say let 'er rip!" Following the older man's lead, Kennedy's group of advisers broke their silence and voiced their continued support of the plan.

Though he said nothing at the meeting, Arthur Schlesinger, Kennedy's Special Adviser and his close personal friend for over a dozen years, informed the President in private just afterward that the plan made sense only if one focused on Cuba and nothing else. When one considered "the hemisphere and the rest of the world," Schlesinger hastily wrote to Kennedy in a memo, "the arguments against this decision begin to gain force." He pointed out that the U.S. involvement would be obvious and that the political and diplomatic repercussions would be severe. "At one stroke," Schlesinger wrote, "it would dissipate all the extraordinary good will which has been rising toward the new Administration through the world." Putting it bluntly, Schlesinger wrote, "This operation is a terrible idea."

Now President Kennedy was deeply conflicted, and there was only a week until the launch of Operation Zapata. Dulles saw that Kennedy was wavering and pushed harder, telling the President, "We have a disposal problem. If we have to take these men out of Guatemala, we will have to transfer them to the United States, and we can't have them wandering around the country telling everyone what they have been doing." Dulles' subsequent words of action sounded virile next to Schlesinger's political concern that the United States not be seen as a bully. Kennedy didn't want to be remembered as a weak President who couldn't follow through with Eisenhower's plan for protecting the country. He decided to trust the more experienced CIA Director over Senator Fulbright, his friend Schlesinger, and his own State Department. He would allow Operation Zapata to move forward.

Dulles, convinced that the march to Cuba would be "a military cakewalk," left Washington to spend the invasion weekend at an exclusive club in Puerto Rico. All was going according to plan when Operation Zapata went into effect on April 15. The vintage B-26s flew from Nicaragua to attack Castro's air force. Reports came back to Washington that the strike was successful and that Castro's air capability had been 80 percent eliminated. The CIA canceled all air support for the beach, as it would be unnecessary if Castro had no planes.

Two days later the moment of invasion arrived. On April 17, just after midnight, the CIA-trained brigadistas boarded ships bound for Cuba. When the landing point came into sight, however, the beach glowed with light instead of the deserted houses the men had expected. In fact, several families were living in the area, constructing houses for a new development Castro had planned. The brigade captains reacted instantly to this U.S. intelligence oversight, making plans to imprison the civilians on shore. But even as they were in the process of doing so, another intelligence failure devastated them—their boats crashed against rocks and coral reefs. The razor-sharp protrusions punctured the bottoms of two ships, causing one to sink. Wet, tired, and scraped up, when the men finally arrived on shore, they discovered materiél from a reconnaissance team, including a warm radio. It was clear Castro had been warned.

When Castro received a distress signal from the Bay of Pigs at 3:15 a.m. on Monday, April 17, he wasn't the least bit surprised. As Kennedy predicted, Castro had used the information he gleaned from American newspapers to take precautions against an invasion. For months he told the Cubans that "an aggression" was coming and had aired training videos on television to prepare his citizens against attack. Cuban children were playing "Cubans and Yankee invaders" instead of "Cowboys and Indians." To make matters worse, not only was the Bay of Pigs far from the deserted beach the CIA had planned for, it was Castro's favorite fishing spot as well. As Castro mobilized his fighters in a war against the United States, he had the incalculable advantage of being intimate with the difficult terrain of battle.

While Adlai Stevenson, the U.S. Ambassador to the United Nations, tried to defend his country against allegations of unprovoked attack, Castro himself led Cuba's defense of the Bay of Pigs. Contrary to CIA intelligence estimates, the advance air strikes had destroyed only a handful of Castro's planes. The rest of his air force was fully functional, and though the brigadistas fought hard for their toehold, they were outnumbered and had no defense against Castro's aerial bombardments. And local Cubans were hardly rising to help; in fact, they were fighting against the exile force. In another clever move, Castro had rounded up thousands of people identified as potential rebels and imprisoned them days before the invasion.

In Washington, Kennedy and his staff gave the illusion that it was a day like any other. But behind White House walls, the President and his advisers agonized over every detail of the attack. It was clear that the invasion was failing, but in its frenzy to maintain secrecy, the CIA had provided only spotty means for the brigadistas to contact Washington. As a result, transmissions from the beach had to go through several channels and were often a few hours old by the time they reached Kennedy and his men. When messages finally did get through, the news coming from Cuba was bad.

But to maintain cover, President Kennedy had to keep his
schedule. That evening, he and the First Lady threw the Annual
Congressional Reception. Some 450 men and women arrived at
the White House for the white tie affair, and President Kennedy
appeared as genial and charming as ever. When the last of his
guests left after midnight, however, Kennedy rushed to the Cabinet
Room to join officials from the CIA, the State Department, and
the Joint Chiefs. The President and most of the others were still
in formal party attire.

The attitude in the room was grim. No one understood why
the mission had gone awry. The most powerful men in the world
had botched the invasion of a disorganized, third-world island.
"The limits and dilemmas of power," Kennedy would later write
of that evening, "the relationship of power to the fate of human
beings was never more clear or poignant." All Kennedy and his
staff could do was to wait for the trickle of bad news that was
obsolete by the time it reached them.

Admiral Arleigh Burke, the Chief of Naval Operations, was
desperate to salvage the invasion and save Brigade 2506. He
paced the room, muttering "Balls!" to himself over and over. The
brigade was repeatedly and emphatically broadcasting desperate
messages for help. But President Kennedy could do nothing now,
and their pleas were repeatedly and emphatically denied.

"Can I send in an air strike?" Burke asked Kennedy.

"No."

"Can we send in a few planes?"

"No, because they could be identified as United States."

"Can we get something in there?"

"No."

"If you'll let me have two destroyers, we'll give gunfire support and we can hold that beachhead with two ships forever."

"No."

"One destroyer, Mr. President?"

"No."

Earlier that day, Kennedy had received a letter from Chairman Khrushchev threatening a Soviet military response if he intensified U.S. intervention in Cuba. "I hope that the Government of the U.S.A. will consider our views dictated by the sole concern not to allow steps which could lead to a military catastrophe," Khrushchev's letter concluded. It was a threat Kennedy had to take seriously. He had gambled on the invasion and was losing; the stakes were far too high to increase his bet by engaging the Soviets. But he had to do something. In a last-minute compromise, Kennedy authorized one hour of air support to try to save the men on the beach.

A CIA operative alerted Pepe San Román, who had just watched one of Castro's tanks run over a 16-year-old fighter.

"Where have you been, you son of a bitch? Where the hell have you been? You have abandoned us," Pepe said.

"I know that you have your problems, but I've had mine," answered the CIA contact. "We will go in tonight."

"That's what you said yesterday and you didn't come."

In a final blunder of unbelievable proportions, the six fighter jets Kennedy authorized arrived too late. No one had remembered to calculate the one-hour time difference between Washington, D.C., and Nicaragua. By then the invasion was finished. As the Cuban brigadistas watched the sun rise the next morning, Kennedy cried in his bedroom. He would have to leave the force in Cuba to be captured or to die.

With the death of an entire squadron of men on his conscience, the Soviets breathing down his neck, and his most experienced advisers exposed as incompetent and sloppy, Kennedy realized that it was time to start making his own decisions.

When it came time to face the press later that day, Kennedy ignored questions about who was to blame. "There's an old saying that victory has a hundred fathers and defeat is an orphan. What matters," he told the gathered crowd of reporters, "is only one fact, that I am the responsible officer of this government." President Kennedy had learned that he alone could decide what happened in his White House, and from now on he was determined to make those decisions count.

When Dulles returned to Baltimore from his resort trip, a CIA agent informed him of Operation Zapata's fantastic failure. "We're hanging on by our fingernails," he told the Director, "this thing is all going to hell." But Dulles refused to call the President until the next afternoon, preferring instead to lock himself up in his home with a bottle of scotch. Bissell attributed the failure in Cuba to "my inexperience in paramilitary matters and over involvement in presenting and pressing the case on behalf of the agency." Kennedy didn't need excuses, and he didn't need men like this anymore. Kennedy fired Dulles and Bissell.

The President installed his most trusted friends and staff in foreign policy positions. It was the dawn of a new political era, and Kennedy planned to put far more weight on diplomacy than on unilateral military action. And for that, Kennedy would need reason and competence in his advisers, not the haughty know-it-all attitude of his former CIA men.

Just over a year later, President Kennedy's newly installed

staff would face their own first crisis. As a final consequence of the Bay of Pigs fiasco, Castro's fear of the United States had pushed him into an alliance with the Soviet Union. The Soviets now moved nuclear missiles into Cuba in defense of their newfound ally. Khrushchev belligerently challenged the United States, and Kennedy's Joint Chiefs clamored for war.

For 13 tense days, the world watched as President Kennedy skillfully dismissed the militant tendencies of his Joint Chiefs and Khrushchev. Though Kennedy immediately ordered a naval blockade of the island, he relied far more on diplomacy than military action. "Our goal is not the victory of might, but the vindication of right," Kennedy told the nation in a radio address, "not peace at the expense of freedom, but both peace and freedom." In the end, he calmly and confidently negotiated the delicate situation and accomplished both.

In 1986, 25 years after the Bay of Pigs fiasco, the last imprisoned member of Brigade 2506 was released from a Havana jail at the request of Kennedy's brother, Senator Edward Kennedy. Though old and weak, 57-year-old Ramon Conte Hernandez stood firm in his dedication to overthrowing Castro. "I don't want to say that the fight is over. Cuba is not free. . . . I'll continue to be a soldier of freedom here and everywhere." Hernandez, accompanied on his flight to Miami by his 82-year-old mother, was one of nine brigadistas who had not been returned to the United States in a political deal that Kennedy brokered in 1962—$53 million in food and medical supplies for the prisoners' release. "I thank the Americans for all they've done," Hernandez said, "and I'll continue to be a soldier of freedom here and everywhere."

Mr. Catledge, members of the American Society of Newspaper Editors, ladies and gentlemen:

The President of a great democracy such as ours, and the editors of great newspapers such as yours, owe a common obligation to the people: an obligation to present the facts, to present them with candor, and to present them in perspective. It is with that obligation in mind that I have decided in the last 24 hours to discuss briefly at this time the recent events in Cuba.

On that unhappy island, as in so many other arenas of the contest for freedom, the news has grown worse instead of better. I have emphasized before that this was a struggle of Cuban patriots against a Cuban dictator. While we could not be expected to hide our sympathies, we made it repeatedly clear that the armed forces of this country would not intervene in any way.

Any unilateral American intervention, in the absence of an external attack upon ourselves or an ally, would have been contrary to our traditions and to our international obligations. But let the record show that our restraint is not inexhaustible. Should it ever appear that the inter-American doctrine of non-interference merely conceals or excuses a policy of nonaction—if the nations of this Hemisphere should fail to meet their commitments against outside Communist penetration—then I want it clearly understood that this Government will not hesitate in meeting its primary obligations which are to the security of our Nation!

Should that time ever come, we do not intend to be lectured on "intervention" by those whose character was stamped for all time on the bloody streets of Budapest! Nor would we expect or accept the same outcome which this small band of gallant Cuban refugees must have known that they were chancing, determined as they were against heavy odds to pursue their courageous attempts to regain their Island's freedom.

But Cuba is not an island unto itself; and our concern is not ended by mere expressions of nonintervention or regret. This is not the first time in either ancient or recent history that a small band of freedom fighters has engaged the armor of totalitarianism.

It is not the first time that Communist tanks have rolled over gallant men and women fighting to redeem the independence of their homeland. Nor is it by any means the final episode in the eternal struggle of liberty against tyranny, anywhere on the face of the globe, including Cuba itself.

Mr. Castro has said that these were mercenaries. According to press reports, the final message to be relayed from the refugee forces on the beach came from the rebel commander when asked if he wished to be evacuated. His answer was: "I will never leave this country." That is not the reply of a mercenary. He has gone now to join in the mountains countless other guerrilla fighters, who are equally determined that the dedication of those who gave their lives shall not be forgotten, and that Cuba must not be abandoned to the Communists. And we do not intend to abandon it either!

The Cuban people have not yet spoken their final piece. And I have no doubt that they and their Revolutionary Council, led by Dr. Cardona—and members of the families of the Revolutionary Council, I am informed by the Doctor yesterday, are involved themselves in the Islands—will continue to speak up for a free and independent Cuba.

Meanwhile we will not accept Mr. Castro's attempts to blame this nation for the hatred which his onetime supporters now regard his repression. But there are from this sobering episode useful lessons for us all to learn. Some may be still obscure, and await further information. Some are clear today.

First, it is clear that the forces of communism are not to be underestimated, in Cuba or anywhere else in the world. The advantages of a police state—its use of mass terror and arrests to prevent the spread of free dissent—cannot be overlooked by those who expect the fall of every fanatic tyrant. If the self-discipline of the free cannot match the iron discipline of the mailed fist—in economic, political, scientific and all the other kinds of struggles as well as the military—then the peril to freedom will continue to rise.

Secondly, it is clear that this Nation, in concert with all the free nations of this hemisphere, must take an ever closer and more realistic look at the menace of external Communist intervention and domination in Cuba. The American people are not complacent about Iron Curtain tanks and planes less than 90 miles from their shore. But a nation of Cuba's size is less a threat to our survival than it is a base for subverting the survival of other free nations throughout the hemisphere. It is not primarily our interest or our security but theirs which is now, today, in the greater peril. It is for their sake as well as our own that we must show our will.

The evidence is clear—and the hour is late. We and our Latin friends will have to face the fact that we cannot postpone any longer the real issue of survival of freedom in this hemisphere itself. On that issue, unlike perhaps some others, there can be no middle ground. Together we must build a hemisphere where freedom can flourish; and where any free nation under outside attack of any kind can be assured that all of our resources stand ready to respond to any request for assistance.

Third, and finally, it is clearer than ever that we face a relentless struggle in every corner of the globe that goes far beyond the clash of armies or even nuclear armaments. The armies are there, and in large number. The nuclear armaments are there. But they serve primarily as the shield behind which subversion, infiltration, and a host of other tactics steadily advance, picking off vulnerable areas one by one in situations which do not permit our own armed intervention.

Power is the hallmark of this offensive power and discipline and deceit. The legitimate discontent of yearning people is exploited. The legitimate trappings of self-determination are employed. But once in power, all talk of discontent is repressed; all self-determination disappears, and the promise of a revolution of hope is betrayed, as in Cuba, into—a reign of terror. Those who on instruction staged automatic "riots" in the streets of free nations over the efforts of a small group of young Cubans to regain their freedom should recall the long roll call of refugees who cannot now go back—to Hungary, to North Korea, to North Viet-Nam, to East Germany, or to Poland, or to any of the other lands from which a steady stream of refugees pours forth, in eloquent testimony to the cruel oppression now holding sway in their homeland.

We dare not fail to see the insidious nature of this new and deeper struggle. We dare not fail to grasp the new concepts, the new tools, the new sense of urgency we will need to combat it—whether in Cuba or South Viet-Nam. And we dare not fail to realize that this struggle is taking place every day, without fanfare, in thousands of villages and markets—day and night— and in classrooms all over the globe.

The message of Cuba, of Laos, of the rising din of Communist voices in Asia and Latin America—these messages are all the same. The complacent, the self-indulgent, the soft societies are about to be swept away with the debris of history. Only the strong, only the industrious, only the determined, only the courageous, only the visionary who determine the real nature of our struggle can possibly survive.

No greater task faces this country or this administration. No other challenge is more deserving of our every effort and energy.

Too long we have fixed our eyes on traditional military needs, on armies prepared to cross borders, on missiles poised for flight. Now it should be clear that this is no longer enough—that our security may be lost piece by piece, country by country, without the bring of a single missile or the crossing of a single border.

We intend to profit from this lesson. We intend to reexamine and reorient our forces of all kinds—our tactics and our institutions here in this community. We intend to intensify our efforts for a struggle in many ways more difficult than war, where disappointment will often accompany us.

For I am convinced that we in this country and in the free world possess the necessary resource, and the skill, and the added strength that comes from a belief in the freedom of man. And I am equally convinced that history will record the fact that this bitter struggle reached its climax in the late 1950s and the early 1960s Let me then make clear as the President of the United States that I am determined upon our system's survival and success, regardless of the cost and regardless of the peril!

PRESIDENT GEORGE W. BUSH DELIVERS THE COMMENCEMENT ADDRESS AT WEST POINT, 2002.

© Reuters / CORBIS

CHAPTER 16

THE MUSHROOM CLOUD

———————•———————

George W. Bush and the Iraq War

On June 7, 1981, a squadron of desert-camouflaged Israeli F-16s raced across Saudi Arabia's northern desert floor, escorted by F-15 fighters. At sunset, the formation penetrated Iraqi airspace and, several minutes later, banked hard north, up the Euphrates Valley.

As the jets pressed toward their target, the F-15s pulled up to establish a defensive perimeter high in the sky. The F-16s, retrofitted especially for this mission, closed in on a gigantic dome south of Baghdad. In choreographed order, each F-16 bled airspeed, pulled straight up above the massive cupola, and as the aircraft went vertical, dropped two 2,200-pound gravity bombs in a "sling" maneuver. Eight passes, 16 bombs, and they accelerated away—a fiery concrete-steel shell collapsed in their wake.

That fiery shell had been a $275-million French-built Tammuz 1 nuclear reactor, weeks away from going "hot." One French technician was killed in the attack.

The Israeli strike was vehemently condemned in the Arab world, the Soviet Union, across Europe, at the U.N. Security Council, and by the White House in the United States.

Israel bristled at the international censure following its attack. Prime Minister Menachem Begin referred to the bombing raid as "anticipatory self-defense." He pointed out that France had started to provide weapons-grade uranium to the Iraqis, which Saddam Hussein (then a little-known dictator in power for only two years) could use to manufacture "in the near future, between three and five Hiroshima-type nuclear bombs." A major oil-producing country certainly did not need a large-scale atomic reactor for energy.

Leaders and governments worldwide vilified Israel, but behind closed doors, they let out a collective sigh of relief.

Almost 22 years later, two matte black American F-117 stealth fighters penetrated Iraqi airspace in the dead of night. Traveling at subsonic speed without escort, they also vectored for a target south of Baghdad, Dora Farm. The mission had been prompted by Rokan, one of the CIA's "Rock Star" informants operating inside Iraq. Rokan had been one of the best and most reliable of supersecret sources. Others of the Rock Stars had been lately uncovered by Saddam's security apparatus—these men were tortured and executed, as were their families. This had deterred many of the in-country operatives, but not Rokan. He called on his satellite phone frequently with reams of crucial information.

On March 19, 2003, Rokan delivered the most urgent intelligence yet. Secretary of Defense Donald Rumsfeld and CIA Director George Tenet raced to the White House. Inside the President's small dining room just off the Oval Office they briefed George W. Bush on the Rock Stars operation and Rokan's report in particular. The well-placed agent had a "real-time" location for Saddam and his sons. As Bush's war council discussed the potential for a "decapitation" strike against Saddam, another report came in—Rokan had eyes on Uday and Qusay Hussein at that very moment, and it seemed the father would be returning late that night.

Ordering a strike on Saddam's Dora Farm compound might throw the Iraqi military into chaos and prevent the looming war, but it would definitely be a risky operation for the pilots; the attack might kill only wives and children, and U.S. forces were not yet in place if Saddam retaliated by launching missiles at Israel or setting oil fields afire. George W. Bush decided to make the play.

That Bush had become the man to make that decision came as a surprise to many, including perhaps the President himself. "Right now, I should be in a bar in Texas, not the Oval Office," he told a group of religious leaders in September 2002. "I found faith. I found God. I am here because of the power of prayer."

An evangelical Christian and a man whose drinking problem provoked him to go sober at age 40, George W. had turned his life around.

Bush had once described his existence as "drinking, and carousing, and fumbling around." The grandson of a Senator and son of a President, he had much to live up to and always fell short. His father excelled as a scholar and athlete at Yale—George W. maintained a C average and lived the life of a dissolute frat boy. His father, the youngest combat pilot in the World War II Navy, was shot down in the Pacific and rescued by submarine— George W. joined the Air National Guard and lost his flying privileges because he stopped showing up. His father had made a tidy fortune in the Texas oil business—George W. drilled holes and lost millions. And his father had served in some of the most important posts for the U.S. government—George W. failed in a quixotic run for Congress. Young George made the effort, sort of, but it just never worked out. "Life takes its own turns, makes its own demands, writes its own story," he would say, "and along the way, we start to realize we are not the author."

Though they shared a name, the father and son were very different men. George H. W. Bush was an establishment patrician from Greenwich, Connecticut, while George W. saw himself as a West Texas good ol' boy. According to one Bush cousin, "Dubya" always felt he was too coarse and rough-edged for his father. Even during the elder Bush's presidency, the first son was told to sit at the opposite end of the table when the British royals arrived and was ordered not to speak to them. At lunch, when Queen Elizabeth II asked the First Lady what made her son the black sheep of the family, Barbara Bush mentioned that George W. spoke a little too bluntly and always wore what he wanted—like cowboy boots with "Texas" or "God Bless America" on them. (When the queen asked George W. which pair he would wear to the state dinner that evening, he told her, "Neither. Tonight's pair will say 'God Save the Queen.'")

But then something changed. While other men his age suffered midlife crises striving to be younger, George W. experienced his own crisis of conscience and suddenly . . . matured. The drinking stopped, he accepted Christ as his personal savior, and he started running. He ran every day—a steady demanding pace with a slight acceleration toward the end. The once prodigal son became a model of self-discipline.

George W. worked hard to help his father win election in 1988. That success burnished young George's image to others and himself. Four years later, his father's loss for a second term made him intensely angry: "Those were such strong emotions for me, to see a good man get whipped." But somehow it only further focused and propelled George W.—first to the Texas governorship, then to an overwhelming reelection, and from there, straight to the White House. (In the meantime, he also made a fortune selling his stake in the Texas Rangers baseball team.) It was as if his father's first real failure had driven George W. to astonishing success.

Not that George H. W. Bush hadn't played a crucial role in his son's rise. "Poppy" Bush's colleagues and advisers served in many of the highest posts in George W.'s presidential campaign, the subsequent election controversy, and then in his administration. Notwithstanding, the younger Bush had a very different take on himself and his presidency—his Texan attitude and positions had more in common with Ronald Reagan than his own father. After he moved into the White House, he did not allow the burdens of office to vary a rigid routine that included ample time for exercise and plenty of sleep. As former Bush speechwriter David Frum described, "Bush was not a lightweight. He was, rather, a very unfamiliar type of heavyweight. Words often failed him, his memory sometimes betrayed him, but his vision was large and clear. And when he perceived new possibilities, he had the courage to act on them."

When I first met George W. Bush at a small luncheon for reporters, the reality was a sharp contrast to the popular image. During a policy discussion, the President was in charge—in command of facts, of the nuances of policy, and of the room. Though Vice President Dick Cheney sat directly across the table from him, Bush barely acknowledged Cheney, who said little. "Politics is all about perception," Bush once told his campaign advisers, and apparently he made a point never to repeat his father's mistakes.

As for the man himself, again Frum, who spent many hours with the President, may have captured him best—"George Bush is a very unusual person: a good man who is not a weak man. He has many faults. He is impatient and quick to anger; sometimes glib, even dogmatic; often uncurious and as a result ill-informed; more conventional in his thinking than a leader probably should be. But outweighing the faults are his virtues: decency, honesty, rectitude, courage, and tenacity."

The decision to go to war in Afghanistan was not a hard one for President Bush. After the events of September 11, 2001, the American people and many nations of the world rallied behind the White House commitment to root out terrorism. True to his cowboy image, George W. vowed to take Osama Bin Laden "dead or alive" and "smoke [his terror network] out of their caves." Critics scorned the President's crude notion of frontier justice, but, actually, Bush showed remarkable restraint before launching an attack. Many Americans wanted immediate action, but Bush waited almost a month before dropping the first bombs over Afghanistan. And when he told the world that "we will make no distinction between the terrorists who committed these acts and those who harbor them," he rewrote the rules for international relations.

The 9/11 attacks gave Bush popularity, stature, and most important, a clarity of purpose for his presidency. "My job is to protect America," he said, "and that's exactly what I'm going to do." The born-again Christian President, who opened every Cabinet meeting with a prayer, described the war on terror as "a monumental struggle between good and evil." New York Senator Charles Schumer remarked, "He told me several times that he is staking his entire presidency on this, that the mark of whether he's successful is whether he can succeed in his goal of wiping out terrorism."

But the President's "eureka moment," as one administration official called it, came when American soldiers made a harrowing discovery in Afghanistan: al-Qaeda had been actively seeking weapons of mass destruction (WMD). Vice President Dick Cheney had long been obsessed with the subject, believing the gravest threat facing America was a chemical, biological, or nuclear attack on an American city. In that context, 9/11 was just a wake-up call.

With this in mind, Bush and his war Cabinet developed a new policy—the United States would take action to eliminate threats to national security before an attack. "I will not wait on events while dangers gather. I will not stand by as peril draws closer and closer," Bush said at a West Point commencement. The United States would preempt the enemy—no more free first shots. National Security Adviser Condoleezza Rice explained the new thinking in an interview: "We don't want the smoking gun to be a mushroom cloud."

If al-Qaeda sought WMD, one man came to mind who might provide them. And if "the sins of the father are to be laid upon the children," then this would be an appropriate piece of unfinished business for George W. to dispatch. Texan Bush would clean up what Connecticut Bush had left behind. If there was ever a time to trump everything the old man had ever accomplished, here it was.

In late February 1991, after six weeks of air bombing and only two days of ground operations, the decimated Iraqi military was trying to get out of Kuwait City as fast as possible. But first, they looted everything they could—cars, suitcases of clothes, bags of flour, children's books, even a white wedding dress. Iraqi military vehicles, trucks, and stolen compacts made for Highway 6 toward Basra. It was a chaotic nighttime convoy along four lanes of unlit roadway.

As the caravan made its dash for the border, a dozen American F-15s converged on the "target-rich environment." Bombing the front and rear of the caravan, the warplanes trapped and then hammered thousands of vehicles in the desert darkness. Trucks crashed into one another and cars drove off the pavement, getting stuck in the sand. Terrified Iraqis ran for their lives.

When the media reached the scene a day later, pictures of charred, dismembered bodies in pools of blood circulated worldwide. It would become known as the "Highway of Death," and human-rights groups were outraged by America's attack on helpless victims.

As Chairman of the Joint Chiefs of Staff, General Colin Powell told then-President Bush that it would be "un-American and unchivalrous" to continue fighting the Iraqis. Bush, attuned to the media's impact on recent events, agreed. He wanted a cease-fire and believed that domestic forces in Iraq would topple Saddam Hussein. Bush told his commander in the field, General Norman Schwarzkopf, "We're starting to pick up some undesirable public and political baggage with all those scenes of the carnage. . . . Why not end it?" The Gulf War would be a "clean" victory. To stop the war after only 100 hours would be a courageous decision by the Commander in Chief, reflecting the will of his advisers, the Congress, the media, the American people, and the world at large.

Only the decision badly misread the situation on the ground in Iraq—it became a misstep with profound implications for years to come. The "Highway of Death" may have been smoldering rubble, but most of the Iraqi military had actually survived by jumping and running; the result was much less lethal than it had first appeared. By ending the war prematurely, two Iraqi Republican Guard divisions, up to 700 tanks, and a lethal fleet of attack helicopters were allowed to escape safely back to Iraq. In the immediate aftermath of the Gulf War, those tanks and helicopters killed tens of thousands of Shiites in Basra and Kurds in the north as Saddam reestablished control over his country.

Over the next 12 years, Saddam flouted America's cease-fire terms and U.N. sanctions, becoming ever more emboldened.

Just as the senior Bush had unilaterally stopped a war with Iraq, George W. was thinking of starting one. Poppy had considered marching into Baghdad as "not prudent"; George W. wanted to head straight for Baghdad with the intention of capturing or killing Saddam and his henchmen. "If you know what you believe," President Bush said at an elementary school, "decisions come pretty easy. If you're one of those types of people that are always trying to figure out which way the wind is blowing, decision-making can be difficult. But I find that I know who I am. I know what I believe in, and I know where I want to lead the country." George W. would redeem the error of his father's ways.

From the intelligence he received, Bush believed Iraq possessed WMD as well as links to al-Qaeda. The President's resolve became singular in its mission: prevent the devastating act of state-sponsored terrorism that seemed all too inevitable. He asked Secretary Rumsfeld and General Tommy Franks to plan for options in Iraq.

With or without WMD, Bush also became convinced that Saddam was a thug who needed to be ousted for humanitarian reasons alone. *The New York Times* reported that "Saddam Hussein, in his 23 years in power, plunged [his] country into a bloodbath of medieval proportions, and exported some of that terror to his neighbors." According to Human Rights Watch, by war and terror, Saddam had killed a million Iraqis—290,000 civilians (50,000 to 100,000 Kurds by nerve agents and mustard gas in 1987–88) and the rest attributable to the wars he caused in Iran and Kuwait. Witnesses and victims cataloged the atrocities of the secret police: raping wives and daughters to force confessions, eye-gougings, electrocutions, acid baths, and assassinations. Many more victims had been tortured and maimed. In 1999, to curtail complaints of prison overcrowding, possibly thousands of inmates were systematically executed. According to Britain's Prime Minister Tony Blair, speaking in 2003, 400,000 children had died in Iraq in the previous five years as a result of the regime stealing or preventing the delivery of food and medical supplies from the international community. A U.S. congressional investigation uncovered that Saddam himself stole $11 billion from the United Nations' oil-for-food program. That Saddam venerated Joseph Stalin came as no surprise. Bush told Australia's Prime Minister John Howard, "Every speech I give, I remind them of the atrocities of the regime."

In his State of the Union address in January 2002, the President identified Iraq as part of an "axis of evil, arming to threaten the peace of the world." One *Washington Post* columnist called the President's "astonishingly bold" speech "just short of a declaration of war." Bush rallied America for the difficult job ahead. "The American people want a big bang," explained the President. "I have to convince them that this is a war that will be fought with many steps."

War-planning meetings on Iraq now took place regularly, with the President in attendance. A rift quickly developed between the State Department and the Pentagon. Secretary of State Colin Powell believed the Pentagon had swayed Bush to go to war, but really he had always been on Cheney's and Rumsfeld's side. Once, when National Security Adviser Condoleezza Rice met in her office with three U.S. Senators to discuss international support for a firm stand against Saddam, the President ducked his head in. "Fuck Saddam. We're taking him out," said Bush as the Senators laughed uncomfortably. Even so, Powell was able to convince Bush to offer a resolution to the United Nations to send weapons inspectors back to Iraq.

The U.N. resolution passed. Now the President could push forward on the paths of both the State Department and the Pentagon. On each front he maintained a steady, demanding pace.

Though Chief U.N. Weapons Inspector Hans Blix claimed not to find any WMD in Iraq, CIA intelligence indicated he was withholding information in his reports—many of Bush's closest advisers believed Blix was lying. When Bush asked CIA Director George Tenet if Iraq had these weapons, Tenet told him it was a "slam dunk." Saddam had actually used WMD in the 1980s, was known to have hidden them in the 1990s, and, now, as Vice President Cheney asked, if he had no WMD, "Why in the world would he subject himself for all those years to U.N. sanctions and forgo an estimated $100 billion in oil revenue? It made no sense!" Even Egypt's President Hosni Mubarak confirmed that his own intelligence network had located WMD labs.

Powell kept up the drumbeat for diplomacy. He argued that the Middle East seethed with anti-Americanism and that an attack by the United States would only give Islamic terrorists another recruiting tool. Powell believed that if America committed to war, at the very least, it needed a coalition of allies, comparable to what Bush's father had built before in the Gulf War. Also, the Secretary of State and others noted that from a military point of view, Saddam might use chemical or biological weapons against U.S. troops. He could set oil fields on fire, disrupting world supply at a time when the American economy was still struggling. He might withdraw his forces into Baghdad, forcing American troops to fight an urban war that could result in huge casualties. Or the dictator could try to spread the war to other countries, lobbing Scud missiles at Israel or Saudi Arabia. On top of all that, Powell believed the war plans needed significantly more troops than the Pentagon had provided for. To add to the almost Freudian drama, Brent Scowcroft, National Security Adviser and close associate to Bush's father, wrote in *The Wall Street Journal* that an invasion would turn the Middle East into a "cauldron." Was Scowcroft actually stating the position of George H. W. Bush?

Shortly after the start of 2003, President Bush brought Powell to the Oval Office. "Time to put your war uniform on," he told the former general.

As Bush prepared to go to war, he maintained his disciplined schedule. He went to bed early, woke up early, and reserved an hour for running and exercise. His father had told him that he did not get enough sleep during the Gulf War, a fact he later regretted. Bush would not make the same mistake. But, interestingly, the President did not seek counsel from his own father, who had been in such a similar situation. "You know," said Bush, "he is the wrong father to appeal to in terms of strength. There is a Higher Father that I appeal to."

As war appeared imminent, millions of people in the United States, Europe, and across the world took to the streets in mass protests against U.S. policy in Iraq. Demonstrators called Bush a butcher and a murderer. Some U.S. allies spoke openly against invasion. Prime Minister Tony Blair, who supported Bush, risked losing his government over the matter.

But Bush believed fiercely that going to war was less of a gamble than waiting for Saddam to either use his weapons of mass destruction or share them with terrorists. "[I]f we wait for threats to fully materialize, we have waited too long," he said. He also believed that the toppling of Saddam might help reshape the Middle East: "Freedom is God's gift to everyone in the world." Bush's hallmarks would be preemption and the aggressive promotion of democracy, and he was not about to relent on either.

In early March 2003, Bush called leaders of nations on the U.N. Security Council, trying to gather their votes for a second resolution to authorize force in dealing with Saddam, but it was no use. After months of diplomacy, Bush was more isolated than ever. "If we have to go it alone, we'll go it alone," said Bush, "but I'd rather not." America would have to invade with significant troops from only Britain and Spain. There would be no grand coalition like his father's. Bush was not deterred.

"Whether you agree with him or not," said Senator Charles Schumer of the President, "one of Bush's strengths is that he goes with his instincts. And at a time like this, when the winds are swirling around in all different directions, a president is well served who has his own internal gyroscope."

At 8 p.m. on March 17, Bush issued an ultimatum giving Saddam 48 hours to leave his country. Early on March 19, with the deadline drawing near, the President convened his war Cabinet in the White House. U.S. commanders in the Middle East were hooked up by video link. "You could have heard a pin drop," said one person who was present. Saddam had stayed put, so the President read his order: "For the peace of the world and the benefit and freedom of the Iraqi people, I hereby give the order to execute Operation Iraqi Freedom." He then stood, saluted his commanders, and walked out of the room with tears in his eyes. He took a walk outside and prayed.

Under a starlit desert night, the two F-117 stealth fighters sped toward Dora Farm. The jets had each been loaded with a pair of EGBU-27 bunker-busting bombs. The pilots engaged their laser-guided targeting mechanisms and then bore down for the pass. Their mission would be followed by a strike package of 16 sea-launched Tomahawk cruise missiles.

In Washington, President Bush was getting television makeup put on in a study next to the Oval Office when the Deputy National Security Adviser informed him that the F-117s had successfully delivered their payloads but were still in Iraqi airspace. At 10:16 p.m., President Bush addressed the country to announce that the war against Saddam Hussein had begun. "This will not be a campaign of half measures," he told the nation.

Back at Dora Farm, an eyewitness reported that Saddam's sons had survived the attack. But Saddam himself had been hurt and had to be dug out of the wreckage and put into an ambulance. "Rock Star" Rokan, the crucial source leading to the strike, was killed by a cruise missile while still at his post.

Militarily, the war succeeded. Saddam did not use chemical or biological weapons on American troops because it seemed he had none. Oil fields did not burn. Instead of withdrawing into Baghdad for a last stand, the Iraqi Army melted away, and the capital fell only three weeks after the start of the war. In December 2003, American soldiers captured Saddam in a hole near a farmhouse outside his hometown.

However, rebuilding Iraq after the war proved far more difficult than the President and his team had anticipated. Unrest, and then violence, ripped through the country. Many more American soldiers died during the postwar occupation than perished during combat. No weapons of mass destruction have been found in Iraq to date. Notwithstanding, Bush would stay the course—even if he shifted the primary rationale for the invasion. In his 2004 State of the Union address, he stated, "For all those who love freedom and peace, the world without Saddam Hussein's regime is a better and safer place."

But the American public grew just as divided over the war in Iraq as they had been about much of the Bush presidency. Much of the intelligence that prompted the war turned out to have been mistaken. Critics argued that by invading Iraq, Bush had endangered the United States on two fronts: he had neglected the more important war against al-Qaeda worldwide, and he had incited the Arab masses against America, which could result in more terrorism. At the very least, the planning for postwar Iraq had been inadequate and naive. Secretary of State Colin Powell had famously told Bush the "Pottery Barn rule" regarding the invasion: "You break it, you own it." Now Bush—and his nation—were responsible for the creation of a stable, secure, and pluralistic society in a faroff land.

The President seemed comfortable with that daunting challenge. He adamantly refused to concede mistakes in policy or planning, and very rarely in execution (the systematic abuse of Iraqi prisoners being a notable exception). He had a vision for protecting America, and he was more than willing to risk his presidency for what he believed was right. And as the 2004 presidential campaign came into focus, it seemed ever more likely that Bush's political fortunes were directly linked to his policies in Iraq.

Other Presidents before him had risked their own presidencies for what they believed was right for the nation. Jefferson kept the country out of war by introducing an oppressive embargo. Lincoln drew fire from the people of two nations—the Union and the Confederacy—when he declared the Emancipation Proclamation. Truman, against the advice of his military and risking World War III, made the Soviet Union blink first in Berlin. And Ronald Reagan, who so many considered an unsophisticated cold warrior, made the world dramatically better and safer through the force of his vision and will. The history of the office, the importance of its decisions, and the resolve demanded of our leaders is not likely lost on President Bush. Indeed, the desk he sits behind was also used by Franklin Roosevelt and John Kennedy.

On May 21, 2003, President Bush flew a Navy warplane
toward a landing on the deck of the *USS Abraham Lincoln*
aircraft carrier in the Pacific to declare the end of "major combat
operations." He wore a Navy flight suit. It was possibly the first
time a sitting President had worn military garb since George
Washington led his troops to suppress the Whiskey Rebellion
and preserve the young nation's fragile fabric two centuries
earlier. By boldly confronting what he believed to be a grave
danger, the President had done what so many other Presidents
had done before him. As the Navy jet flew west over the Pacific,
with Bush at the controls, he must have known the future was
never something to be awaited—it must be met.

President George W. Bush
Remarks at the Graduation Exercise of the
United States Military Academy
West Point, New York

June 1, 2002

THE PRESIDENT: Thank you very much, General Lennox. Mr. Secretary, Governor Pataki, members of the United States Congress, Academy staff and faculty, distinguished guests, proud family members, and graduates: I want to thank you for your welcome. Laura and I are especially honored to visit this great institution in your bicentennial year.

In every corner of America, the words "West Point" command immediate respect. This place where the Hudson River bends is more than a fine institution of learning. The United States Military Academy is the guardian of values that have shaped the soldiers who have shaped the history of the world.

A few of you have followed in the path of the perfect West Point graduate, Robert E. Lee, who never received a single demerit in four years. Some of you followed in the path of the imperfect graduate, Ulysses S. Grant, who had his fair share of demerits, and said the happiest day of his life was "the day I left West Point." During my college years I guess you could say I was a Grant man.

You walk in the tradition of Eisenhower and MacArthur, Patton and Bradley—the commanders who saved a civilization.

And you walk in the tradition of second lieutenants who did the same, by fighting and dying on distant battlefields.

Graduates of this academy have brought creativity and courage to every field of endeavor. West Point produced the chief engineer of the Panama Canal, the mind behind the Manhattan Project, the first American to walk in space. This fine institution gave us the man they say invented baseball, and other young men over the years who perfected the game of football.

You know this, but many in America don't—George C. Marshall, a VMI graduate, is said to have given this order: "I want an officer for a secret and dangerous mission. I want a West Point football player."

As you leave here today, I know there's one thing you'll never miss about this place: being a plebe. But even a plebe at West Point is made to feel he or she has some standing in the world. I'm told that plebes, when asked whom they outrank, are required to answer this: "Sir, the Superintendent's dog—the Commandant's cat, and all the admirals in the whole damn Navy." I probably won't be sharing that with the Secretary of the Navy.

West Point is guided by tradition, and in honor of the "Golden Children of the Corps," I will observe one of the traditions you cherish most. As the Commander in Chief, I hereby grant amnesty to all cadets who are on restriction for minor conduct offenses. Those of you in the end zone might have cheered a little early. Because, you see, I'm going to let General Lennox define exactly what "minor" means.

Every West Point class is commissioned to the Armed Forces. Some West Point classes are also commissioned by history, to take part in a great new calling for their country. Speaking here to the class of 1942—six months after Pearl Harbor—General Marshall said, "We're determined that before the sun sets on this terrible struggle, our flag will be recognized throughout the world as a symbol of freedom on the one hand, and of overwhelming power on the other."

Officers graduating that year helped fulfill that mission, defeating Japan and Germany, and then reconstructing those nations as allies. West Point graduates of the 1940s saw the rise of a deadly new challenge—the challenge of imperial communism —and opposed it from Korea to Berlin, to Vietnam, and in the Cold War, from beginning to end. And as the sun set on their struggle, many of those West Point officers lived to see a world transformed.

History has also issued its call to your generation. In your last year, America was attacked by a ruthless and resourceful enemy. You graduate from this Academy in a time of war, taking your place in an American military that is powerful and is honorable. Our war on terror is only begun, but in Afghanistan it was begun well.

I am proud of the men and women who have fought on my orders. America is profoundly grateful for all who serve the cause of freedom, and for all who have given their lives in its defense. This nation respects and trusts our military, and we are confident in your victories to come.

This war will take many turns we cannot predict. Yet I am certain of this: Wherever we carry it, the American flag will stand not only for our power, but for freedom. Our nation's cause has always been larger than our nation's defense. We fight, as we always fight, for a just peace—a peace that favors human liberty. We will defend the peace against threats from terrorists and tyrants. We will preserve the peace by building good relations among the great powers. And we will extend the peace by encouraging free and open societies on every continent.

Building this just peace is America's opportunity, and America's duty. From this day forward, it is your challenge, as well, and we will meet this challenge together. You will wear the uniform of a great and unique country. America has no empire to extend or utopia to establish. We wish for others only what we wish for ourselves—safety from violence, the rewards of liberty, and the hope for a better life.

In defending the peace, we face a threat with no precedent. Enemies in the past needed great armies and great industrial capabilities to endanger the American people and our nation. The attacks of September the 11th required a few hundred thousand dollars in the hands of a few dozen evil and deluded men. All of the chaos and suffering they caused came at much less than the cost of a single tank. The dangers have not passed. This government and the American people are on watch, we are ready, because we know the terrorists have more money and more men and more plans.

The gravest danger to freedom lies at the perilous crossroads of radicalism and technology. When the spread of chemical and biological and nuclear weapons, along with ballistic missile technology—when that occurs, even weak states and small groups could attain a catastrophic power to strike great nations. Our enemies have declared this very intention, and have been caught seeking these terrible weapons. They want the capability to blackmail us, or to harm us, or to harm our friends—and we will oppose them with all our power.

For much of the last century, America's defense relied on the Cold War doctrines of deterrence and containment. In some cases, those strategies still apply. But new threats also require new thinking. Deterrence—the promise of massive retaliation against nations—means nothing against shadowy terrorist networks with no nation or citizens to defend. Containment is not possible when unbalanced dictators with weapons of mass destruction can deliver those weapons on missiles or secretly provide them to terrorist allies.

We cannot defend America and our friends by hoping for the best. We cannot put our faith in the word of tyrants, who solemnly sign non-proliferation treaties, and then systemically break them. If we wait for threats to fully materialize, we will have waited too long.

Homeland defense and missile defense are part of stronger security, and they're essential priorities for America. Yet the war on terror will not be won on the defensive. We must take the battle to the enemy, disrupt his plans, and confront the worst threats before they emerge. In the world we have entered, the only path to safety is the path of action. And this nation will act.

Our security will require the best intelligence, to reveal threats hidden in caves and growing in laboratories. Our security will require modernizing domestic agencies such as the FBI, so they're prepared to act, and act quickly, against danger. Our security will require transforming the military you will lead—a military that must be ready to strike at a moment's notice in any dark corner of the world. And our security will require all Americans to be forward-looking and resolute, to be ready for preemptive action when necessary to defend our liberty and to defend our lives.

The work ahead is difficult. The choices we will face are complex. We must uncover terror cells in 60 or more countries, using every tool of finance, intelligence, and law enforcement. Along with our friends and allies, we must oppose proliferation and confront regimes that sponsor terror, as each case requires. Some nations need military training to fight terror, and we'll provide it. Other nations oppose terror, but tolerate the hatred that leads to terror—and that must change. We will send diplomats where they are needed, and we will send you, our soldiers, where you're needed.

All nations that decide for aggression and terror will pay a price. We will not leave the safety of America and the peace of the planet at the mercy of a few mad terrorists and tyrants. We will lift this dark threat from our country and from the world.

Because the war on terror will require resolve and patience, it will also require firm moral purpose. In this way our struggle is similar to the Cold War. Now, as then, our enemies are totalitarians, holding a creed of power with no place for human dignity. Now, as then, they seek to impose a joyless conformity, to control every life and all of life.

America confronted imperial communism in many different ways—diplomatic, economic, and military. Yet moral clarity was essential to our victory in the Cold War. When leaders like John F. Kennedy and Ronald Reagan refused to gloss over the brutality of tyrants, they gave hope to prisoners and dissidents and exiles, and rallied free nations to a great cause.

Some worry that it is somehow undiplomatic or impolite to speak the language of right and wrong. I disagree. Different circumstances require different methods, but not different moralities. Moral truth is the same in every culture, in every time, and in every place. Targeting innocent civilians for murder is always and everywhere wrong. Brutality against women is always and everywhere wrong. There can be no neutrality between justice and cruelty, between the innocent and the guilty. We are in a conflict between good and evil, and America will call evil by its name. By confronting evil and lawless regimes, we do not create a problem, we reveal a problem. And we will lead the world in opposing it.

As we defend the peace, we also have an historic opportunity to preserve the peace. We have our best chance since the rise of the nation state in the 17th century to build a world where the great powers compete in peace instead of prepare for war. The history of the last century, in particular, was dominated by a series of destructive national rivalries that left battlefields and graveyards across the Earth. Germany fought France, the Axis fought the Allies, and then the East fought the West, in proxy wars and tense standoffs, against a backdrop of nuclear Armageddon.

Competition between great nations is inevitable, but armed conflict in our world is not. More and more, civilized nations find ourselves on the same side—united by common dangers of terrorist violence and chaos. America has, and intends to keep, military strengths beyond challenge—thereby, making the destabilizing arms races of other eras pointless, and limiting rivalries to trade and other pursuits of peace.

Today the great powers are also increasingly united by common values, instead of divided by conflicting ideologies. The United States, Japan and our Pacific friends, and now all of Europe, share a deep commitment to human freedom, embodied in strong alliances such as NATO. And the tide of liberty is rising in many other nations.

Generations of West Point officers planned and practiced for battles with Soviet Russia. I've just returned from a new Russia, now a country reaching toward democracy, and our partner in the war against terror. Even in China, leaders are discovering that economic freedom is the only lasting source of national wealth. In time, they will find that social and political freedom is the only true source of national greatness.

When the great powers share common values, we are better able to confront serious regional conflicts together, better able to cooperate in preventing the spread of violence or economic chaos. In the past, great power rivals took sides in difficult regional problems, making divisions deeper and more complicated. Today, from the Middle East to South Asia, we are gathering broad international coalitions to increase the pressure for peace. We must build strong and great power relations when times are good; to help manage crisis when times are bad. America needs partners to preserve the peace, and we will work with every nation that shares this noble goal.

And finally, America stands for more than the absence of war. We have a great opportunity to extend a just peace, by replacing poverty, repression, and resentment around the world with hope of a better day. Through most of history, poverty was persistent, inescapable, and almost universal. In the last few decades, we've seen nations from Chile to South Korea build modern economies and freer societies, lifting millions of people out of despair and want. And there's no mystery to this achievement.

The 20th century ended with a single surviving model of human progress, based on non-negotiable demands of human dignity, the rule of law, limits on the power of the state, respect for women and private property and free speech and equal justice and religious tolerance. America cannot impose this vision—yet we can support and reward governments that make the right choices for their own people. In our development aid, in our diplomatic efforts, in our international broadcasting, and in our

educational assistance, the United States will promote moderation
and tolerance and human rights. And we will defend the peace
that makes all progress possible.

When it comes to the common rights and needs of men and
women, there is no clash of civilizations. The requirements of
freedom apply fully to Africa and Latin America and the entire
Islamic world. The peoples of the Islamic nations want and
deserve the same freedoms and opportunities as people in every
nation. And their governments should listen to their hopes.

A truly strong nation will permit legal avenues of dissent
for all groups that pursue their aspirations without violence. An
advancing nation will pursue economic reform, to unleash the
great entrepreneurial energy of its people. A thriving nation will
respect the rights of women, because no society can prosper while
denying opportunity to half its citizens. Mothers and fathers and
children across the Islamic world, and all the world, share the same
fears and aspirations. In poverty, they struggle. In tyranny, they
suffer. And as we saw in Afghanistan, in liberation they celebrate.

America has a greater objective than controlling threats and
containing resentment. We will work for a just and peaceful world
beyond the war on terror.

The bicentennial class of West Point now enters this drama.
With all in the United States Army, you will stand between
your fellow citizens and grave danger. You will help establish a
peace that allows millions around the world to live in liberty and

to grow in prosperity. You will face times of calm, and times of crisis. And every test will find you prepared—because you're the men and women of West Point. You leave here marked by the character of this Academy, carrying with you the highest ideals of our nation.

Toward the end of his life, Dwight Eisenhower recalled the first day he stood on the plain at West Point. "The feeling came over me," he said, "that the expression 'the United States of America' would now and henceforth mean something different than it had ever before. From here on, it would be the nation I would be serving, not myself."

Today, your last day at West Point, you begin a life of service in a career unlike any other. You've answered a calling to hardship and purpose, to risk and honor. At the end of every day you will know that you have faithfully done your duty. May you always bring to that duty the high standards of this great American institution. May you always be worthy of the long gray line that stretches two centuries behind you.

On behalf of the nation, I congratulate each one of you for the commission you've earned and for the credit you bring to the United States of America. May God bless you all.

AUTHOR'S NOTE

First and foremost, I want to proudly acknowledge the contribution of the late Professor Richard Neustadt, author of *Presidential Power,* founding Dean of the Kennedy School of Government, and adviser to Presidents. One of the world's great authorities on the subject, Dick took the time nine months before he died to discuss the concept of a book on presidential courage. He talked passionately about a number of Presidents and the controversial decisions they made in the face of daunting pressures. I first met Richard Neustadt back in the 50s when I went to grade school with his son. I remember fondly visiting their home on the Upper West Side of Manhattan, when he was a professor at Columbia. His enthusiasm for this project propelled me to try to live up to his vision. Professor Neustadt—and I will always feel that's what I should call him—was a wonderful man who will be greatly missed.

A book, like a news show, has many people toiling behind the scenes. The team for this book did most of the heavy lifting. I cannot express my full gratitude to the people who made this project possible: Bruce Bennett, Jeremy Blachman, Tom Folsom, Nkomo Morris, Justin Shoemake, Peter Wolfgang, and Carolin Young. I have the deepest admiration for their energy, scholarship, patience with my directions, and most of all, their commitment to getting these stories right.

Finally, I must thank the two men who were most responsible for this book. Bill Adler called me one day and suggested I write a book. I had toyed with the idea for a long time. Bill's special genius is to take some ill-formed thoughts and help shape them into an exciting concept. It is his own special brand of alchemy.

Bill did me another great service. He put me together with Rugged Land and its splendid editor, Webster Stone. Until you've worked with a first-rate editor, you can't imagine all the ways in which he or she can help a writer—with big ideas about how to organize a sprawling enterprise like this; with endless creative suggestions about how to tell these stories in an engaging, informative way; with the ten thousand choices that go into any book. Web—now I know. Thank you.

BIBLIOGRAPHY

INTERNAL STRIFE

1. SADDLE UP George Washington and the Whiskey Rebellion

Baldwin, Leland D. *Whiskey Rebels: The Story of a Frontier Uprising.* Pittsburgh: University of Pittsburgh Press, 1939.

Ferling, John E. *The First of Men: A Life of George Washington.* Knoxville: University of Tennessee Press, 1988.

Flexner, James Thomas. *Washington: The Indispensable Man.* Boston: Back Bay Books, 1974.

Slaughter, Thomas P. *The Whiskey Rebellion: Frontier Epilogue to the American Revolution.* Oxford, England: Oxford University Press, 1986.

2. TO THINE OWN SELF BE TRUE Abraham Lincoln and the Emancipation Proclamation

Bates, David Homer. *Lincoln in the Telegraph Office.* Lincoln: University of Nebraska Press, 1995.

Burlingame, Michael, ed. *Lincoln Observed: Civil War Dispatches of Noah Brooks.* Baltimore: Johns Hopkins University Press, 2002.

Gould, William B. *Diary of a Contraband.* Palo Alto, Calif.: Stanford University Press, 2003.

McPherson, James M. *The Negro's Civil War.* New York: Vintage Books, 2003.

3. CONSTITUTION BE DAMNED Grover Cleveland and the Pullman Strike

Brodsky, Alyn, and Truman Talley. *Grover Cleveland: A Study in Character.* New York: St. Martin's Press, 2000.

Jeffers, H. Paul. *An Honest President: The Life and Presidencies of Grover Cleveland.* New York: HarperCollins, 2000.

John F. Kennedy School of Government Case Program C14-86-715.0.

Prepared by Thomas Green, under Professor Richard E. Neustadt for use at the John F. Kennedy School of Government, Harvard University (1184). 1984.

McElroy, Robert M. *Grover Cleveland, the Man and Statesman.* Vols. 1 and 2. New York: Harper and Brothers Publishers, 1923.

Papke, David R. *The Pullman Case: The Clash of Labor and Capital in Industrial America.* Lawrence: University Press of Kansas, 1999.

EXECUTIVE ACTION

4. BREAKING THE BANK Andrew Jackson and the Second National Bank

Ellis, Richard E. *Andrew Jackson.* Washington, D.C.: CQ Press, 2002.

Gammon, Samuel Rhea, Jr. "The Presidential Campaign of 1832." Ph.D. diss., Johns Hopkins University, 1922.

Remini, Robert V. *The Jacksonian Era.* Arlington Heights, Ill.: Harlan Davidson, 1989.

Schlesinger, Arthur M., Jr. *The Age of Jackson.* Boston: Little, Brown, 1988.

Taylor, George Rogers, ed. *Jackson vs. Biddle's Bank: The Struggle over the Second Bank of the United States.* Lexington, Mass.: DC Heath, 1972.

5. MR. JOHNSON GOES TO WASHINGTON Andrew Johnson and His Secretary of War

Compilation of the Messages and Papers of the Presidents, 1789–1897. Edited by James D. Richardson. 10 vols. Washington, D.C.: Government Printing Office, 1896–99.

Nash, Howard Pervear, Jr. *Andrew Johnson: Congress and Reconstruction.* Rutherford, N.J.: Dickinson University Press, 1972.

Schroeder-Lein, Glenna R., and Richard Zuczek. *Andrew Johnson: A Biographical Companion.* Santa Barbara, Calif.: ABC-CLIO, 2001.

Trefousse, Hans L. *Andrew Johnson: A Biography.* New York: Norton, 1989.

6. GUNS AND BUTTER Lyndon Johnson, the Vietnam War, and the Great Society

Beschloss, Michael R, ed. *Reaching for Glory: Lyndon Johnson's Secret White House Tapes, 1964–1965.* New York: Touchstone Books, 2002.

Califano, Joseph A., Jr. *The Triumph and Tragedy of Lyndon Johnson: The White House Years.* New York: Simon and Schuster, 1991.

Dallek, Robert. *Flawed Giant: Lyndon Johnson and His Times, 1961–1973.* Oxford, England: Oxford University Press, 1998.

Goodwin, Doris Kearns. *Lyndon Johnson and the American Dream.* New York: Harper and Row, 1976.

Goodwin, Richard. *Remembering America: A Voice from the Sixties.* Boston: Little, Brown, 1988.

THE MAP FOR PEACE

7. A GENERAL SKIRTS WAR Ulysses Grant and Cuba

Foner, Philip S. *A History of Cuba and Its Relations with the United States.* New York: International Publishers, 1962.

Grant, Ulysses S. *Personal Memoirs of U.S. Grant.* Cambridge, Mass.: Da Capo Press, 2001.

Nevins, Allan. *Hamilton Fish: The Inner History of the Grant Administration.* New York: Frederick Ungar, 1937.

Smith, Jean Edward. *Grant.* New York: Simon and Schuster, 2001.

Thomas, Hugh. *Cuba: The Pursuit of Freedom.* New York: Harper and Row, 1971.

8. PEACE WARRIOR Theodore Roosevelt and the Russo-Japanese Peace Plan

Beale, Howard K. *Theodore Roosevelt and the Rise of America to World Power.* Baltimore: Johns Hopkins University Press, 1956.

Esthus, Raymond A. *Double Eagle and Rising Sun: The Russians and Japanese*

Morris, Edmund. *The Rise of Theodore Roosevelt.* New York: Coward, McCann, and Geoghegan, 1979.

Morris, Edmund. *Theodore Rex.* New York: Random House, 2001.

Roosevelt, Theodore. *An Autobiography.* New York: Charles Scribner's Sons, 1913.

9. MISSION FROM GOD Woodrow Wilson and the League of Nations

Axson, Stockton. *"Brother Woodrow": A Memoir of Woodrow Wilson.* Princeton, N.J.: Princeton University Press, 1993.

Clements, Kendrick A., and Eric A. Cheezum. *Woodrow Wilson, World Statesman.* Washington, D.C.: CQ Press, 2003.

Link, Arthur. *Woodrow Wilson: Revolution, War, and Peace.* Arlington Heights, Ill.: Harlan Davidson, 1979.

Miller, William D. *Pretty Bubbles in the Air: America in 1919.* Champaign: University of Illinois Press, 1991.

Smith, Gene. *When the Cheering Stopped: The Last Years of Woodrow Wilson.* New York: William Morrow, 1964.

10. THE CHINA CARD Richard Nixon and the People's Republic of China

Foot, Rosemary. *The Practice of Power: U.S. Relations with China since 1949.* Oxford, England: Oxford University Press, 1995.

Hersh, Seymour M. *The Price of Power: Kissinger in the Nixon White House.* New York: Summit Books, 1983.

Hoff, Joan. *Nixon Reconsidered.* New York: Basic Books, 1994.

Nixon, Richard M. *RN: The Memoirs of Richard Nixon.* New York: Grosset and Dunlap, 1978.

O'Brien, Cormac. *Secret Lives of the U.S. Presidents.* Philadelphia: Quirk Books, 2004.

11. THE ZERO OPTION Ronald Reagan and the Soviet Union

Gaddis, John Lewis. *The United States and the End of the Cold War: Implications, Reconsiderations, Provocations.* Oxford, England: Oxford University Press, 1992.

Garthoff, Raymond L. *A Journey through the Cold War: A Memoir of Containment and Coexistence.* Washington, D.C.: Brookings Institution Press, 2001.

Mandelbaum, Michael, and Strobe Talbott. *Reagan and Gorbachev.* New York: Vintage Books, 1987.

Reagan, Ronald. *An American Life.* New York: Simon and Schuster, 1990.

Robinson, Peter. *How Ronald Reagan Changed My Life.* New York: Regan Books, 2003.

AGAINST THE ENEMY

12. LIFE, LIBERTY, AND THE PURSUIT OF SMUGGLERS Thomas Jefferson and the Embargo Acts

Mapp, Alf J., Jr. *Thomas Jefferson: Passionate Pilgrim: The Presidency, the Founding of the University, and the Private Battle.* Lanham, Md.: Madison Books, 1991.

Sears, Louis Martin. *Jefferson and the Embargo.* New York: Octagon Books, 1966.

Spivak, Burton. *Jefferson's English Crisis: Commerce, Embargo, and the Republican Revolution.* Charlottesville: University Press of Virginia, 1979.

Wills, Garry. *Negro President: Jefferson and the Slave Power.* New York: Houghton Mifflin, 2003.

13. THE GARDEN HOSE Franklin Roosevelt and the Lend-Lease Act

Churchill, Winston. *Their Finest Hour.* New York: Houghton Mifflin, 1949.

Kimball, Warren F. *The Most Unsordid Act: Lend-Lease, 1939–1941.* Baltimore: Johns Hopkins University Press, 1969.

Meacham, Jon. *Franklin and Winston: An Intimate Portrait of an Epic Friendship*. New York: Random House, 2003.

Moss, Norman. *Nineteen Weeks: America, Britain, and the Fateful Summer of 1940*. New York: Houghton Mifflin, 2003.

Ward, Geoffrey C. *A First-Class Temperament: The Emergence of Franklin Roosevelt*. New York: HarperCollins, 1989.

14. ALWAYS DO RIGHT Harry Truman and the Berlin Airlift

Andreas-Freidrich, Ruth. *Battleground Berlin: Diaries, 1945–1948*. Translated by Anna Boerresen. New York: Paragon House, 1990.

Haydock, Michael D. *City Under Siege: The Berlin Blockade and Airlift, 1948 - 1949*. Washington, D.C.: Brassey's, 1999.

Huschke, Wolfgang J. *The Candy Bombers: The Berlin Airlift, 1948 - 1949. A History of the People and Planes*. Berlin, Germany: Metropol, 1999.

McCullough, David. *Truman*. New York: Touchstone Books, 1992.

Pearcy, Arthur. *Berlin Airlift*. Shrewsbury, England: Airlife Publishing, 1997.

15. DEFEAT IS AN ORPHAN John Kennedy and the Bay of Pigs

Dallek, Robert. *An Unfinished Life: John F. Kennedy, 1917–1963*. Boston: Little, Brown, 2003.

John F. Kennedy School of Government Case No. 279.0, "Kennedy and the Bay of Pigs." Prepared by Stephen Bates, Richard Neustadt, and Joshua Rosenbloom for use at the John F. Kennedy School of Government, Harvard University. 1980.

Johnson, Haynes Bonner. *The Bay of Pigs: The Leader's Story of Brigade 2506*. New York: W.W. Norton and Company, 1974.

Kornbluh, Peter, ed. *Bay of Pigs Declassified: The Secret CIA Report on the Invasion of Cuba*. New York: New Press, 1998.

Schlesinger, Arthur M., Jr. *A Thousand Days: John F. Kennedy in the White House*. Boston: Mariner Books, 2002.

Triay, Victor Andres. *Bay of Pigs: An Oral History of Brigade 2506*. Gainesville: University Press of Florida, 2001.

Wyden, Peter. *The Bay of Pigs: The Untold Story*. New York: Vintage/Ebury, 1979.

16. THE MUSHROOM CLOUD George W. Bush and the Iraq War

Bruni, Frank. *Ambling into History: The Unlikely Odyssey of George W. Bush*. New York: HarperCollins, 2002.

Frum, David. *The Right Man: An Inside Account of the Bush White House*. New York: Random House, 2003.

Minutaglio, Bill. *First Son: George W. Bush and the Bush Family Dynasty*. New York: Three Rivers Press, 1999.

Woodward, Bob. *Bush at War*. New York: Simon and Schuster, 2002.

Woodward, Bob. *Plan of Attack*. New York: Simon and Schuster, 2004.